a
THE LOVE OF GOD

THE LOVE OF GOD

AN ESSAY IN ANALYSIS

BY

DOM AELRED GRAHAM

MONK OF AMPLEFORTH

" At eventide they will examine thee in love—"
St John of the Cross: *Spiritual Maxim.*

LONGMANS, GREEN AND CO.
LONDON : NEW YORK : TORONTO

LONGMANS, GREEN AND CO. LTD.
39 PATERNOSTER ROW, LONDON, E.C.4
17 CHITTARANJAN AVENUE, CALCUTTA
NICOL ROAD, BOMBAY
36A MOUNT ROAD, MADRAS

LONGMANS, GREEN AND CO.
55 FIFTH AVENUE, NEW YORK
221 EAST 20TH STREET, CHICAGO
88 TREMONT STREET, BOSTON

LONGMANS, GREEN AND CO.
215 VICTORIA STREET, TORONTO

NIHIL OBSTAT: D. STEPHANUS MARRON, S.TH.D.
CENSOR CONGREG. ANGLIAE O.S.B.
IMPRIMATUR: RR. DD. SIGEBERTUS TRAFFORD
ABBAS PRAESES

NIHIL OBSTAT: GEORGIUS CAN. SMITH, S.TH.D., PH.D.
CENSOR DEPUTATUS
IMPRIMATUR: E. MORROGH BERNARD
VIC. GEN.
WESTMONASTERII, DIE 7A NOVEMBRIS, 1939

PRINTED IN THE UNITED STATES OF AMERICA

TO
ALL WHO
WOULD LOVE GOD

ACKNOWLEDGMENT

A DEBT of gratitude is due to all those who so kindly helped with their advice, and in other ways, while this book was being prepared for publication. The debt is especially heavy to Mr. Walter Shewring, who read it both in MS. and in proof, making many valuable suggestions; to Fr Conrad Pepler, O.P., for his constructive theological criticism; and to Dom Felix Hardy, who corrected the final proofs.

INTRODUCTION

It is with some misgiving that the title " The Love of God " has been given to this book. The handling of such a theme might justly be regarded as the peculiar province of the masters of the spiritual life. Indeed, had the times been more propitious and the witnesses to Christian truth at this unhappy hour as numerous (and as vocal) as could be wished, the present writer would have been well content to wait until he had earned a less disputable right to attempt even such an outline as this. Taking refuge, however, in the Chestertonian paradox that if a thing is worth doing at all it is worth doing ill, he has ventured to publish this essay, despite the imperfections which greater maturity might have removed. Not that there is here implied a desire to disarm criticism in advance, to avoid the consequences of one's folly (if such it be), but only to offer some explanation for what might otherwise appear unwarrantable presumption.

If eminence in practice and profound personal experience were indispensable qualifications for discussing the subject, these reflections would assuredly be based on the flimsiest foundations. Fortunately this is not so. There is a distinction as old as Aristotle between the man who knows a science empirically, from his own dealings with the subject-matter, and one who has some theoretical acquaintance with its underlying principles. The saints and mystics write of the love of God pre-eminently, though by no means exclusively, from the first of these standpoints; in the pages which follow we shall approach it from the second.

It must be admitted that the works which have come to be known as " spiritual classics " are the fruit of the writers' own experience. Their teaching is largely the outcome of a saintly life; it is in fact just this which forms a great part of its appeal. One advantage, however, attaches to what we may call the analytical method which is perhaps lacking to the other. It enables us to see the subject dealt with in its general context, objectively; we have not to surrender our minds entirely to the viewpoint of the writer before we can acquiesce in what he has to say. Contemplative souls, treating of divine charity, persuade by their sincerity, and often charm by their eloquence, but the warmth of their love sometimes leads them to take for granted what the rest of us would wish to have discussed.

Although this book was written while the war-clouds were as yet gathering, its message surely takes on a heightened significance now that the storm has burst upon us. If the religion of Christ be true then the love of God to which it invites us is still the most important thing in life. At a time when men's minds are filled with foreboding at the prospect of the future, and that peace which is the tranquillity of order seems almost an idle dream, there is some comfort to be found in turning our thoughts to the two abiding realities: God and our own souls. When we are embarked upon a war of unforeseeable horrors, threatened with the disruption of civilised society and a spectacular, albeit ephemeral, triumph has been achieved by the powers of darkness it is well for us to be fortified by the vision of timeless things. The kingdoms of the world may pass away, but the truths by which the mind lives endure. If we are to be asked to submit to privation and suffering we may fairly lay claim to the one consolation that is not cowardice. For to view calamity in the light of supernatural belief is not to take an unworthy refuge from the harsh realities of life; it is only to penetrate more deeply their meaning. In order to show this we should not have to appeal to the beauty of the Faith, or even to its ethical value, but simply to its truth. The aesthetic and moral approach to religious problems can have little permanent effect if it is not founded upon a groundwork of sound doctrine, that is, upon what is universally true. As Jörgensen so strikingly observes in his admirable *Saint Catherine of Siena* [1] :

All Christian life, all self-denial, all work of charity and love depends on faith, hangs from it as the globe of the earth and all the gods of Olympus hung in the chain which Zeus held in his almighty hand. For what does it avail me that it is *beautiful* to be a Christian, that it is *good* to be a Christian, if Christianity is

[1] p. 59.

not *true*? Here neither aestheticism nor pragmatism is of any use. If the Word has not become flesh, if the Virgin has not borne the Child, then let the ringing of the Angelus bells be never so lovely when the sky is golden behind the black cypresses of Italy —those bells must be silent, or they must become a mere sound of Nature—like the singing of birds or the soughing of the wind among the leaves of the olive trees! Truth is the most precious possession of human-kind, and no one has the right to betray it for the sake of a poetical mood. We dare not imitate those pagan orators and poets who, during the last centuries of antiquity, raved poetically about the deserted temples. Nor do we dare to think like those kings and emperors who thought that religion was useful for the people and ought to be maintained. Nothing but the truth is of any use either to you or me or the people! Christ has therefore asserted most emphatically that He is the Truth. If He were not, how, then, could He save us? No perfect Christian life is possible without a perfect conviction of this. At all decisive moments, at the parting of the ways, at the turning points, doubt will otherwise arise: " Is it true after all, what I believe, so that I do not risk anything by acting upon it? " If you take your stand on a half-belief you cannot act with conviction.

And truth comes to us by knowledge. That it is more important to love God than to know Him is one of the convictions which inspire these pages. Yet love presupposes knowledge. Not blindly must the Beloved be approached, but with enlightened understanding. Short of the experimental knowledge of the mystics, on which it would be presumptuous folly to rely, perhaps the means best calculated to ensure fulfilment of the greatest of the commandments lie in our trying to appreciate, however imperfectly, what God is, to discern thereby something of His innate lovableness; and, we may add, what man is, and how great his need for God.

Accordingly the attempt is here made to consider man's love for God, both in itself, and in its relation to human life as a whole. The command to love God above all else is given to every Christian; it is not the exclusive concern of those who dedicate themselves to the priesthood or take vows of religion. With this in view we have ventured some general reflections, as touching such problems as art, education, sex, in so far as they fall within the wider context of divine charity. For it is the man who is interested in these various things, that is to say, every man who thinks at all, who must see them in relation to the main business of life: his standing right with his Creator. Nor does experience run counter to the theory. Nothing is more encouraging (and how frequent it is!) than to discover a highly intelligent interest in the questions which underlie our relations with God among those who feel no incompatibility between life in the modern world and unflinching fidelity to the practical demands of religion. It is to the laity then, especially to the young and thoughtful (of whom we know many), as much as to the priest and religious, that these reflections are addressed. That they may bring something of light and encouragement to those who are being called upon to suffer and enter danger is the hope which is now uppermost in the mind of their author.

Nevertheless, since it has not been possible to treat of the subject without incursions into the realm of metaphysics, it is too much to hope that parts at least of the chapters which follow will not make difficult reading. Each section could of itself be expanded to form a book, and much compression has been called for. But this notwithstanding, the widespread revival of interest in St Thomas and his thought is perhaps a sign that it is not as necessary as some suppose to "adapt" his teaching to the mentality of the layman. The general background against which this work is set is, as it must necessarily be, revealed truth. But the glass, so to say, through which revelation has been viewed is that provided by the immortal *Summa Theologica*.[1]

"A perfect harmony between the demands of reason and those of the most exacting religious feeling, such is the secret of St Thomas."[2] It is because we profoundly share this view that we have chosen to discuss the love of God in the light of Thomist principles rather than make miscellaneous selection from authorities who, though possessing greater

[1] During his student days the author enjoyed the happy privilege of traversing this incomparable work from end to end under the able guidance of the English Dominican Fathers at Oxford. It is no more than fitting that he should record in this Introduction his deep indebtedness to his former masters.
[2] Étienne Gilson, *Saint Thomas Aquinas*: Annual Lecture on a Master Mind (Henriette Hertz Trust of the British Academy), 1935, p. 13.

emotional appeal, are not so fundamentally satisfactory. What originality can be claimed for an essay which moves over these deep, though well-charted, waters must be left to the judgment of others. At any rate, such lack of variety and picturesqueness as results may be compensated for in some degree by the effort at intellectual consistency. Inevitably other great names have been appealed to—notably, St Augustine and St John of the Cross—but as witnesses to a unity of thought rather than as contributors to a spiritual anthology.

One further point calls for mention. It may be felt, by those more learned and of deeper theological insight than the present writer, that sufficient indication has not been given of legitimate divergence of view on many of the questions touched upon. For example, the nature of the theological virtues, the gifts of the Holy Spirit, the relation of grace to mystical experience, the experience itself. In reply to such criticism it will be enough to admit its justice, while pointing out that limitations of space and the wish to avoid anything that could fairly be described as *odium theologicum* made any other course extremely difficult. As it is, a sincere adherence to the principle *Amicus Plato sed magis amica veritas* has perhaps suggested an occasional note which may sound out of harmony with the general theme. The few points in dispute to which reference is actually made hide no challenging or controversial intention; they might well have been indicated more gracefully by another, less unskilled in the use of words, but it would surely have been disingenuous to pass them over altogether. Happily St Thomas knows how to temper the Aristotelian vindication of the rights of truth with the warmth of Christian charity. " The concord," he says, " which is the effect of charity results from a union of wills, not from a unanimity of opinions."[1] It is in this spirit that the chapters which follow are offered as a slight contribution to the task all have in common—that of " bringing into captivity every understanding unto the obedience of Christ."[2]   A.G.

Ampleforth Abbey,
  York.   October, 1939.

[1] IIa IIae, q. 37, a. 1.   [2] 2 *Corinthians* x, 5.

ANALYTICAL CONTENTS

PAGE

I. THE NATURE OF THIS LOVE . . . 1

I. *THE ONE WHO IS LOVED*

The ineffability of God—p. 3. The Hebrews were concerned with doing God's will rather than knowing His nature—p. 3. Nevertheless God has revealed Himself and men have rightly tried to penetrate the meaning of His revelation—p. 4. God to be thought of, as well as worshipped, in spirit and in truth—p. 4. God reveals His name—p. 5. The significance of this name: *Ipsum Esse Subsistens*—p. 5. God is complete actuality—p. 7. The distinction between essence and existence—p. 8. God, since He is Creator, contains within Himself all creaturely perfections—p. 8. His care for the individual —p. 10. The way in which the things we know exist in God—p. 10. The divine Personality—p. 12. All that can be said of God can be said of the Person of Jesus Christ—p. 13. Summary—p. 15.

II. *THE ONE WHO LOVES*

All things can be said to love God—p. 16. The dignity of man—p. 16. Man a rational animal—p. 17. Relation between body and soul—p. 17. Importance of this classical conception of man's nature—p. 18. The modern view of man—p. 19. Implications of man's nature as a rational animal—p. 21. Reflection and knowledge—p. 21. Relation between knowledge and love— p. 22. The will and its object—p. 23. The nature of freedom—p. 24. Obstacles to liberty: the Fall—p. 25. Possibility of exaggerating its evil effects— p. 25. Man's moral activity—p. 26. Over-emphasis on one of its departments —p. 27. The three constituents of the human act: object, circumstances and end—p. 28. Relation between means and ends—p. 28. Good will and prudence—p. 30. The natural law—p. 31. Man's longing for God—p. 33.

III. *THE LOVE ITSELF*

Difficulty of discussing love in rational terms—p. 34. GOD'S LOVE FOR US:— God's dealings with mankind those of a bridegroom with his bride—p. 34. The preliminaries of this marriage belong to God alone—p. 35. Creation His first act of love—p. 35. The nature of God's love for creatures—p. 36. The difference between His love and ours—p. 36. The purpose of creation— p. 37. *Bonum est diffusivum sui*—p. 38. Exemplified in the Blessed Trinity— p. 38. The Incarnation—p. 39. God's self-giving here is absolute—p. 39. The consummation of the union between God and His people—p. 40. OUR NATURAL DESIRE FOR GOD:—Distinction between natural and supernatural love of God—p. 41. We naturally love God more than ourselves—p. 42. This is based on the truth that God is our final end—p. 42. Plato has given it classical expression—p. 43. What is the precise object of this love?—p. 44. The nature of our natural desire for God—p. 45. St Thomas's teaching— p. 46. The scope of his argument: our desire subject to a polarity—p. 47. St Thomas distinguishes between our natural and supernatural desire for God—p. 48. We naturally desire God as the Author of nature, not as He is in His intimate life—p. 49. The vagueness and uncertainty of this conception— p. 49. OUR SUPERNATURAL LOVE OF GOD: DIVINE CHARITY:—Charity includes all that is implied by natural love and immeasurably more—p. 49. A sharing in the love wherewith God loves Himself—p. 50. A friendship with God—p. 50. The love which is to be preferred to knowledge—p. 51. A

xv

personal possession—p. 51. None of the virtues complete without charity—p. 52. Charity regulated by the gift of wisdom—p. 53. The soul's kinship with God—p. 54. Charity increases in intensity—p. 54. Its maximum and minimum—p. 55. God first of all loved and then creatures in Him—p. 55. Charity distinct from philanthropy and humanitarianism—p. 56. But our love for God is human as well as divine—p. 57. THE LOVE OF OURSELVES IN GOD:—The importance of rightly-ordered self-love—p. 58. The problem of pure love—p. 58. Love of God includes the true love of self—p. 59. Love of spiritual goods unites men, love of material things divides them—p. 60. In desiring rightly our own perfection we love God more than ourselves—p. 60. St Augustine on the all-embracing reality of the love of God—p. 61.

II. THE CONDITIONS OF THIS LOVE . . p. 63

I. *KNOWLEDGE*

Importance of the principle that nothing is loved unless it is first known—p. 65. Our Lord's insistence on the factor of knowledge—p. 65. Knowledge and truth—p. 66. In knowledge joined with love we have the only lasting riches—p. 67. Distinction between knowledge and learning—p. 67. Truth and education—p. 68. The object of education—p. 69. The limitations of the modern system—p. 69. Contemporary education engenders habits of mind which are unfavourable to the reception of revealed religion—p. 70. The mind diverted from its true path—p. 70. This is exemplified in the field of literary studies—p. 71. The limitations of the physical sciences as an educational discipline—p. 72. Qualifications of for going criticism—p. 73. Philosophical roots of educational disorder—p. 74. Cause of the modern attack on Christianity—p. 74. The responsibility of those charged with the education of the young—p. 75. Importance of understanding the realist and contemplative nature of the intelligence—p. 76. Our knowledge of God derives from two sources—p. 76. The scope of reason and faith—p. 77. Historic Christianity can be considered from two points of view—p. 78. Faith both rational and supernatural—p. 78. Faith is the substance of things hoped for—p. 79. It is knowledge—p. 79. The authority behind faith—p. 80. Intimate relationship between God and the soul which faith implies—p. 81. In regard to the Hypostatic Union—p. 82. This elevated conception of faith scriptural and traditional: St John and St Paul—p. 83. Lost sight of by certain theologians—p. 84. Evident in the *Summa* of St Thomas—p. 85. Implications of transcendent and mystical quality of faith—p. 86. Confirmed by St John of the Cross—p. 87. And St Catherine of Siena—p. 88.

II. *DRAWING NEAR TO GOD*

Twofold aspect of our approach to God—p. 89. Importance of understanding Catholic notion of grace—p. 89. Christianity transcends as well as includes ethical perfection—p. 90. Grace: a participation in the divine nature—p. 91. Unfortunate over-emphasis on one of its functions—p. 92. The *reality* of grace—p. 92. St Thomas's view—p. 93. Grace distinct from the infused virtues—p. 94. Grace is a *nature*—p. 95. Charity the creature's highest endowment—p. 96. The meaning of *habit*—p. 97. Misunderstood by the moderns—p. 97. The theological virtues perfect the natural faculties of the soul—p. 99. The gifts of the Holy Spirit—p. 100. How the supernatural life develops—p. 102. The Sacraments—p. 102. The Eucharist supreme among the sacraments—p. 104. The sacrament of charity—p. 105. How charity increases—p. 106. Importance of making acts of charity—p. 107. Modern world has lost faith and charity—p. 108. Charity should increase progressively until the Beatific Vision is reached—p. 109.

III. *UNWORLDLINESS*

Necessity of co-operating with grace—p. 110. Possibility of misunderstanding the principle: *gratia perficit naturam*—p. 111. The way in which grace perfects nature—p. 111. Unworldliness: the meaning of "the world"—p. 113. Detachment achieved by the practice of the virtue of temperance—p. 114. Mr Aldous Huxley on non-attachment—p. 114. Nature of the liberty implied by detachment—p. 115. The place of the senses—p. 116. Function of temperance: to produce tranquillity of spirit—p. 117. Nature of temperance—p. 118. Threefold disorder remedied by temperance—p. 120. Importance of abstinence—p. 121. How it uplifts the mind—p. 122. Human affections—p. 123. The sex-instinct—p. 124. The dignity of chastity—p. 125. Marriage compatible with detachment—p. 126. The disorder of pride—p. 127. The place of humility—p. 128. Compatible with magnanimity—p. 129. Humility and charity—p. 130. The Mother of God, model of humility—p. 131. The spirit of the evangelical counsels—p. 132.

III. THE EXPRESSION OF THIS LOVE   p. 133

I. *PRAYER*

Possibility of confusion on the subject—p. 135. Prayer an activity of the virtue of religion—p. 136. Important distinction between religion and charity—p. 136. Prayer an activity of the practical intellect: a petition—p. 137. Prayer the work of the reason—p. 137. How prayer produces its effect—p. 138. An instrument of God's providence—p. 139. What we ought to pray for—p. 139. The inspiration to pray indicates that what we pray for is part of God's plan—p. 141. Prayer for temporal needs—p. 141. A means of raising our hearts to God—p. 142. The best of all prayers: the Our Father—p. 142. The excellence of prayer in common—p. 144. The Church's own prayer—p. 144. Modern vogue of mental prayer—p. 145. Liturgy the most perfect form of worship—p. 146. But the activities of the supernaturalised soul not merely liturgical—p. 147. Over-simplification by liturgical enthusiasts—p. 148. Fallacy of exalting social worship at the expense of the personal element in religion—p. 148. Catholic orthodoxy meets the needs of both—p. 148. Danger inherent in all forms of ritualism—p. 150. How we take part in the liturgy—p. 151. Liturgists' lack of sympathy for certain aspects of the Church's devotional life—p. 151. The modern psychological attack—p. 151. No incompatibility between orthodoxy and personal religion—p. 152. Liturgy not so immediately concerned with God as faith and charity—p. 152. Theological virtues concerned with God immediately—p. 153. Religion ruled by prudence—p. 154. Not so the theological virtues—p. 154. Contemplation: an activity of faith and charity and the gift of wisdom—p. 155. Contemplation and liturgy should harmonise—p. 156. The Exercises of St Ignatius—p. 157. Père Lallemant on contemplation—p. 158.

II. *SELF-ABNEGATION*

The need for purification—p. 159. Self-abnegation here considered as an expression of love—p. 160. Nature of suffering—p. 160. The Passion—p. 160. The essence of Christ's sacrifice—p. 162. Need for clear ideas about evil and suffering—p. 162. Problem of evil—p. 162. Its nature—p. 163. An example—p. 164. Sin—p. 165. What is God's responsibility for the evil which occasions suffering?—p. 165. He wishes us to enter into the mystery of pain—p. 165. Value of suffering depends on the moral worth of the sufferer—p. 166. Evil and pain fall within the scheme of divine providence—p. 167. God in no way the cause of sin—p. 167. God's part in physical evil—p. 168.

The finger of God in human affliction—p. 169. Opposition to our desire the *ratio* of pain—p. 170. Herein lie its potentialities as a purifying force—p. 170. Passive purifications the most efficacious—p. 171. The purgation of the senses and the spirit: the teaching of St John of the Cross—p. 173. As compared with St Thomas—p. 173. The place of contemplation—p. 174. The night of the senses—p. 175. The passage from meditation to contemplation—p. 176. The stripping of the soul implied by these purifications negative in name only—p. 177. The night of the spirit—p. 179. The soul must walk in the purity of faith—p. 179. The reward of complete self-abnegation—p. 180.

III. ACTION

Charity shows itself in action—p. 181. Nevertheless action is subordinate to contemplation—p. 182. The " two lives "—p. 182. Action the ritual of contemplation—p. 183. Why contemplation is superior to action—p. 185. Our deeds must conform to charity—p. 186. Artistic activity—p. 186. Its non-moral character—p. 187. The relation between art and prudence—p. 187. And beauty—p. 188. The value of great art—p. 190. The Christian artist—p. 191. Detailed consideration of the virtue of prudence—p. 192. Presupposes right desire—p. 192. Distinction between speculative and practical truth—p. 193. The prudent act always an expression of the love of God—p. 194. Prudence concerned with the whole field of human action—p. 195. Analysis of the prudent act—p. 195. The elements which make up prudence: Memory—p. 196. Understanding—p. 196. Reason—p. 197. Docility—p. 197. Shrewdness—p. 198. Foresight—p. 198. Cautiousness—p. 198. Circumspection—p. 199. The gift of counsel perfects prudence—p. 199. Its connection with the Beatitude of mercy—p. 200. The Church's prayer for prudence—p. 201.

IV. THE EFFECTS OF THIS LOVE . . p. 203

I. *THE PRESENCE*

Our Lord's promise of His special presence—p. 205. The effect of His love—p. 205. A sense of God's presence the accompaniment of sanctity—p. 206. God is to be found within our own souls—p. 207. He is naturally present by His ubiquity—p. 207. But we have no intuition of this presence—p. 208. The *mens*: its likeness to the Blessed Trinity—p. 210. How does God's presence by grace differ from His natural presence?—p. 210. St Augustine's awareness of the problem—p. 210. St Thomas's teaching—p. 211. The Lord is not only *in* us but He is *with* us—p. 213. God present as an object of knowledge and love—p. 213. The Word and the Holy Spirit sent into the soul—p. 215. *Verbum spirans amorem*—p. 215. The Eucharistic presence—p. 216. The *reality* of the sacrament—p. 217. The manner of Christ's presence—p. 218. His body not localised—p. 218. His coming into the soul at Communion—p. 220. The Eucharist is the food of our souls—p. 220. Its effects—p. 221. The Bread of angels—p. 221. Fundamental truth of the doctrine—p. 222.

II. *UNION*

The union takes place in " the inmost centre of the soul," i.e. the *mens*—p. 223. No true vision of God in this life—p. 224. Visions and ecstasies no proof of genuine holiness—p. 225. Is mystical experience possible without grace?—p. 225. Difficulties against an affirmative answer—p. 226. The question must be decided by theology—p. 227. Agreement with the conclusions of M. Maritain—p. 228. Authentic mystical experience in the natural order a contradiction in terms—p. 228. Yet such experience is possible outside the visible communion of the Church—p. 229. Mohammedan mystics—p. 229. The experience conditioned by supernatural faith—p. 230. By their faith the apparent infidels are invisibly united to Christ's Church—p. 230. Union with the Church: its necessity—p. 231. Faith provides the intellectual content of the experience—p. 231. A conceptual knowledge—p. 232. Though the mystics may be unaware of this—p. 232. The relation between the cognitive and affective elements in the soul's union with God—p. 233. God known by the effects of filial love—p. 234. A quasi-experimental knowledge—p. 234. How the soul is transformed by the object of its love—p. 235. For complete union our will must correspond with God's on the plane of action—p. 235. Abandonment to the divine will—p. 236. The divine " will of good pleasure " and the " will as expressed "—p. 236. Self-abandonment an act of the theological virtues—p. 238. Practical conclusions of universal application—p. 238. The danger of quietism—p. 238. The contrary danger—p. 239. Abandonment rooted in faith, though the union is effected by love—p. 239. St John of the Cross on the transforming union—p. 240.

III. *THE MIND OF CHRIST*

We most resemble Our Lord by possessing the " Mind of Christ "—p. 241. Christ's own knowledge the basis of the absolute conformity of His will with the Father's—p. 242. His intense love for the Father the exemplar-cause of charity—p. 242. Grace and charity the first beginnings of the " Mind of Christ "—p. 243. The imitation of Christ—p. 243. Point of communication with Christ outside space and time: the *mens*—p. 245. The Mystical Body of Christ—p. 245. Possibility of misunderstanding the doctrine—p. 246. The essential truth: the life which is proper to Christ is communicated to His followers in a multiplicity of ways—p. 247. Basis of the doctrine: the theology of grace—p. 248. The building up of the Body of Christ—p. 249. The place of the " weaker brethren "—p. 249. All contribute to the harmony and beauty of the finished plan—p. 250. The need for " ordinary " Christians as well as for the saints—p. 251. The " Mind of Christ " perfected in love—p. 252.

Part I
THE NATURE OF THIS LOVE

I
THE ONE WHO IS LOVED

"Thus shalt thou say to the children of Israel: He Who Is hath sent me to you."—*Exodus iii*, 14.

GOD is ineffable. That is to say, no words are able to describe Him. Human language, for all the richness and subtlety it has acquired through centuries of development, must still wait upon our thought. And our thought in its turn has its limitations; it is generated, to speak somewhat loosely, by the senses and the imagination. In our present mode of existence thought must always bear the signs of its origin; our ideas are expressed in and bounded by imagery. The fusion of idea and image is natural to our way of thinking; only by reflection and a certain effort do we learn to separate them and consider the idea, the concept, in detachment from the particular embodiment of it which forms the object of sense-knowledge; the notion of man, for example, in isolation from the individuals with whom we are acquainted.

Language can be, and has, in fact, been purified from all but the minimum of imaginative adornment to form a medium of expression for philosophers and scientists. But the resultant terminology, without warmth or aesthetic appeal, excites little interest and inspires no enthusiasm among the mass of mankind. If God is only to be approached through the cold abstractions of philosophy then we might be pardoned for holding back in dismay. Happily it is far otherwise. We have but to recall that God's unique self-revelation was made to a people whose genius found expression in practice as distinct from theorizing, in action rather than in thought. The Hebrews, unlike the Greeks, were more concerned with doing God's will than with seeking to know His inmost essence. If we except the later Wisdom literature and, in the New Testament, St John and St Paul—exceptions, however, of the highest significance—the inspired books show little evidence of "philosophy." Poetry, on the other hand, abounds. Yahwe is portrayed in imagery sometimes picturesque, sometimes otherwise, almost always anthropomorphic. Not that we need be surprised at this; for the minds of simple and primitive people respond easily to poetry. God revealed His secrets in order that they might in some measure be understood, and condescended to the mentality of those who were to receive His revelation.

Nevertheless it was clearly in accordance with His will that the inner content of that revelation should be brought to light in terms other than those in which it was first set down and its objective validity for the whole world made clear. Man could not presume to add to or improve upon, but he could at least attempt to search into, the meaning of what God had revealed. He might legitimately strive to realize its implications and demonstrate its bearing upon his everyday life. Such was to be the work of theology. It began at the opening of the Christian era, in the New Testament writings, and has continued in the Church down the centuries. To assist them in their work of explanation the fathers and theologians made use of the philosophers. At first Plato, and later Aristotle, was appealed to in the immense task of expressing in human modes of thought truths that were essentially divine. The Church, in her anxiety to penetrate more deeply into " the Faith once delivered to the saints," has never hesitated to utilize the instruments forged by a purely rational philosophy. Accordingly we should be false to the traditional Christian method, and courting failure in advance, were we to attempt a discussion of our subject without reference to the hard-won philosophical concepts in which a universal religion must necessarily express itself.

The fact that God is a spirit suggests not only that we should worship Him, but also think about Him, in spirit and in truth. Any approach towards an understanding of Him requires an intellectual as well as a moral purification. Unhappily contemporary culture and modern methods of instruction are unfavourable to concentration upon the great realities. Linguistic versatility and cultivated eclecticism, the fairest fruits of our present-day educational system, engender habits of mind little adapted to the contemplation of universal ideas. Indeed contemplation—by which, for the moment, no more is meant than thoughtfulness and reflection—is only to be achieved at a price which few can be induced to pay. The times in which we live cry out for such an effort but no other encouragement is offered. Yet if we are to approach God in thought, and such is an indispensable preliminary to our approaching Him in love, the effort must be made. To think of Him requires no intellectual technique. The philosophy of the Church is not an esoteric doctrine; it is nothing more formidable than exalted common sense and requires for its understanding only patience and mental simplicity. Indeed, experience shows that scholarship and imaginative brilliance can often be obstacles rather than aids to anything deeper than a verbal appreciation of the *philosophia perennis*. Here. as in another context, the things hidden from the wise and prudent are revealed to babes.

From out of the burning bush God spoke His name to Moses. " I am Who am."[1] The ultimate metaphysical import of that formula doubtless escaped the mind of the Hebrews. They would have held it more profitable to show honour to God than to rest content with defining His essence. The task of the chosen people, of those who kept faith with Yahwe, was to serve Him in hope and holy fear until the great day of His coming. They were not called upon to work out a theology. But the day was to come when that also would have to be undertaken. When, in the fulness of time, divine revelation had been perfected, the moment must arrive for the attempt to systematize, and thus embrace more firmly, the knowledge so acquired. And first, what of God Himself, the author of revelation? What name could best distinguish Him from the creatures He had made?

God *is* what He is. So much had been learned from the name He had given to Himself. The Greek philosophers had thought of Him as the Good, the object of all desire; or else as subsisting self-consciousness, knowledge of knowledge. While these conclusions of philosophy were by no means set aside, it was God's own witness to Himself, the notion of Him as subsisting being, which was at length to prevail as the least inadequate statement of what He is. *Ipsum esse subsistens* : in this short phrase we have perhaps the nearest approach to

[1] Exodus iii, 14.

a definition of God that man can devise. Let us attempt to see something of its significance.

From even the most casual observation of the world around us one fact stands out with self-evident clearness: the fact of change, of mutability. The passage through the heavens of the sun and stars and our own earth, the change of the seasons, the growth of crops followed by autumnal death and decay, the ebb and flow of the tides exemplify the truth on the grand scale. But nothing, however diminutive, falls outside this law. The corn in blade, a grain of dust, no less than the mountain ranges crumbling as they stand, witness to nature's radical instability. We ourselves, albeit fashioned for immortality, are subject unceasingly to mutations of place and time. Masters of the material universe, we look before and after, but we do not embrace even all that we know in a single glance, *tota simul*. Development, the march towards perfection, proclaim the absence of what we have yet to acquire. The achievement of our final destiny will truly fulfil each of our potentialities, leaving nothing further to be longed for; but such a consummation comes to us as a gift from without, it is not ours by right. We shall be enriched above measure, but never to the point of self-sufficiency.

So universal is this law of change that some philosophers have mistakenly regarded it as the ultimate reality underlying all things. But, as Aristotle long ago pointed out, change is inconceivable without a being which undergoes the change. Movement does not exist apart from something which moves. Bound up with the impermanency inherent in change and movement there must exist the static element which forms, as it were, the substratum of the evolutionary process. Thus we are led into the world of fixed essences. Each being, just in so far as it is, is itself and nothing else. An acorn may be in the way of becoming an oak tree, but, in itself, it is an acorn and no other thing. It is *actually* an acorn but *potentially* an oak tree. And so universally: things are themselves in act, though something else in potentiality—whether the potentiality in question implies the complete corruption of one form and the generation of another, as with the acorn, or a merely " accidental " change, as, for example, in local motion.

The significance of the distinction between actuality and potentiality in our present context can hardly be exaggerated. It enabled Aristotle, who was the first to see its ramifications, to establish the existence of a first unmoved mover which was itself pure actuality to the exclusion of all potentiality. Movement, change, could only be accounted for by the existence of some being which already possesses the perfection to be acquired by the transition. Otherwise there would be no means whereby what is potential could realize itself and become actual. Nothing passes from potentiality to actuality save at the instigation of what is actual.

Nor is the opposition, or, more accurately, interrelation, between these two realities, potentiality and actuality, restricted to the closed system of the material universe. The Christian doctrine of creation showed its application to the whole created order of things as it stood over against the Creator. The idea of creation *ex nihilo* does not seem to have entered into Greek philosophy. Matter existed eternally and the world, though perpetually subject to change, never had a beginning. True, the evidence of potentiality everywhere was enough to show the need of positing a first unmoved mover, pure act, or, at least, a series of first movers each supreme within its own order, to account for the actualization of beings subordinate to them. But it would appear that the first mover was not needed to give precisely *existence* to what it moved or actualized. The beings it influenced had in fact existed as long as the first mover itself.

Now it was here that the Christian thinkers took a step further. From the truth that the world had not enjoyed eternal existence a conclusion follows of immense consequence: creatures must be in potentiality to their existence. Assuredly they exist, but they do not of themselves account for that fact. That which produced them out of nothing, and continues to preserve them from falling back into their original nothingness, was not themselves. " I asked the heavens, sun, moon, stars, ' Nor (say they) are we the God whom thou seekest.' And I replied unto all the things which encompass the door of my flesh: ' Ye have told me of my God, that ye are not He; tell me something of Him,'

And they cried out with a loud voice, 'He made us'."[1]

The implications of this distinction between the essences of created things and their existence—it has been well named the fundamental truth of Christian philosophy—are so vast that we must restrict ourselves to those which bear upon our subject. If no created thing exists of itself, if existence is contingent to it, then it must owe its being to something which is self-existing, that is to the self-subsisting being, *ipsum esse subsistens*, namely, God. That which is most intimate to everything we know, the actuality by which it exists, comes to it from God. By His creative fiat He produced the world from no pre-existing material and, by His continued act of conservation, preserves it in being. We ourselves can make something (we cannot create) and set it aside with the assurance that it will be there when we wish to find it. Not so with God. For us this is possible because we do not confer existence on what we make, we merely shape some pre-existing material into a form of our own fashioning. But God works in the first place without material; and when it has been produced even He cannot give to it self-existence (which would imply the contradiction of making a created thing not to be created) but must continue to bestow existence upon it. If God is the creator He must needs look after His world on pain of it ceasing to exist. Here we have the metaphysical foundation for the reality of divine providence. This most consoling truth, that God is preoccupied with His creatures, was foreign to the thought of the ancient world. Plato and Aristotle had glimpsed something of God's dignity and truth, but little of His condescension and lovingkindness.

These considerations, despite their abstruseness, cannot be too much dwelt upon. Apart from the knowledge brought to us by any subsequent revelation, they throw significant light upon the divine nature itself. If all things owe their existence to God, if He is not only the artificer of the universe but its creator also, then each of these things must exist in Him more really, more substantially, than it exists in itself. Stripped of the imperfections inherent in creaturehood and identified with the simplicity of the divine essence,

[1] Augustine: *Confessions*, bk. 10, vi.

the world we know, all that is of substance and value in it from what is least and most trivial to what is most glorious, is present in the mind of God, transfigured and raised above itself, in its whole physical reality.

Things spiritual and intangible leave us unmoved only because we do not give them sufficient thought. In fact they are more satisfying, have greater ontological stability, than anything we can see or touch or handle. Compared with the existence they enjoy in God, the objects which delight our senses and afford us mental exultation are but shadows of their proper selves. The rose in flower, the tints of autumn leaves, a nightingale at song, sunrise in early winter, the sight of distant hills on spring mornings, all that moves us in our hearts to say that it is good to be alive are no more than faint symbols of the eternal beauty. Man's own handiwork, the products of his "creative imagination," contain no heights and depths which are not embraced by God. Shakespeare's dramatic skill, the strength and delicacy of Mozart, the painters and sculptors whose works compel our admiration, reproduce on an immeasurably lower plane the productive activity of the first among artists. Nor, though we may sometimes overlook it, should God's practical genius cause us less wonder than His creative and artistic power. The realization of God's changelessness may hide from us the precision with which He guides His creatures on their course. We marvel at the strategic ability of Alexander or Napoleon, at the capacity for rulership of some great king or pope; in scholarship, at a patient life's work of research, implying a seemingly infinite care for detail and minutiæ; at the triumphs over the intransigence of matter, space and time achieved by modern science. But what are these compared to the Wisdom which stretches from end to end mightily ordering all things sweetly, the Providence by whose solicitude the hairs of our head are numbered?

God, as we should expect, carries out His government of the world in the grand manner. He is incapable of taking petty views, of working only for immediate ends. But never should the divine magnificence blind us to God's tender regard for the particularities of His creation. Unlike His creatures, the Creator has not the defects which so often accompany good qualities. In human affairs a capacity for large views, administrative skill, having to take account of many factors at once, not seldom implies insensibility and even ruthlessness in dealing with the individual; contrariwise, due consideration for the personality of each, the endeavour to respect and legislate for the peculiar needs of every member of the community, may well involve real inefficiency and a breakdown in practical government. The limitations of human nature being what they are, this dilemma is almost unavoidable. But with God it is not so. In His Kingdom the individual has not to be sacrificed for the good of the community nor the community rendered ineffective for the benefit of the individual. Divine wisdom knows how to compass the good of the whole without detriment to the perfection of each part. No truth of Christian philosophy is better calculated to encourage than this, that providence extends to things not as classes but as individuals. God deals not with humanity but with man.

Thus the reality behind our innocent passing joys, the good humour which breaks the tedium of every-day life, the pleasures of friendship and human intercourse, these also have in Him their true reality. We speak of heaven as our homeland and no word could be more accurate. The theologians, absorbed in their abstractions, fail perhaps to show the attractiveness of God to those who cannot think theologically. And yet we have only to deduce the consequences of their own principles. How often does it occur to us that the sense of good health and physical well-being, the felicities of family life, such things as the warmth of winter firesides, the thrill of reunions after long absence, the uniqueness of love between man and woman, all have their cause in God and therefore are to be found in Him, not attenuated by their spiritual mode of being, but heightened and intensified beyond description?

And with what truth can it be said that creatures exist in God? To attempt to answer this question we should have to discuss the divine attributes in some detail. Here, however, it is impossible to do more than select the one most relevant to our purpose. Let us consider the attribute of immutability. At first sight none of God's characteristics makes less appeal than that of His changelessness. But only at first sight; on examination it proves the one best able to bring home to us some idea of the immeasurable riches of His nature. We habitually associate absence of change with stagnation and inertia. It seems to us only natural that things should change and so acquire perfections which they do not already possess. Evolution and progress have the appearance of being so bound up with life itself that we may feel loth to deny them to God who is the Author of life. We must note, however, that the sort of change we see around us implies in the thing which undergoes the change power of development, a capacity to acquire some different state of being. Assuredly a changelessness such as this, arising from an original poverty of being, or, it may be, a powerlessness to respond to the influence of some higher agent, implies imperfection. But supposing that the immutability is of an entirely different order, a changelessness due to the possession of every conceivable perfection, leaving nothing further to be acquired, then it will itself be a perfection of the highest kind.

This is the immutability we attribute to God; unlike anything in our experience, it arises from the fact that He is actually all that He can be and potentially nothing whatever. To realize what this means must bring solace to the mind grown weary of watching in a distracted world the mere sequence of events—" the moving image of eternity," as Plato called it. By nature we wish for greater stability than is compatible with the order of time. For the *nunc fluens* in which we are immersed so faintly represents the *nunc stans* of the divine changelessness. Eternity, in the great definition of Boethius, is the " simultaneously full and perfect possession of interminable life."[1] This is to be the reward of those who see the face of God.

Such reflections as these bring home to us that God must be the fulfilment of all creaturely desire. There is nothing to be wished for which is not contained in Him; which is but another way of saying that He is intrinsically lovable. Add to what has been said the truth that He is also a Person, " the

[1] Boethius, *De Consolatione*, V. 6. Cf. St Thomas Aquinas, *Summa Theologica*, Ia, q. 10, a. 1.

most perfect thing in all nature," *id quod est perfectissimum in tota natura.*[1] We know indeed from revelation that the divine nature superabounds mysteriously in a Trinity of persons; but reason alone could satisfy itself that God must, of His nature, be endowed with the perfection of personality.

Oddly enough, the ascription of personality to God has proved a stumbling-block to many minds in other respects not unsympathetic to Christianity. They regard such a notion as grossly anthropomorphic, an unfortunate inheritance bequeathed to the Church from its Hebrew ancestry. Such criticism is beside the mark. Apart from revelation, orthodoxy can defend itself on merely rational grounds. By a simple application of the law of causality it becomes evident that the perfection by which creatures can be called persons must pre-exist in God. It is true—and the theologians are the first to insist on the point—that personality exists in God in a manner which is beyond our conception.[2] But the divine transcendence cannot exclude perfections which are not of their nature creaturely. God is infinitely above any mode of being or individuality of which we have experience, *super ens et super unum*; nevertheless it is impossible to deny being and individuality to Him. He is the source and origin of all being, necessarily distinct from His creation. Supremely individual, to Him most of all must be accorded the dignity of personality. *I, the Lord; I am the first and the last.* With better right than any creature can God make use of what is at once the shortest and greatest of words: " I."

In comparison with the divine, human personality is scarcely worthy of the name. We speak, with some truth, of the " development " of personality. It is to this end that our educational efforts are directed. Mental and moral training, the distribution of book-learning, physical exercise, the provision of favourable surroundings and atmosphere—all aim, though often with but little success, at making each member of the community what in childhood he is only potentially, a responsible individual, capable of leading a life at once human

[1] Ia, q. 29, a. 3.
[2] The Church has made clear that whatever affirmations are made about God which are true also of creatures indicate, notwithstanding, a greater dissimilitude between the two realities than they do similarity: *inter creatorem et creaturam non potest tanta similitudo notari quin inter eos maior sit dissimilitudo notanda.* Conc. Lateran. IV; Denzinger, 432.

and rational and therefore patient of being supernaturalized by grace. When we speak of someone as a "personality," we mean that he possesses striking qualities which set him apart from his fellows. He is unique, not from oddness or eccentricity, but by reason of distinctive intellectual and moral endowments. It is in virtue of these that one man is better than another; in proportion to the depths of our awareness and our capacity for love are we more alive, more responsible, more truly men. Education, it need hardly be said, does not bestow such gifts; it brings to light and enhances what already lies latent. We are born persons, but, being creatures, achieve our full stature only with the passage of time.

Transferred to God the notion of personality is indescribably rich. Development here is out of the question. He is all that He can be. Vitality, understanding, generosity, magnanimity, those characteristics we associate with the highest type of personality, are there in an infinite degree. In the light of the Incarnation the significance for mankind of this truth is heightened beyond measure. Space and the selected method of treatment forbid more than an indication of what might form the subject of a volume. The unique fact about Christ Our Lord is that He is God. All that He did and continues to do through His Church and by the instrumentality of the sacraments takes its value from His Godhead. Of the grace and redemption that pour out upon the world the sacred humanity of Christ is truly the instrument (*instrumentum conjunctum*), but it is the divinity that is the origin and cause. *Deum de Deo, lumen de lumine, Deum verum de Deo vero.* These words of the Creed proclaim the ancestral faith of Christians. To reject them means the rejection of Christianity.

All then that can be said of God can be said of the Person of Jesus Christ. In His humanity He was subject to limitations but not in His Godhead. The hypostatic union, the unity which is so close as to permit of only one personality, and that divine, while excluding any confusion between the two natures, is the richest and most consoling mystery of our faith. As man, Our Lord was born at Bethlehem in Juda and, for some thirty years, was encompassed by the restrictions of space and time; as God, He enjoyed an eternal existence and, throughout the years of His earthly life, was master of the universe He had created. His humanity was so perfect that He can truly be described as the most human of the sons of men, and yet the unique reality which made Him a person was not human but divine. By this fact the " first born among many brethren"[1] possesses a dignity which raises Him infinitely above them all. In the counsels of eternal Wisdom it had been decreed that, unlike the rest of mankind, this Humanity should not have a human personality; this Human Nature was to be endowed with the personality of the Godhead. Justifiably then, during His days on earth, could Christ use the word " I "—the index of personality—as no man would dare to use it. " *I* am the resurrection and the life "[2]; " *I* am the way, and the truth and the life "[3]; " For this was *I* born, for this came *I* into the world, that *I* should give testimony to the truth."[4]

To approach Christ in all the attractiveness of His humanity is at the same time to draw near to the God Who " inhabiteth light inaccessible."[5] Though devotion may dwell, human-wise, upon the mysteries which reveal His manhood, we should never forget that it is strictly unorthodox to consider Our Lord's human nature apart from the Godhead with which it is inseparably united. We must pass " by the wounds of His humanity so as to reach the intimacy of the divinity."[6] The same truth is taught us by the Preface for the Mass of Christmas: " so that while we acknowledge Him as God seen by men, we may be drawn by Him to the love of things unseen." It is in this connection that St Thomas makes the following observation: " Matters concerning the Godhead are, in themselves, the strongest incentives to love and consequently to devotion, because God is supremely lovable. Yet such is the weakness of the human mind that it needs a guiding hand, not only to the knowledge,

[1] Romans viii, 29.
[2] John xi, 25.
[3] John xiv, 6.
[4] John xviii, 37.
[5] 1 Timothy vi, 16.
[6] St Albert the Great, *De Adhaerendo Deo*, c. 2. (N.B.—The ascription of this work to St Albert is in fact disputed by some scholars. The truth of an observation, however, is not affected by its authorship.)

but also to the love of divine things by means of certain sensible objects known to us. Chief among these is the humanity of Christ . . . Wherefore matters relating to Christ's humanity are the chief incentive to devotion, leading us thither as a guiding hand, although devotion itself has for its principal object matters concerning the Godhead."[1]

It is now time to summarize these reflections. To begin with we noticed that the ineffability of God does not preclude a knowledge of Him which is true within its limits though inadequate. God is subsistent being. The formula: " I am Who am ", in which this truth is expressed, though itself revealed by God, is recognized by reason alone to do Him least injustice. It expresses in ultimate terms, better than the imagery of the poets, better even than the rhapsodies of the mystics, God's infinite ontological richness. The things we know and feel to be desirable exist in Him with a higher reality, a greater desirability, than in their own mode of being. From this there follows the immense lovableness of God. And we must add also that He has the dignity of being a Person; He is not a vague amorphous entity, a " spirit of the universe," but vitally, uniquely, a Person—or rather, a Trinity of Persons identical in their nature. And finally, the divine Personality has been manifested to the world through the Incarnation; not that thereby God might become more lovable, for that were impossible, but in order to draw us to Himself in a way that should make any rejection of Him inexcusable. We should need no threats or moral exhortations to lead us to love God. We have only to realize what He is.

[1] IIa IIae, q. 82, a. 3, ad 2.

II

THE ONE WHO LOVES

"What is man that Thou art mindful of him? Or the son of man that Thou visitest him? Thou hast made him a little less than the angels: Thou hast crowned him with glory and honour, and hast set him over the works of Thy hands. Thou hast subjected all things under his feet...."—*Psalm viii*, 5-8.

"O GOD," exclaims St Augustine in a memorable phrase, "Who art loved knowingly or unknowingly by everything capable of loving."[1] There is indeed a sense in which all things can be said to love God. As we have seen, everything depends on Him for its existence, and this law of dependence permeates the universe. From this viewpoint the whole of nature is to be conceived as loving God, stretching out its hands towards the Creator in silent acknowledgement of His act of creation. Man also, being a part of the cosmos, tends towards God in this way. In this chapter, however, we shall attempt to state certain truths about man's nature which throw light upon a capacity for a love-union with God which belongs to him alone.

In the first place it is well to insist on human dignity. It is an error to suppose that we glorify God by belittling His creation. Not a few of the expressions of the masters of spirituality, and even of the saints, if taken too literally, could lead us astray in this respect. The essence of the virtue of humility lies not in self-depreciation but in a practical realization of our complete dependence on God. "... What hast thou that thou hast not received? And if thou hast received, why dost thou glory as if thou hadst not received?"[2] asks St Paul. Truly. But we are not thereby justified in denying the worth of what we have in fact received. "Acknowledge, O Christian, thy dignity," writes the great St Leo, "and, being made sharer in the divine nature, do not fall back into thy former degeneracy."[3] But even the lowly state from which we have been uplifted denotes a weakness in action, in our capacity to know what is

---

[1] Augustine, *Soliloquia*, I, i, 2.   [2] 1 Corinthians iv, 7.
[3] S. Leo Papa, *Sermo I de Navitate Domini*.

true and do what is good, rather than essential corruption. Grace does not destroy but perfects nature and the supernatural life is built upon a natural structure that is fundamentally sound.

"What a piece of work is a man! how noble in reason! how infinite in faculty! in form and moving how express and admirable! in action how like an angel! in apprehension how like a god! the beauty of the world! the paragon of animals!" So Shakespeare, through the mouth of Hamlet, expressing no doubt the mood of the Renaissance, proclaims man's confidence in his own worth. It is permissible to think that St Thomas himself, notwithstanding his acknowledgement of original sin and the fall, would have had but little qualification to make of this eulogy of man.

The conception of human nature preserved by the Christian philosophical tradition can be stated quite simply: man is a rational animal. He is a being sharing with the animals many of their activities: he is born by the processes of physical generation and dies from physical decay; he enjoys a life of the senses and imagination; the need for food, susceptibility to heat and cold, the effects of environment and heredity, of changes of time and place—in all these he is subject to much the same laws as the animal world. He is nevertheless outside that world by reason of a vital unifying principle which places him nearer to the angels than to the brute creation. He possesses a spiritual soul. Or, to be more exact, he *is* a spiritual soul informing and giving substance to a material body. His body is not an animal body indwelt by an alien substance which we call the soul; it is a human body, designed by nature to be united to, and vivified by, a principle of undying life. We speak commonly of the body possessing the soul, of the soul being within the body, but a more accurate description is the reverse of this: the soul is the rightful master of the body, the body is within the soul—not indeed spatially, but in virtue of its relation to it as instrument.

The last point should not, however, be pressed too far. Man is a complete unity and his body must not be imagined as being a mere means for the soul's self-perfection. Such a view of the body's function has appealed to many noble minds but has been rejected by the central tradition of Christian thought. The Incarnation and the doctrine of the resurrection have made it clear that the body is to share the soul's immortal destiny. Neither can achieve its due perfection apart from its union with the other. Such apparent conflict as may exist between these two principles, the warfare of flesh against spirit, cannot be ascribed to their mutual incompatibility. It is due, as we shall have occasion to remind ourselves on a later page, to human nature's fall from grace. The original harmony has been disturbed, though by no means irreparably, as a result of Adam's sin.

The importance of this classical conception of man's nature—a union of body and spirit, the second element dominating and giving significance to the first—cannot be overstressed. It is not in favour with the materialism of our day and is tacitly ignored by much that goes by the name of psychology. With disastrous results. Human problems are no longer discussed by the standards of ultimate truth, in relation to an indestructible reality known as human nature, but in terms of an empiricism which, notwithstanding its pragmatic successes, has no claim to be called a science, still less a philosophy. Once the effort to understand the inner nature of man, and his activities as determined by that nature, is abandoned there is no limit to the aberrations which can follow.

All data—not excluding human nature—of which we have knowledge through our senses can be considered in two ways: formally and materially, from the point of view of their formal and material causes. Both these causes must be understood if the data in question are to be explained; but, of the two, the first is of incomparably greater importance. It is the formal cause which makes a particular thing to be what it essentially is, but not without the material cause does it receive individual characteristics and accidental modifications. To apply this to man: As will have been gathered from the foregoing remarks, his formal cause is the spiritual soul, the principle of rationality which makes him to be just precisely a man and distinguishes him from the whole order of animals; the body and all that is not spiritual within him play the rôle of the material cause, manifesting his individuality and, incidentally, exhibiting many of the phenomena which he shares with the lower animals. These two causes coalesce to form human nature in the individual and give it its status in the order of creation, above the animal world and a little lower than the angels.

A moment's reflection will make clear that any study of man's nature which concentrates on one of these aspects to the prejudice or complete exclusion of the other will lead to conclusions that are false and one-sided. To over-emphasize the formal element, our essential spirituality, is the more pardonable error and indicates a deeper insight, but it is an error nevertheless. Plato himself might be indicted on this charge and Plotinus certainly. Excessive idealism, which looks for the realization of an absolute order of things regardless of the complexities of time and place and circumstances, is one of the commonest fruits of this mistake. In Christian times the habit of certain ascetical writers of legislating for man as if he were a disembodied spirit exemplifies the same tendency. Not least among the services rendered to the Church by St Thomas was his correction of all this. By reinstating Aristotle and Christianizing his teaching on prudence he was able to lay down moral principles which could harmonize the most uncompromising pursuit of perfection with the conditions of life as we know it.

It is, however, the opposite error to the one just indicated which dominates our modern ways of thought. Anthropology and biological studies in general, divorced from natural philosophy and metaphysics, have led to an almost complete materialization in the popular mind of the conception of human nature. Nor do the efforts of some among the modern physicists to effect an apparent "spiritualization" of matter point towards a restoration of man to his due place. Whatever be the end to which we are moving, they tell us, there can be no doubt about whence we have come; we have been evolved from the lower animals. In consequence we are a part of the material creation, by nature subject to the laws which govern matter. The existence of a spiritual principle within us may be conceded as a possibility, but little account is made of it. We have the evident tangible fact of our kinship with the other animals; let us be content to draw our conclusions from that.

Be it noted that we are not concerned to deny that man's body may have evolved from a species of irrational animal—the possibility is recognized by some of the Church fathers and theologians—nor that much light has been thrown on human behaviour by modern psycho-analysis and experimental psychology. What is here deplored is the appeal to an empiricism of this kind for an answer to the ultimate questions about our nature and activities. To do so is not only to be profoundly unphilosophical but to flout common-sense. The last word on any human problem rests with the philosopher—not to say the theologian—rather than the psychologist. We shall learn immeasurably more about ourselves, our needs and aspirations, from the pages of Aristotle's Ethics than from the writings of Sigmund Freud.

We may illustrate this point by the most obvious example. Instead of the human sex-instinct receiving its explanation with reference to the natural impulse for union with something other than self, and ultimately with a Being who can satiate every desire, exactly the opposite has taken place; man's natural worship of truth, goodness and beauty, the longing for the vision of God rooted in his heart, is regarded as a manifestation of the " pan-sexualism " which motivates all his actions. This is precisely that materialization of man's essential activity, by nature spiritual, to which we have alluded. By the same method worship, sacrifice, self-abasement before God, penance after wrong-doing—all impulses fundamentally rational—are reduced to the categories of sadism and masochism. Disinterestedness, generosity and the pursuit of noble ideals, since they can only be explained by the very spiritual principle which is left out of account, are dismissed as the sublimation of activities which are basically animal.

Let it be repeated that we have no wish to disparage the labours of the psycho-analysts. The more reputable among them acknowledge the limitations of their province. Moreover practical good sense is a fairly adequate safeguard against the aberrations of the extremists. Unfortunately the press and modern methods of propaganda have given to these researches a publicity out of all proportion to their value. As a result, what is at best a branch of the science of medicine is in danger of attaining to the status of a philosophy. It is to guard against any notion of this kind that we have ventured upon these remarks which might otherwise appear out of place.

Having cleared the ground a little, we may now go on to elaborate our concept of man as a rational animal. This is not the place to state the proofs for the spirituality and consequent immortality of the soul; it must suffice to point to certain of its operations which can only be explained by the existence of powers which transcend the limitations of matter. Chief among these is the power of reflection; we not only know the external world, but we know that we know it. In other words the intellect, the soul's principal faculty, is able to double back on itself, to watch itself watching something else. This is an activity of which material things are incapable; they can turn back part against part but they cannot be detached spectators of their own acts: brushes don't brush themselves, knives don't cut themselves, still less can they be aware of their own brushing and cutting.

Knowledge itself is something so mysterious that no philosopher has succeeded completely in explaining it. Even sense-knowledge is, within limits, immaterial and intellectual knowledge entirely so. How does the black lettering which your eyes are reading at this moment enter the sphere of your sense-consciousness? What is the medium of transition between the printed page and the organ of sight? Nor is it merely a case of the words impinging on the retina of the eye as on a mirror; that would not account for your vital awareness of the words as significant facts. More wonderful still, by what insight do you discern in these words, themselves no more than printer's ink patterned on paper, the train of thought here being expressed? With what power are we endowed that we can read so much meaning in so little matter? These and kindred questions are an abiding fascination to the reflective mind. In the attempt to answer them the great thinkers have been led to investigate the nature of knowledge. They have discovered that it consists essentially in a union between the subject knowing and the object known. With us this union takes place on the parallel planes of senses and intelligence; by the senses we make superficial contact with the things which surround us, by the intelligence we realize their significance and know them for what they are. So unanimous is the Graeco-Christian tradition in pointing to the intellect as the instrument of what is at once our noblest and most characteristic activity that the desire of all men for knowledge has come to be regarded as axiomatic.

To seek for explanation, truth, and finally for the vision of the First Cause wherein is contained all truth and explanation, is natural to man. That this is denied, in theory, by some, and in practice, it would seem, by very many, is due to some such one-sided view of human activity as has been touched on above or else to an incomplete analysis of the facts. We shall return to this second point on a later page.

Corresponding to the intelligence and the organs of sense-knowledge there exist the will, that is, the reason's desire, and the sensitive appetite. By these we love the things that are good for us, seek for them when absent, enjoy them when present. Through knowledge, apprehension, we draw external things to ourselves and make them our own. *Anima est quodammodo omnia*, the soul is in a manner all things; by the light of intelligence it is in potential possession of the whole universe. Love and desire, on the other hand, lead us to the objects as they are in themselves. By love we take leave of ourselves, as it were, and make our abode with the beloved object. Where knowledge stands detached and aloof, love goes out to seek and find. With knowledge we begin the journey, only by love do we reach the end.

By these two activities, knowing and loving, and by the faculties from which they proceed, our lives are ruled from start to finish. Everything we do as men is a function of one or both. This is no less true of our least worthy than of our noblest pursuits. Selfishness and sinful conduct in general, though often due to the usurpation of reason by sensuality, can still be analysed in terms of knowledge and desire. The profligate, intent on sense-gratification and the pleasures of the hour, is still, pathetically enough, the seeker after knowledge and the lover. The knowledge in this case is no more than animal experience and the love a preoccupation with self, but they are still evidence of the guiding principles of all our life.

Our domination by these forces can be seen clearly enough in the sphere of the arts and the sciences, but it is no less real in our seemingly insignificant every-day occupations. Commerce and industry are demonstrably governed by the desire for money and power. The millions who toil on at the dehumanizing and apparently futile tasks to which so many are condemned, unable to give any account of the reason for their labours, at least give expression to the will to live; they work in the knowledge that if they cease working they will starve. But the point is obvious and need not be laboured. It must be constantly borne in mind, however, in the light of what is to follow. We shall see that every human action, of no matter how little consequence, has a part to play in the expression of our love for God. That this is so is due to the fact that the intelligence and will are directly supernaturalized by grace: in this condition, by virtue of that natural supremacy on which we have been insisting, they can confer a supernatural character on all the activities which proceed from them, that is, on every individual act we perform. We shall attempt to develop these thoughts in a later chapter.

For the moment we must turn our attention to the will. The will is essentially a tendency towards goodness; not to goodness of a particular sort but to goodness in general—*bonum in universali*, as the philosophers call it. The things which present themselves to the intellect to be apprehended by it in terms of truth, being so apprehended, offer themselves in turn as desirable to the will under the aspect of goodness. The mind is not, in fact, completely adjusted to its object until both these faculties are engaged, until knowledge has issued forth in love. As the intelligence remains in potency, and therefore unsatisfied, until it attains to the vision of all truth, so can the will experience no satiety until it embraces the totality of goodness, that is to say, God. In this inexhaustible capacity of intellect and will we have the secret of the will's freedom—a freedom, be it noted, which has its roots in the intelligence. By the intelligence we are carried into the universal order of things, liberated from the bondage of particularities and given insight into the general scheme. It is in virtue of this insight that our wills can remain undetermined and consequently free in any concrete situation.

The practical importance of this interrelation between intellect and will is often overlooked. The stress which is laid by moralists on the will in its imperative function (*quoad exercitium*) at the expense of its fundamental nature as rational desire (*quoad specificationem*) may well account for this. In this connection we may note in passing how the Kantian " categorical imperative "—duty for duty's sake regardless of all desire—has cut across the stream of Christian ethical teaching and muddied its waters. It is sometimes forgotten that a free act is no exception to the law of causality. In many minds caprice, eccentricity, motiveless diversity are taken to be the characteristics of freewill while the root of the matter is ignored. Free action, since it is rational, is invariably motivated. Freedom lies precisely in the control of motive; we *choose* the motive to which we shall respond. Confusion can arise from the multiplicity of meanings attaching to the English word " will "; the Latin phrase *liberum arbitrium*, free choice, is much more exact. We judge the situation, set the stage, as it were, for our actions, select the reasons for our conduct. We are masters in our own house and nothing within or without can supplant us from our rightful place. Only the sight of the supreme good, the vision of God, can prove for us irresistibly attractive. Confronted by anything less, the will of its nature retains its indetermination and detachment.

It will be obvious that in practice this ideal state of things is seldom to be found. The necessary insight and awareness, without which we are but partially free, are by no means always at our command in the moment of need. We act by instinct and on impulse when we should pause to deliberate. Prejudices arising from heredity, upbringing, environment cloud our judgment and prevent us from seeing things as they are. By affection, interest, lack of mental tranquillity we are impeded from making that impartial choice which is the essence of liberty. These defects, it will be observed, belong to the intelligence rather than the will; but they cut at the roots of freedom. What is called weakness of will is often no more than an incapacity to isolate and focus the mind upon the motives which should guide our actions, a deficiency as much intellectual as volitional.

Moreover there is another and more radical obstacle to true freedom, in a large measure the cause of those just mentioned. As children of Adam we have fallen from grace, we are no longer in our original state. The worst effect of original sin has been to deprive us of a supernatural inheritance, a life of union with God given to us by grace entirely above the exigencies of our nature. But this spoliation of gifts to which we had no title has brought with it a wounding in nature itself. The happy state of subordination of our lower instincts to reason, of matter to spirit, enjoyed by our first parents was in its turn the result of the complete subjection of the mind to God. This harmony of the mind with the divine order of things was the effect not of nature but of grace. With its loss there followed as a consequence the partial destruction of that balance and poise in our natural faculties which depended on it.

The tragedy of man's loss of grace is not to be described in words. Calvary is its most fitting commentary. It is possible, however, to exaggerate the evil effects wrought by original sin upon our purely natural faculties. The Church has always resisted excessive pessimism in this matter; even the writings of St Augustine, wherever they depreciate man's natural capacity for good, have been accepted only with qualifications. The reasons for this are worth considering. They have been summed up in the dictum of St Thomas that any disparagement of the natural perfection of the creature reflects by implication on the divine power; *detrahere . . . perfectioni creaturarum est detrahere perfectioni divinae virtutis.*[1] It is true that grace (*gratia sanans*) heals the wounds of nature, but this, in a sense, is its incidental effect; its essential function is to endow us with supernatural life and raise us (*gratia elevans*) to a participation in the divine nature.[2] This was the truth ignored by Luther and later by the Jansenists. To suppose that human nature demands the life of grace as a complement to its own intrinsic deficiencies

[1] *Contra Gentiles*, lib. iii, c. 69.   [2] 2 Peter i, 4.

is to lower what is supernatural to the natural level and misconceive the meaning of the good news brought to us by Christ. On such a view the Incarnation becomes no more than an act of justice and the Redemption a payment of a debt. The fall of man, instead of being recognized as an evil permitted by God that He might draw therefrom a greater good, the *felix culpa* of the Easter liturgy, becomes a meaningless and inexplicable frus ration of the divine plan.

In reality the life and death of Jesus are tokens not of God's justice but of His friendship and lovingkindness. Even the attribute of divine mercy, with its faint suggestion of patronage and aloofness, is withheld from our eyes in order that we may perceive more clearly what it means to be beloved of God. Equality is the keynote of the Incarnation; for by it we are no longer, or not only, the King's servants, we are also His friends. To this we shall return; it is mentioned here by way of emphasizing the gratuitousness of grace. Without a realization of this we can understand neither the significance of the supernatural life nor the innate potentialities of the human nature which that life elevates and perfects.

A word must now be said about man's activities viewed in their moral aspect. This is in fact the ultimate point of view, the final court of appeal. By the moral goodness or badness of our actions do we have status as men, by them shall we be judged in eternity if not also in time. As we shall attempt to show later, religion and the love of God are above the plane of the moral virtues—it is better to have charity than to be merely prudent—but, far from excluding them, they derive from those virtues almost all their constancy and operative force. It is notorious that religion can make an emotional and intellectual appeal while leaving the moral character practically untouched. A liturgical revival, for example, is not necessarily a sign of a renewal of religious spirit nor an interest in Catholic philosophy a proof of the divine predilection; even a taste for " mysticism " and the refinements of spirituality is compatible with lapses from obvious duty which are curiously unimpressive. Only when we have laid firm hold of the infused virtues of prudence, justice, fortitude and temperance may we safely set our course for the stars. Charity, as well as faith, must die without good works. And good works are themselves the issue of moral character.

Morality, it is useful to recall, is a quality of every human act. Unfortunately the word has come in many contexts to be associated exclusively with a particular department of moral conduct, that of sex; with unhappy results. It is often assumed that once a tolerable standard of sexual purity has been attained nothing further is to be hoped for. There are occasions when one might be pardoned for supposing that all the resources of religion have been placed at our disposal for no other purpose than to provide an armoury against this sort of temptation. Nor does the treatment of the matter in some of the modern manuals of moral theology do much to dispel this impression. Experience no doubt justifies the authors' preoccupation with the subject, but it is surely desirable that the practice were more widespread of treating sexual immorality as an infringement of the virtue of temperance. It is so handled by St Thomas, who thus gives it its rightful place in the exhaustive outline of Christian ethics which forms the second part of the *Summa Theologica*. In this way we are allowed to view a restricted field of moral activity in its due perspective.

No one would wish to minimize the importance of the questions which arise in this connection. From concupiscence and the struggle against it no man is granted immunity and it would be foolish to treat the matter lightly. We shall consider in a succeeding chapter how directly it impedes the soul's union with God. Of our threefold adversary, the world, the devil and the flesh, it is the last which scores the greatest number of victories. But it is possible to live in too great fear of even our most redoubtable enemy and thereby give him an unnecessary advantage; by doing so in the present case we weaken our powers of resistance and are in danger of becoming victims of a quite erroneous conception of our relations with God.

Freedom from habitual sins of intemperance is an indispensable condition of leading the truly Christian life; but it is a condition and not its end and object. The end, to be achieved in some measure at least even in this world, is a union with God in knowledge and love by comparison with which the closest of earthly unions is but a shadow and a symbol. This is the fundamental truth of Christian morality; it should be the light of all our seeing. The shedding of vices and acquirement of virtues, the more or less painful processes of asceticism which are part of the law of life, take on a new meaning when seen from this angle. They are no more than the tests of the lover in search of his beloved, the trials of the wayfarer on his journey home. The strife and stress of our present existence are not to be avoided on the plea that we are citizens of another world, but they must be viewed in relation to that world: *sub specie aeternitatis*, with an eye to eternity. Grace surrounds our actions with an eternal weight of glory, but it never substitutes itself for them. Even though we be raised to a participation in the divine life we have as yet no security of tenure. The vision by which each man lives, the love in his heart, and the deeds which reveal both are the surest sign-posts of the way in which he is travelling. Our every-day actions are the instruments by which we fashion for ourselves an immortal destiny and climb to the summit of the everlasting hills.

There are three elements in each of our conscious acts which combine to make them morally good or evil. First, the object with which the act has to do, taken in its moral, as distinct from its merely physical, context—e.g. walking, considered not simply as a case of local motion but as the rational activity of a responsible agent. Secondly, the circumstances in which the act is performed, again, in their moral aspect—not whether the day be wet or fine, but with reference to our obligations to ourselves and others at the time in question. And finally, the end or final object which motivates the act. If these three—object, circumstances and end—are together approved by the judgment of reason and conscience then the act is morally good, if any one fails to pass this scrutiny the act is morally bad. The circumstances, provided they do not change the whole nature of the act, affect it only in an incidental way; an action whose end or object is evil does not lose its evil character though done under the happiest conditions. Nor does an otherwise good act become essentially bad owing to the unfavourable circumstances in which it is performed: a work of charity is still charity even when marred by tactlessness. The circumstances, however, play an integral part in moral conduct, enhancing or derogating from its worth. In practice they often affect more than they should our judgments on the value of men's behaviour. Social conventions, the way in which things are done, not seldom appear more important than the activities themselves. But it would be wrong to react too strongly against this attitude; the graces and adornments of life are the pleasant instruments on which charity can play. Where they are lacking charity may be forced to stand idle and grow cold.

The thing which is actually being done and the motive or end for which it is done are of the essence of morality. Here there are no qualifications to be made. No good action can retain its good qualities if done directly for an evil end; it is vitiated throughout. Similarly the noblest of motives is powerless to ennoble an action not of itself good. The end can justify indifferent means but never those that are evil. This last point must always prove a stumbling-block to those who take only a pragmatic view of morality and refuse to examine its immutable foundations. Even the children of light have sometimes failed to realize its consequences. And yet the position, when rightly understood, is irrefutable. The reason why a good end cannot legitimate the evil means which appear necessary for its attainment is because, morally speaking, the two are unrelated. An intrinsically evil act can never produce directly a good effect. The emergence of good results from apparently unworthy antecedents is due to the operation of forces which are strictly proportioned to their effects but hidden from view under accompanying, though incidental, evils. Normally the attempt to excuse wrong actions on the grounds that they subserve a good end can be ascribed to mental confusion or malice. The relation which is imagined to exist between ends and means does not in fact exist at all or has been arbitrarily imposed by the mind. The realities of the case have been ignored and the situation falsified. Thus there can be no relation of means to ends between the bombing and wholesale destruction of innocent people and the maintenance in being of the Catholic Church, between tyrannical forms of government and the happiness and good estate of the community at large, between aggressive nationalism and the general peace of the world.

All this has its bearing on the field of individual conduct. A right intention, which means having a good end or motive, is not sufficient grounds for action. We must be sure that our actions here and now are of a sort which bring that intention into effect. Granted that the end has been settled, we are not now at liberty to choose any means to achieve it; the means to be chosen are in large measure dictated by the nature of the end. It is idle to talk of having good motives, of meaning well, when what we are doing bears no essential relation to the object proposed. To behave thus is, at worst, sinful, at best, a waste of energy. Nor can we be content with proposing to ourselves some such ultimate motive as the will of God or His greater glory. While never losing sight of that end which should give point to all we do, we are bound in conscience to pay heed to those ends which are immediate and transient. By attending to these we approach our final objective and cause what as yet is only an intention to become an accomplished fact. God's will in our regard is shown us for the most part by our circumstances and state of life. Entirely submissive to the divine good pleasure, we must work out our salvation within a limited range of activities. Among these we have to discern the subordination of means to ends and conform our conduct to it with complete fidelity.

The foregoing remarks in no way lessen the importance of good will and right intentions. With these we can be saved even when we fail in perception. To have a rightly ordered will is for man the most vital of all necessities. The love of God, in the last analysis, is no more than good will towards Him. Emphasis has been laid on awareness and insight, partly because their place in moral activity is often unduly neglected, partly because they condition good will. It is possible to exaggerate the importance of intelligence in our relations with God, but it is also possible to under-estimate it. The intellect is man's highest faculty; failure to appreciate its bearing on our conduct must rule out any real understanding of human nature. St Paul, who had little patience with mere worldly wisdom, gave no countenance to a zeal for God which was not " according to knowledge."[1] The surest safeguard of good will and rightness of intention is a well-instructed conscience. To have this we need the virtue of prudence, the *recta ratio agibilium*, insight into what is to be done here and now. Without prudence we are incapable of self-government and at the mercy of extrinsic rules of conduct; the unenlightened legalism of the " probable opinion " becomes a substitute for personal responsibility. We shall examine the virtue of prudence at close quarters on a later page; for the moment, however, it should be noted that, although it is essentially an intellectual virtue, it depends for its functioning upon good will. Without this latter quality a man can be a competent artist or mathematician—that is, good as regards a specified field of action—but he cannot be prudent, that is to say, good precisely as a man. Prudence, unlike the other intellectual virtues, presupposes the rectitude of the appetite; since it is directed to practice, it requires the fixity of the will on its due end and a corresponding ordination of the lower appetitive powers. In other words, prudence assumes the possession of the other moral virtues, justice, fortitude and temperance; it unites them and gives them the light by which they act. Through prudence our conduct has significance, not merely within a limited sphere of activity, but with reference to life taken as a whole and in view of its ultimate end: *prudentia est bene consiliativa de his quae pertinent ad totam vitam hominis et ad ultimum finem vitae humanae.*[2]

The general background against which each of our actions must fall into place is the natural law. St Thomas's conception of the natural law is inspiring and profound. It is the rational creature's participation of the eternal law as existing in the divine mind: *lex naturalis nihil aliud est quam participatio legis aeternae in rationali creatura.*[3] Quoting the verse of the fourth psalm, " Who sheweth us good things? " he takes it in its moral implication, as asking the question: from whom shall we learn to do good deeds? The psalm itself gives the answer, " The light of Thy countenance, O Lord, is signed upon us." The light of natural reason by which we discern,

[1] See Romans x, 2.   [2] Ia IIae, q. 57, a. 4, ad 3.   [3] ibid., q. 91, a. 2.

as it were by native instinct, what is good and evil is nothing less than an impress of the divine light upon our minds: *nihil aliud sit quam impressio divini luminis in nobis.* Thus we are illuminated, in the measure corresponding to the needs of our nature, by the eternal law in the light of which God governs the universe. The first precepts of morality—good must be done, evil avoided—innate within us are reflections on a lower plane of the principles to which the activities of God Himself must conform in virtue of His being Eternal Truth. The dictate of conscience is in a very real sense the voice of God; it is a more certain guide in the moment of action than any reliance on the detached processes of the speculative reason or the subtleties of moral casuistry. Through it those eternal sanctions, which are the laws of our life, present themselves to consciousness and we know experimentally whether what we do is right or wrong.

From what has just been said it will be evident that the natural law is not a code of conduct arbitrarily imposed upon us from without. Since it formulates the principles by which we as persons attain to full stature it is obvious that it can be in no way opposed to nature. As each element of the universe reaches its due perfection through conformity to the laws of its own development so likewise do we by compliance with this law immanent in our being. The ten commandments, for example, which are but particular determinations of the natural law, are not intended as an irksome discipline for the endurance of which we receive a prize. They are means proportioned to the end, direct contributions to the enlargement of human personality.

But it is time to bring these general reflections to a close. We find that man is a composite creature of body and spirit, limited in all manner of ways as regards the body but with spiritual potentialities which are boundless. His characteristic activities are knowledge and love; these must always be operative or he ceases to act humanly. By knowledge in the intelligence and love in the will the whole of his conduct is ruled. Through knowledge his actions are begun and directed on their course, from the will they receive their unity and driving force. Good will alone, which is another name for love, gives final significance to all he does. Fixed upon a timeless and unchanging object, which the philosophers call the *summum bonum,* and the more enlightened God, the will endows the passing events which engage its attention with something of the permanence and stability of what it clings to. But these events are not of a kind to prove all-absorbing. The will, the source of every desire, can never desert its first love, which draws it in secret before consciousness wakens it to lesser though inevitable claims. By a seeming paradox the best assurance of our own good will is to have at least some faint awareness of the divine discontent, the heart's ill-ease at finding nothing that can satisfy a longing for it knows not what. " I will rise and go about the city. In the streets and broad ways I will seek him whom my soul loveth. I sought him and I found him not."[1]

[1] *Canticle* III, 2.

III

THE LOVE ITSELF

"In this is charity: not as though we had loved God, but because He hath first loved us, and sent His Son to be a propitiation for our sins."—*1 John, iv. 10.*

LOVE, the most fascinating of themes, is the most difficult of all to discuss in rational terms. This may be accounted for by its essentially volitional character. Words can be a marvellously subtle and harmonious instrument of thought, they are well adapted to expressing intellectual concepts, but they tend to lose their exact significance when used as the vehicle of strong emotion. The language of lovers and mystics is metaphorical; they seek modes of self-expression from the poets rather than the philosophers. By such means they transmit to others, in some measure, their experiences, but not always a clear understanding of the causes which produced them. Notwithstanding this difficulty, the nature of love has been submitted to philosophical analysis with no little success. We shall now attempt, in the light of the Christian revelation, to place some of the principles and conclusions which have emerged in the context of our relations with God.

GOD'S LOVE FOR US

It is scriptural and philosophically justifiable to think of God's dealings with mankind, whether collectively or individually, as those of a bridegroom with his bride. Our Lord, when on earth, was pleased to suggest such a relationship Himself and the idea has become a part of Catholic tradition. One has but to recall the influence of Solomon's Song of Songs on the language of spirituality for confirmation of this. The saints have seen something inherently fitting in illustrating God's presence in the hearts of those who love Him by comparisons drawn from the closest of earthly unions. Nor do the metaphors used exaggerate the reality they signify: they fail by deficiency rather than excess. Language is, in fact, too crude an instrument to convey the intensity and depth of the soul's absorption in God while at the same time avoiding any suggestion of pantheism, that is, of ontological identity between the creature and the Creator.

The preliminaries of the great marriage between heaven and earth belong, as might be expected, to God alone. It is the part of the bridegroom to make the first advances. The thing began with a gesture of liberality to which the generosity of a human lover can offer no parallel. *Ipse solus est maxime liberalis.*[1] God freely created the object of His love. This truth is so significant that we must dwell upon it. The marvel here, be it noted, is not precisely the fact that of all the objects God might have created His choice has fallen on the order of beings, including ourselves (though this should excite our unceasing gratitude), we know to exist. The wonder consists in the act of creation itself. To create, as we have already insisted, is an operation to which God alone is equal. Although it involves no effort on His part it nevertheless engages completely His omnipotence.

Creation means the production of something without any pre-existing material. It is not a change or modification of what is already present but the conferring of existence where there was none before. If the reader be tempted to think that the idea of creation is self-evident and easy to grasp, let him reflect that it escaped the notice of the greatest minds of antiquity and has been analysed only by the Christian philosophers in the light of the truth that God created the world in time. The divine act of creation points to a conclusion highly significant in our present context. The fiat by which it is put into effect is an act of God's will motivated by nothing but His own generosity. We have already seen something of the importance of the will in the activity of love; to say that the will tends towards an object is another way of saying that it loves it. The creative act is the initial movement of divine love.

The reason why there is often so little response to these ideas—themselves of stupendous significance—is because of the difficulty of making real to ourselves, even within the limits possible, the distinctive character of the divine operations. Through an incorrigible anthropomorphism, we tend to think of creation as a form of making, of God's love as a

[1] 1a, q. 44, a. 4, ad 1.

movement towards an object desirable apart from His own act of will, and so fail to grasp what distinguishes His activities from our own. Reflection may be left to clarify the meaning of creation; of the characteristics of God's love for creatures something more must be said.

Amor Dei est infundens et creans bonitatem in rebus:[1] the love of God infuses and creates the goodness which is present in things. In these words St Thomas states the principle underlying God's love for the creatures which owe Him their existence. His love is active and creative; in this it is distinguished from our love for Him and for our fellows. When we love it is because we discern something lovable in the beloved object which evokes a movement of desire in our wills. With God this is not so; He rather imparts desirable qualities to things and this is precisely His love for them. Our love is in its essence passive, a response, a movement, an emotion elicited from without; hence its ecstatic quality; it implies self-forgetfulness, a seeking after, a melting into the being of what is loved. In God there can be nothing passive; He cannot be stirred by a goodness lower than Himself and submit, as it were, to its attractions. Whatever is attractive in the universe does not draw forth God's love but is rather its effect. It is not because God has found us lovable that He loves us; it is because He has loved us that we are lovable in His sight.

From this it is easy to see the gratuitous and selfless quality of God's love as well as its strength and intensity. He has nothing to gain by loving the works of His hands; He does so from sheer benevolence. We, for our part, do gain beyond telling by loving Him and by our worthy human loves. Apart from the mutual services which friends render each other, friendship itself—above all, friendship with God— breaks down the barriers and limitations of individual selfhood and gives us a share in the lives of others. But God, containing all life within Himself, acquires no new experience by loving us; He cannot share in what is His already. Thus He is the lover Who alone is supremely free, yet choosing His loves by the counsels of eternal wisdom. Paradoxically enough the infinite freedom and disinterestedness of the

[1] Ia, q. 20, a. 2.

divine love implies not a less but an immeasurably higher degree of intensity in regard to its object than can be known by creatures. Compared with the constancy of God all human fidelity is fluctuating and unstable. Once He has chosen His love He is incapable of desertion. The love of God permeates its object to its inmost depths, creating and diffusing within it all the goodness it possesses. "For our God is a consuming fire."[1]

In the supernatural order, that of grace, God can be said to withdraw from the creature, following upon the latter's rejection of Him by sin, but in the natural order, that of simple existence, He continues to love every element of good there present. Were He to withhold His love from us for an instant we should cease to exist. In the last analysis, it is by His creative love that He drew us out of our original nothingness, and by that continued act of love He preserves us from falling back into the state from whence we came.

At this point the thought may well suggest itself: Why, if God acquires nothing by His creative act that is not already His, did He create anything at all? Put in this form the question is extremely difficult, if not impossible, to answer. The universe is not a necessary consequence of God being what He is; it came into being by a free choice of His will. Now the reason for those things which depend solely upon God's will and are not presupposed by His justice cannot be known to us except by revelation.[2] More properly then the query might be put thus: granted the divine wisdom and accepting the existence of the world as we find it (postulates whose truth can hardly be questioned), what is the end for which it has been created? To this question the reply of Christian tradition has been unanimous. God made the heavens and the earth to show forth His own truth and goodness and beauty. "The Lord hath made all things for Himself."[3] Not from divine egoism, but by a self-communication of boundless generosity, He manifests Himself in all that He has made. "The heavens show forth the glory of

---

[1] Hebrews xii, 29.
[2] Ea enim quae ex sola Dei voluntate proveniunt supra omne debitum creaturae, nobis innotescere non possunt nisi quatenus in Sacra Scriptura traduntur, per quam divina voluntas nobis innotescit.—IIIa, q. 1, art. 3.
[3] Proverbs xvi, 4.

God."[1] Egoism is vicious in a creature because it is a glorification of self at God's expense, a direction of activity towards a subordinate, in place of the ultimate, end. Applied to God the word has no meaning; here self and the supreme good which is the final end of all things are identified. It would be tantamount to a mortal sin in God to have made the world for any other object than as subserving the absolute goodness which He is.

It is the nature of what is good to communicate itself to others. *Bonum est diffusivum sui.* This is not merely a conclusion of philosophy but a fact of experience. Good-natured people are selfless, they give themselves to their fellows. Generosity, expansiveness, a power to enter into the thoughts and feelings of the people around them, are the qualities of those we think of as good men. An absence of such qualities or their replacement by self-centredness, insensibility, incapacity for friendship and sympathy with others, are recognized defects of character. Little reflection is needed to perceive that this principle, whereby what is good tends naturally towards self-diffusion, has its perfect verification in God. So struck have certain philosophers been by this fact that they have deduced from it the false conclusion that God was obliged in virtue of His own nature to create the world. This view has been resisted as false by the Christian thinkers on the grounds that it leads logically to pantheism and virtually denies to God the perfection of freedom. The divine nature itself, involving as it does the generation of the Person of the Son from the Father and the spiration of the Holy Spirit from both, exemplifies the truth on a scale which is infinite. The inner life of the Blessed Trinity—the complete self-giving to the Son of His own nature by the Father and their united act of self-giving which is the Holy Spirit—is the first model and exemplar cause of any of the created modes of self-communication. But if God was not bound of necessity to create there is an unquestionable aptness and suitability (*convenientia*) in His having done so. When an artist is possessed of abounding riches and measureless power it is fitting that at times he should use them.

[1] Psalm xviii, 1.

The foregoing remarks should have prepared us for another consideration. The perfect manifestation of God's love for man is contained in the Incarnation of the Second Person of the Blessed Trinity. "For God so loved the world as to give His only begotten Son: that whosoever believeth in Him may not perish, but may have life everlasting."[1] The mystery of divine love is here so immense that it can scarcely be stated in words. Indeed, four centuries were to elapse before the Church was able finally to formulate in rational terms the belief that had been handed down from the beginning. There is doubtless little profit to be gained from considering the life and death of Christ Our Lord in isolation from His personality but it is well to remind ourselves that everything He did derives its significance from what He was. "What think you of Christ: whose son is he?"[2] That is the most momentous of all questions; if we cannot answer it correctly it is of small avail to know the material facts of His human history. The incomparable graciousness of His earthly life, the redemption wrought on Calvary, the foundation of the Church, the gift of the sacraments and all they imply, the participation of His own life bestowed on us through grace are so many harmonious consequences of the fact that He was God. But their dependence on that truth is absolute; apart from it they have no meaning. The Incarnation is God's final message to mankind; it is a message whose complete significance will not be realized until the end of time, but essentially there is nothing more to add. "God, Who at sundry times and in divers manners spoke in times past to the Fathers by the prophets, last of all in these days hath spoken to us by His Son, Whom He hath appointed heir of all things. . ."[3]

God's self-communication in the mystery of the Incarnation is of a kind so perfect that nothing more complete can be conceived. In essence it is the giving of the undiminished Godhead; it is not a gift which can be distinguished from the giver, for the giver is Himself His own gift. The noblest acts of human selflessness imply only a limited self-giving. The lover can communicate his own vital spirit to another, he can even sacrifice himself to the point of laying down his

[1] John iii, 16.   [2] Matthew xxii, 42.   [3] Hebrews i, 1-2.

life for his beloved; but he cannot give his own living personality and still continue to exist as an individual. And yet this is precisely what God does. God, in the person of the Son, gives Himself to humanity, as represented by a single individual, in a mode of union to the closeness of which there exists no parallel whatever. Human nature, whose separate existence apart from a human personality giving it subsistence might have been thought inconceivable, here receives its subsistence, the ultimate perfection which renders it incommunicably itself, from a divine Personality. This was the extent of God's giving of Himself to mankind, that upon the human nature of Christ—that nature which He shares with us—should be bestowed the personality of the Godhead. " For in Him dwelleth all the fulness of the Godhead corporeally."[1] Small wonder that St Paul could elsewhere speak of this all but incredible thing in terms which have been mistaken as implying a change within the Godhead equivalent to self-destruction. " For He, though He was by nature God, yet did not set great store on his equality with God: rather, He emptied Himself by taking the nature of a slave and becoming like unto men."[2]

We began these reflections by suggesting that the most apt illustration of the part played by God in regard to mankind is that of the lover and bridegroom. Little insight is needed for us to understand that the Incarnation is the consummation of the union between God and the human race. Centuries before He had pledged Himself to His own by the mouth of Jeremiah: "Yea, I have loved thee with an everlasting love: therefore pityingly have I drawn thee. And I will build thee again, and thou shalt be built, O virgin of Israel."[3] The " bands of love " wherewith He was to draw His chosen one gave place in a later time to the appearance of the Lover Himself. God could approach no nearer to His people than He has done in the Person of Jesus Christ. Looking back on this mystery of divine condescension the great minds of Christendom have never ceased to wonder at it. Perhaps the most moving passage in St Augustine's *Confessions* occurs in the seventh book where he acknowledges having learned

---
[1] Colossians ii, 9. [2] Philippians ii, 6-7 (Westminster Version).
[3] Jeremiah xxxi, 3-4.

from the Platonists the doctrine of the "Word" of God, only to discover that it stopped short of the life-giving truth: ". . . But that that word was made flesh and dwelt among us, I read not there." St Thomas, for all his characteristic restraint of language, speaks of the fact that the Word was made flesh as the "miracle of miracles," *miraculum miraculorum.* "The Incarnation of the Word is the miracle of miracles, as the saints say, because it is greater than all miracles, and to this miracle all the others are ordered: and on this account it not only leads to belief in the others, but these others lead to belief in the Incarnation itself."[1]

OUR NATURAL DESIRE FOR GOD

Having seen how God initiates the intimate love-relationship with ourselves we may now turn to what is the main object of this chapter, namely, to examine the nature of our response in terms of love for Him. We must begin by indicating a distinction of the highest importance. The love of God can be of two kinds: the first, natural, the tendency by which the will goes out in desire towards God in so far as He is known as the Creator and author of nature; the second, supernatural, the love of God as He is known by revelation in His intimate nature. This second and higher form of love can only be possessed by the soul when it is raised by grace to a participation in the divine life; it is, in a word, charity. The existence of a quite natural love of God distinct from charity has been maintained by the Church to the point of an explicit condemnation of the opposite view.[2] Moreover this twofold love is clearly taught by St Thomas. To quote but one text: "Charity loves God above all things more eminently than nature: for nature loves God above all things as He is the beginning and end of natural good, but charity in so far as He is the object of beatitude, and as man has a certain spiritual fellowship with God. . . ."[3]

In this book we are only directly concerned with the love of God which is charity, but in order to grasp the nature of charity it is necessary to say something about the natural love which it intensifies and perfects. Superficially, the dis-

[1] *De Potentia,* q. 6, art. 2, ad 9. [2] Denzinger 1034.
[3] Ia IIae, q. 109, a. 3, ad 1.

tinction here insisted upon might appear no more than a gratuitous piece of theological hair-splitting. On examination, however, it proves but another instance of the Church's care to safeguard human dignity. Grace perfects and does not destroy nature; correspondingly, charity gives new content and richness to our natural power of loving God.

St Thomas maintains in this connection what may appear at first sight an astonishing doctrine; he teaches that we tend by nature to love God more than we love ourselves. He does not deny that this natural tendency fails in practical effectiveness owing to the weakness we inherit from original sin,[1] but the tendency itself is as fundamental and indestructible as nature. What is meant is not, of course, a love of God consciously recognized, but the natural movement of the will towards some object capable of satiating all its desires which, in fact, is God. In practice the individual may misinterpret the longings of his own heart or protest his unawareness of any need for union with an all-sufficient Being. He would nevertheless be compelled to admit that what he wishes for is a state of unending happiness. The things from which he hopes to derive contentment are so many participations of the divine goodness; in every created good that is desired the supreme good is desired still more: *in omni bono summum bonum desideratur.*[2] Like St Augustine he seeks for the God Who " is loved knowingly or unknowingly by everything capable of loving."[3]

This natural love of God has as its root our dependence on Him as our last end and source of ultimate happiness. But for this, St Thomas does not hesitate to say, there would be no reason for our loving Him. " . . . For it would not be in anyone's nature to love God but for the fact that each thing depends upon the good which is God."[4] Succinctly the whole doctrine is summarized: " Because therefore the universal good is God Himself, and beneath this good are comprised also the angel, man and every creature (because every creature in regard of its entire being naturally belongs to God), it follows that from natural love angel and man alike love God before themselves and with a greater love. Other-

---

[1] See Ia IIae, q. 109, a. 3.   [2] II *Sent.*, distinction 1, q. 11, a. 2, resd.
[3] Augustine *Soliloquia*, I, i, 2.   [4] Ia, q. 60, a. 5, ad 2.

wise, if either of them loved self more than God, it would follow that natural love would be perverse and that it would not be perfected but destroyed by charity."[1]

Man's natural desire for God has received its classical expression in Plato's *Symposium*. The following passage from the famous speech of Socrates at Agathon's party shows us the Platonic dialectic of love:

For he who has been brought thus far in the school of love, gazing on beautiful things in due succession, shall draw near at length to the end of that loving art and shall suddenly behold a beauty marvellous of nature, that very same, Socrates, for whose sake were all the toils before. For it always is, and neither comes to be nor ceases to be, neither waxes nor wanes; also it is not in part beautiful, in part unbeautiful, or now beautiful, now not; nor beautiful as towards this, unbeautiful as towards that, nor beautiful here, unbeautiful there. Nor shall he see this beauty in the likeness of face or hands or anything besides wherein body has a portion; nor as any discourse or any knowledge. Nor has it its being in place and in any other thing, whether creature or earth or sky or whatsoever else; but it is of itself, with itself, of one simple form always. And of this are all other beautiful things partakers, in such fashion that though they come to be or cease to be, it becomes not greater nor less nor changes at all. When therefore a man, holding the right course of . . . love, climbs above beauties here and begins to see the beauty there, then indeed he is near his goal. For thus may he rightly go or rightly be led towards the things of love; beginning from beauties here, he must climb always upward, from rung to rung, for the sake of that beauty—from one to two, from two to all beautiful bodies, and from beautiful bodies to beautiful practices, and from those practices to beautiful studies, and from those studies at length to that study which is of that beauty itself and nothing besides; so that he may know at last beauty in essence. Dear Socrates (said the woman of Mantinea) in that reach of life above all others may a man live as a man should, contemplating beauty itself. If once you have sight of this, you will not compare it to gold and garments and the beautiful boys and youths whose sight so enchants you now that you and many another, in sight and continual presence of your darlings, are ready, if that might be, neither to eat nor drink, but only to gaze and still be there. But tell me, what if a man might see beauty

[1] Ia, q. 60, a. 5.

itself, whole, pure and unalloyed, unclogged by human flesh and colour and all such mortal trumpery? What if he might look on the divine simple essential beauty? Would it be a paltry life, think you, to live with one's gaze on that, contemplating that with the proper faculty, communing with that? You must consider (she said) that there alone will it be possible for a man, seeing the beautiful by the faculty whereby it is to be seen, to beget not shadows of virtue, for it is no shadow that he clasps, but true virtue, for he clasps truth. And when he has begotten true virtue and fostered it, then he becomes dear to God. If any man is immortal, this is the man.[1]

It will hardly be questioned that the love here described is the highest flight of desire of which man is capable. Nevertheless it would seem to be strictly within the limits of his natural faculties. It has arisen from the rational consideration of the transient nature of all earthly beauty. The mind, viewing the individual objects of sense-knowledge, has caught a glimpse of their inherent instability and powerlessness to give satisfaction. At length, having freed himself by a process of asceticism from the trammels of sense and imagination, the lover is rewarded by a vision of essential Beauty. This elevated conception of man's relations with the supreme Being proved irresistibly attractive to many of the earlier ecclesiastical writers. Plato was hailed as a Christian before his time, and, when this thesis became difficult to sustain, the alternative was suggested that he had taken his ideas from Moses without acknowledgment. St Augustine, whose Platonism was derived from Neoplatonic rather than original sources, apparently accepted the underlying principles with all but unqualified enthusiasm.

The position, however, was not without its difficulties. The existence of this love no one wished to deny, but what, ontologically considered, was its object? Could it be God Himself? If this were so then it would follow that man was naturally capable of His love of friendship. With such a conclusion what was left of the essentially supernatural character of the Christian virtue of charity? Indeed the unique element in Christianity was imperilled: if we could know and love God by our own powers without being raised to a super-

[1] *Symposium* 210E-212A. I owe this rendering to the kindness of Mr Walter Shewring.

natural life of grace then the Incarnation and Redemption became superfluous. The Church's solution to these difficulties has already been pointed out; it lies in the recognition of a twofold love, the one natural, whereby the soul loves God by its unaided powers, the other supernatural, implying an intensity of love completely beyond the reach of our natural capacities. Yet it has to be admitted that, even within the pale of orthodoxy, opinions have differed as to how this position can best be explained. In what follows we shall confine ourselves to the traditional Thomist teaching on the point as having, in the view of the present writer, the unique advantage of adequately safeguarding both the dignity of divine charity and the reality of the natural love of God which it perfects.

Before setting forth one or two representative texts it may help towards clarity to state in as few words as possible the generally accepted Thomist position with reference to man's natural desire for God. The matter can be put thus: *Man desires naturally, with a desire not innate but elicited, conditional and inefficacious, to see the essence of God as the author of nature.*[1] By saying that this desire is elicited, as distinct from innate, it is meant that it proceeds from a knowledge of the effects of the first cause and is not antecedent to such knowledge. To say that it is conditional implies that it could be expressed in some such hypothetical judgment as : " I desire to possess the vision of God if that were possible, and if He should will to raise me to this vision which surpasses the capacities of unaided nature." As a consequence of its being conditional this desire is inefficacious; that is to say, its object is beyond the reach of our purely natural powers. It would be outside the scope of these remarks to attempt a detailed proof of the carefully qualified statement just given; but, in the light of what has already been said, the thoughtful reader will have little difficulty in seeing its main bearing. To one point, however, attention may be drawn: the fact that the natural desire for God proceeds from the knowledge of the effects of

[1] Garrigou-Lagrange, *De Revelatione*, vol. I, p. 395. So also John of St Thomas, Gonet, Salmanticenses, Billuart and, with some modification, Suarez. See the commentaries of these authors on the *Summa*, Ia, q. 12, a. 1, and in the tractatus " De Gratia " : *utrum status naturae purae fuerit possibilis.* Cf. *The Desire of God in the Philosophy of St Thomas Aquinas* by Dr James O'Mahony, O.S.F.C.; an important and suggestive work.

the first cause and is not innate or infused. We shall examine later some further aspects of the relationship between knowledge and love, but it must be sufficiently obvious at this stage that desire in the will is in vital dependence on the knowledge acquired through the intelligence. We cannot wish for what we do not know.

At the opening of the second part of the *Summa Theologica*, discussing the nature of happiness, St Thomas proposes the question : " Whether man's happiness consists in the vision of the divine essence ? " His reply is as follows:

Final and perfect happiness can consist in nothing else than the vision of the divine essence. To make this clear two points must be observed. First, that man is not perfectly happy so long as something remains for him to desire and seek; secondly, that the perfection of any power is determined by the nature of its object. Now the object of the intellect is *what a thing is*, i.e., the essence of a thing, according to *De Anima* iii, 6. Wherefore the intellect attains perfection in so far as it knows the essence of a thing. If therefore an intellect should know the essence of some effect, whereby it is not possible to know the essence of the cause, *i.e.*, to know the cause *what it is*, that intellect cannot be said to reach the cause simply, although it may be able to gather from the effect the knowledge that the cause is. Consequently when man knows an effect and knows that it has a cause, there naturally remains in him the desire to know about that cause, *what it is*. And this desire is one of wonder, and causes inquiry, as is stated in the beginning of the *Metaphysics* (i, 2). For instance, if a man, knowing the eclipse of the sun, consider that it must be due to some cause, and know not what that cause is, he wonders about it, and from wondering proceeds to inquire. Nor does this inquiry cease until he arrive at a knowledge of the essence of the cause.

If therefore the human intellect, knowing the essence of some created effect, knows no more of God than *that He is*; the perfection of the intellect does not yet reach simply the first cause, but there remains in it the natural desire to seek the cause. Wherefore it is not yet perfectly happy. Consequently for perfect happiness the intellect needs to reach the very essence of the first cause. And thus it will have its perfection through union with God as with that object in which alone man's happiness consists. . . .[1]

[1] Ia IIae, q. 3, a. 8.

The scope of this argument should be noted with care. The greatest Christian theologian here reproduces, admittedly in a form aesthetically less attractive, the essentials of the Platonic dialectic of love; but with a difference. Combining Aristotle's analytical genius with the sweeping vision of Plato, he sacrifices nothing of the latter's elevation of thought while avoiding the ambiguity of his conclusion. He does not lead the mind to an intuition of the first cause but to a recognition of an insatiable desire for it. Furthermore the remarks made here about the object of the intellect must be understood in the context of St Thomas's general doctrine on the functioning of that faculty. The proper object of the human intellect is the essences of material things; these are what it is directly proportioned to know. True, since it is by nature spiritual, the intellect can move in the realm of the universals, of being *qua tale*, unrestricted by its material modes—which fact is the foundation of the possibility of our knowing God at all. Nevertheless, in this life, it can never completely transcend its relationship with matter; always it must tend to interpret its knowledge (even to itself) in terms of the senses. Thus this desire to know the divine essence is subject to a sort of polarity; the mind tends upwards to something beyond its reach, to God, while at the same time it must necessarily seek the realization of this tendency in an experience which is natural to it, namely, such as arises from sense-knowledge.

This apparent cleavage between what is desired and what may be achieved can be understood from a still more fundamental viewpoint. An intellectual creature, whether man or angel, is finite, and, in consequence, even its highest faculties must be limited in the range of their activities. The divine essence, on the other hand, being infinite, can form the natural object of knowledge and love only of God Himself. It is inconceivable that a created intelligence should be naturally capable of the direct vision of the divine essence. Lacking an inherent capacity for such intercourse, the creature cannot be said positively to desire it. But notwithstanding these qualifications, the fact that even the created mind is able to know *being as such*, and therefore, within its limits, all beings—is "in a manner all things," in

Aristotle's phrase—does not exclude the possibility that God, Who is Being *par excellence*, could, if He so willed, endow His creatures with powers whereby they would be made capable of participating in that life of knowledge and love proper to God Himself. This possibility, or, more accurately, this non-impossibility, is called by the theologians the " obediential potentiality " to the reception of divine grace.

As the point has been disputed, even by those who claim acquaintance with his teaching, it is worth while making clear that St Thomas himself is at pains not to confuse the natural desire for God with the desire for the Beatific Vision, of which supernatural grace is a condition *sine qua non*. Indeed, as has been pointed out, it was precisely his capacity to demarcate the boundaries between nature and grace, to give its due value to each without in any way confusing them, which is his greatest contribution to the well-being of the Church. To quote only three texts: " Now everlasting life is a good exceeding the proportion of created nature; since it exceeds its knowledge and desire, according to 1 Corinthians ii, 9: " Eye hath not seen, nor ear heard, neither hath it entered into the heart of man."[1] No less clearly, "The end towards which created things are directed by God is twofold; one which exceeds the proportion and faculty of created nature; and this end is life eternal, that consists in seeing God, which is above the nature of every creature, as shown above. The other end, however, is proportionate to created nature, to which end a created being can attain according to the power of its nature."[2] More explicitly still: " To see God in His essence, wherein the ultimate beatitude of the rational creature consists, is beyond the nature of every created intellect. Consequently no rational creature can have the movement of the will directed towards such beatitude, except it be moved thereto by a supernatural agent; and this is what we call the help of grace."[3]

What man desires naturally is not the vision of God in the intimate life of the three Persons of the Blessed Trinity, as known by revelation, but an understanding of Him sufficient to account for His created effects; that is, the knowledge of

---
[1] Ia IIae, q. 114, a. 2.   [2] Ia, q. 23, a. 1.   [3] Ia, q. 62, a. 2.

God as the author of nature. Unquestionably the Triune God is Himself the author of nature, but we could not appreciate this identity apart from what has been revealed to us. Nature, since it is finite, is not an effect proportionate to the infinity of God. Unlike all human artists, He produces no effect, save the act of conferring existence—itself not a phenomenon we can observe but rather a deduction from data—which is strictly proportioned to His powers. God, so to say, threw off this world as He might have done a million others quite different from it, and none of them revealing anything of that intercommunion between Father, Son and Holy Spirit which is the heart of the Beatific Vision. From the spectacle of nature we can raise our minds, and even our hearts, to what Pascal has called " the God of the philosophers and the learned," but not to the God of Abraham, Isaac and Jacob, Who became man in order to make it possible for us to love Him.

So uncertain, subjectively considered, is the object of the will's natural tendency to its Creator that St Thomas is content to describe it vaguely as the *bonum commune* or *ultimus finis in communi*. " There exists in man an appetite for his final end *in communi*, namely, by which he desires to be completed in goodness. But in what this completion consists, whether in the practice of virtue, or in knowledge, or in pleasure, or the like, is not determined for him by nature."[1]

OUR SUPERNATURAL LOVE OF GOD: DIVINE CHARITY

We are now in a position to discuss with better understanding the supernatural love of God which is charity. Charity includes all that is implied by the natural love of God and immeasurably more. Though perfecting the desire of the will to reach the Author of its being, it is not to be understood as a fulfilment of the will's tendency in its own line, as the eye might be strengthened by a telescope to see beyond its normal range. This would result only in an accidental modification of what would remain an essentially natural love of God. Rather it is an elevation of the will to a manner of loving for which it has, from a natural viewpoint,

[1] *De Veritate*, q. 22, a. 7.

no capacity at all. Just as the essence of the soul is adorned with sanctifying grace so that it participates in the divine nature, in parallel fashion, the will is divinized to enable it to love God and creatures, no longer merely naturally, but in the way in which God Himself loves. Charity is something quite literally divine. It is a sharing by the creature in the mutual love of the Father and the Son. Through charity we show towards God the intimate affection wherewith He loves Himself. That we might be admitted to such a union was the burden of Christ's prayer to His Father on the night before He died. " And I have made known Thy name to them, and will make it known; that the love wherewith Thou hast loved me may be in them, and I in them."[1]

The boldness with which St Thomas applies the Aristotelian psychology of friendship to our relations with God[2] would be disconcerting were it not based on the gospel text itself. " I will not now call you servants . . . But I have called you friends. . ."[3] We are the friends of the Bridegroom. And what is this love of friendship? It is not simply desire; friendship cannot be based on the mere satisfaction of appetite. It is more even than the divine good will, though that is presupposed. This good will must be mutual, for there can never be friendship where affection exists on one side only. Again this good will must be based on some kind of community of life and interest. It is the part of friends, as Aristotle remarks, ." to spend their days together delighting in each other."[4] God admits man to His friendship by granting him a share in His own happiness. " Since therefore there is a communication between man and God, inasmuch as He communicates His happiness to us, some kind of friendship must needs be based on this same communication, of which it is written (1 Corinthians i, 9): ' God is faithful: by Whom you are called into the fellowship of His Son.' The love which is based on this communication is charity:

---

[1] John xvii, 26.
[2] The interest here is heightened by the fact that Aristotle himself explicitly denies the possibility of friendship between man and God on the grounds that the distance which separates them is too great. *Ethica Nicomachea* VIII, 7; 1159a 5. So immense is the change wrought by the Incarnation!
[3] John xv, 15.
[4] *Ethica* VIII, 6; 1158a 9.

whence it is clear that charity is a certain friendship between man and God."¹

By reason of the union of friendship which it effects charity holds first place among the virtues. Although the intellect is in itself a higher faculty than the will, in which charity inheres, there is a difference in their way of operating which accounts for the superiority of charity over every intellectual virtue, not excluding supernatural faith. The intellect draws its object to itself and gives it its own mode of being, but the will tends towards the object as it exists outside the mind. From this it follows that the things which are below us in dignity—e.g., the whole material universe—enjoy a nobler existence in the intellect than in their own mode of being; hence it is better to know them than to love them. But with reference to the things which are above it, the mind perfects itself more by moving towards them through the will than by apprehending them intellectually. Accordingly " the love of those things which are above us, and especially of God, is to be preferred to the knowledge of them; wherefore charity is more excellent than faith."² It is true that hope also is a virtue of the will and is a form of love of God; it differs, however, from charity in that it is a love of something not yet possessed and implies rather a striving after its object than the joy of being united to it. In heaven faith will be transformed into vision and hope into possession but charity yields place to nothing, for it is already perfect. " And now there remain faith, hope and charity, these three: but the greatest of these is charity."³

St Thomas's conception of charity, sublime though it be, makes it clear that this supernatural love of God is a personal possession and not merely a divine activity working through us as its instrument. In this he discerned the mind of the Church better than many of his contemporaries. He resisted strongly the view that charity was no more than the direct operation of the Holy Spirit to which the soul passively submitted. He held, what is now Catholic teaching, that it is a virtue or habit of the soul by which we ourselves, and not God through us, make acts of an essentially supernatural love. Thus the vitalism of charity is preserved. Charity is

---
¹ IIa IIae, q. 23, a. 1.   ² ibid., a. 6, ad 1.   ³ 1 Corinthians xiii, 13.

as intimate to the soul as the soul is to the body. Dependent as we are upon God for His gifts both of nature and grace, once we have received them, the latter permeate our life as deeply as the former. In fact, more deeply; for nature is subordinate to grace.

This surely is the secret of the passionate love for God of the saints and mystics. Their charity was not something extrinsic to themselves, an attitude, but a reality which stirred them to their inmost depths. The concentration of mind and heart on the beloved object, the dedication of the whole personality, which characterize those who are accounted the great lovers of history have in the saints been transferred to the one Being worthy of so complete a self-immolation. It has been pointed out that there is tragedy inherent in merely human love. Setting aside the miseries arising from disordered sensuality, the lover's idealization of the person of the beloved and the complete absorption of each in the other, to the disregard of every mundane interest, are incompatible with the realities of the world in which their lives are cast. The situation must resolve itself into death or disillusionment. The poets and writers of romantic fiction commonly prefer the former alternative; in practice it is the latter which more generally prevails. Human love, the noblest of natural emotions, can be marvellously sanctified by charity, on condition that it resists the temptation to which it is most of all susceptible—that of idolatry. The heart which can only find satisfaction in the vision of the eternal Trinity and the sacred humanity of Christ must go out to its lesser loves conscious of their limitations. We shall return to these thoughts in the pages which follow.

Without the infused virtue of charity it is impossible to possess any of the virtues in their complete form. The individual virtues, such as justice, fortitude, temperance, are complete when they are ordered to our final end. A man may, for example, be just within a limited sphere of reference, but he cannot have that disposition to render to each his due (which is justice) in relation to the whole field of human activities unless his will adheres to the end to which, in the last resort, they are all directed. As a man is, says Aristotle, so does his end appear to him to be; by so much do our personal habits and subjective dispositions tend to govern our moral conduct. And the reverse is equally true: accordingly as we view the end—practically, not merely in theory; behave towards it, not just think about it—so shall we act and so, consequently, shall we build up our moral personality. Now we can adhere to the end of human life only by charity. We may be quite clear, speculatively, about the ultimate purpose of existence; we may accept by faith the whole Christian revelation; but unless our wills are in contact with our final end we are like ships without a rudder, unable to give effective direction to anything we do. The only way to heaven, wrote Newman, is the desire for heaven. We can only reach our end by having our wills fixed upon it, that is, by desiring it, and, once our wills are so fixed, the rest of our actions fall of themselves into their own place.

Charity then should regulate the whole of human conduct. But here a difficulty suggests itself: Charity is a virtue of the will ; our actions, on the other hand, since we are rational beings, must be guided by reason. Only after receiving such guidance is the will justified in acting. It might seem that by abandoning ourselves wholly to the rule of charity we are in danger of being led into dark places. To this difficulty St Thomas replies as follows: " According to the philosopher (*De Anima, iii*), the will also is in the reason: wherefore charity is not excluded from the reason through being in the will. Yet charity is regulated, not by the reason, as human virtues are, but by God's wisdom, and transcends the rule of human reason, according to Eph. iii, 19: ' The charity of Christ which surpasseth all knowledge.' Hence it is not in the reason, either as its subject, as prudence is, or as its rule, as justice and temperance are, but only by a certain kinship of the will to the reason."[1]

Following St Paul, St Thomas rejects human reasoning as a sufficient guide for good action and invokes a wisdom that is divine. Even when equipped with the theological virtues, the reason is unable to repel all the obstacles—ignorance, stupidity, insensibility—which prevent us from acting as we should.[2] We need in addition the gifts of the Holy Spirit. Through these we are led by the *instinctus Spiritus Sancti*, a

[1] IIa IIae, q. 24, a. 1, ad 2.   [2] See Ia IIae, q. 68, a. 2.

kind of supernatural instinct, to carry out the obligations of charity in accordance with a rule which it is beyond reason's competence to lay down. Wisdom, first among the gifts, is the light of charity. Infused into the intelligence, it endows it with an insight which the processes of rational deliberation and prudence could never achieve. It judges of what is to be done, not by the principles of moral or even theological science, but by a certain kinship or affinity with those things about which the decision is to be made. It has vision, intuition, since it reflects the light of the Holy Spirit from which it proceeds. Through wisdom the soul is in sympathy with God. "Thus Dionysius says (Div. Nom. ii) that 'Hierotheus is perfect in divine things, for he not only learns, but is patient of, divine things, *patiens divina*.' Now this sympathy or connaturality for divine things is the result of charity, which unites us to God, according to 1 Corinthians vi, 17: 'He who is joined to the Lord is one spirit.' Consequently the wisdom which is a gift has its cause in the will, which cause is charity, but it has its essence in the intellect, whose act is to judge aright."[1]

This mystical, quasi-experimental quality which the gift of wisdom gives to charity should never be lost sight of. It explains much that might be otherwise obscure in the lives of the saints. The ruthless asceticism and seeming contempt for nature, which are a source of so great embarrassment to the humanist, are dictated by surer instincts than the promptings of reason. Our Lord's triumphant protestation to His Father before He went out to die: "... the world hath not known Thee; but I have known Thee ...,"[2] which has been re-echoed down the centuries by His followers each in his own measure, must hold its secret in the assurance which charity brings through wisdom.

Charity increases, not in virtue of the number of things to which it extends, but in intensity towards its object and in its domination of the soul. The Christian is a wayfarer who journeys along St Paul's "more excellent way." He must progress unceasingly; but progress here takes on its ultimate meaning, that of drawing ever nearer to God. To Him we approach, "not by the steps of the body but by the affections

[1] IIa IIae, q 45, a. 2.   [2] John xvii, 25.

of the soul," *cui non appropinquatur passibus corporis sed affectibus mentis*.[1] Charity can even attain a certain perfection in this life: where the point is reached when we can say with St Paul that we " desire to be dissolved and be with Christ."[2] This is the third and final stage, at which the soul arrives after having passed through the two which precede—the first, that of " beginners," who are chiefly concerned with avoiding sin and resisting concupiscence, and the second, that of " proficients," whose main pursuit is to aim at progress in virtue. The characteristic activity of those who have been admitted to the third and last degree of charity is simply union with and enjoyment of God.

St Thomas's discussion of this point is of great interest as he states in precise terms both the maximum degree of the love of God attainable in this life and the minimum without which, by implication, the soul is in a state of mortal sin. Having dismissed the possibility of our loving God as much as He is worthy of being loved, he continues:

> On the part of the person who loves, charity is perfect when he loves as much as he can. This happens in three ways. First, so that man's whole heart is always actually borne towards God: this is the perfection of charity of heaven, and is not possible in this life, wherein, by reason of human infirmity, it is impossible to think always actually of God and to be moved by love towards Him. Secondly, so that a man devote his attention to giving his time to God and the things of God, while leaving aside all other things except in so far as the needs of the present life demand. This is the perfection of charity which is possible in this life; but it is not common to all who have charity. Thirdly, so that a man give his whole heart to God habitually, viz., by neither thinking nor desiring anything contrary to the love of God; and this perfection is common to all who have charity.[3]

The primary object of charity is God Himself. As a consequence of this first friendship and love of God there comes into being a new relationship with His creatures. They are loved not merely in themselves but in Him. The significance of this will be better understood in the light of what is to be said about that peculiar kind of knowledge on which charity depends, namely, faith; but the main point

---

[1] IIa IIae, q. 24, a. 4.   [2] Philippians i, 23.   [3] IIa IIae, q. 24, a. 8.

is scarcely in need of emphasis. Our love of God must embrace also His creatures according to the dignity they possess in His eyes. Through charity our wills go out to them, not directly as rational beings with creaturely limitations, but as companions and friends beloved of God as we are. They are the brethren for whom Christ died.

St Thomas expresses this thought in coldly metaphysical terms but his meaning is unmistakable. St Francis of Assisi, discerning in every man his divine Master, for all his lyrical enthusiasm, is no more realistic in his conception of charity. St Thomas will not allow that there is any difference in the *kind* of acts by which respectively we love God and our neighbour. An act of charity towards the latter is not, as it were, a new impulse of good will, but an application to a creature of the original movement of the will towards God. Or, to employ his own comparison, as by the same glance we perceive the light of the sun and the coloured object it illuminates, so do we include our neighbour in the act of the love of God.

As stated above habits are not differentiated except their acts be of different species. For every act of the one species belongs to the same habit. Now since the species of an act is derived from its object, considered under its formal aspect, it follows of necessity that it is specifically the same act that tends to an aspect of the object and that tends to the object under that aspect: thus it is specifically the same visual act whereby we see the light and whereby we see the colour under the aspect of light.

Now the aspect, *ratio*, under which our neighbour is to be loved is God, since what we ought to love in our neighbour is that he may be in God. Hence it is clear that it is specifically the same act whereby we love God and whereby we love our neighbour. Consequently the habit of charity extends not only to the love of God, but also to the love of our neighbour.[1]

This conception of charity, evangelical and traditional, raises it far above the level of the philanthropy and humanitarianism with which the virtue is often confused. The rise of humanism and naturalism, following upon the religious apostasy of the sixteenth century, was accompanied inevit-

[1] IIa IIae, q. 25, a. 1.

ably by a substitution of natural for supernatural values. Ironically enough the increased attention given in modern times to man's material well-being has not brought with it a heightened appreciation of human dignity. Social reforms, based upon a noble instinct for justice, have proved powerless to safeguard the worth of personality. Man, unrelated to God and outside the plan of the redemption, is unable to command the respect which is his due by natural right. The exploitation of the masses in the interests of a privileged few, the employment of torture and barbarous cruelty as instruments of government, the spirit of organized inhumanity in which the nations are prepared to engage upon mutual destruction are the measure of the failure of the attempt to replace charity by natural justice. The brotherhood of man is impossible of achievement without the recognition of the fatherhood of God. We cannot love our fellow-men as we should unless we love them first in Him in Whom most of all they are lovable.

We should recall, however, that our love of God is human as well as divine. St Thomas shows his awareness of the familiar truth that charity begins at home. He raises the question: " Whether we ought to love more those who are better than those who are more closely united to us. "[1] Far from replying with an unqualified affirmative, he applies a distinction which answers to the demands of experience and common sense. We should desire for those who are better, and therefore nearer to God, a higher measure of beatitude —in this sense we love them more. Nevertheless the intensity of love depends on our nearness to its object—from this point of view, we love more (*intensiori affectu*) those who are nearer to us; we wish them well with greater feeling. Further, the bonds of union, such as family relationship, likeness of temperament, membership of the same community, which bind us to those whom we are naturally disposed to love, can themselves be informed by charity. In this way our love has greater depth and sincerity towards those who are close to us than towards those whom we may recognize as of greater virtue.

[1] IIa IIae, q. 26, a. 7.

THE LOVE OF OURSELVES IN GOD

Self-love is not normally considered an attractive quality. The reason for this is the opposition it suggests to the love of God and our neighbour. To love self would seem to imply a lack of due love for God. In so far as this is true, self-love is rightly looked upon by the masters of the spiritual life as the direct antithesis of divine charity. We must abandon ourselves in order to find God, lose our lives to save them, as the gospel warns us.

And yet the writers who speak thus are no less insistent upon the need for aiming at self-perfection, an undertaking which presupposes both a knowledge of ourselves and a desire for our own spiritual well-being. Nor have the saints themselves failed to perceive the necessity of paying heed to self. "O God, Who art ever the same, let me know myself, let me know Thee."[1] St Bernard's *De Consideratione* is largely concerned with urging a reigning pope to acquire a true knowledge of himself, and it is interesting to observe that the same saint does not exclude a certain love of self from even the highest degree of the love of God.[2] St Thomas goes so far as to say explicitly that "a man ought, out of charity, to love himself more than he loves any other person."[3]

How then are the claims of God to be reconciled with this needful attention to ourselves? In what way can a harmony be established between divine charity and our instinctive self-love? Is a pure and disinterested love of God an impossible ideal? From these and like questions there arises what has been called the problem of love.[4] It has received concrete expression in the New Testament itself in St Paul's avowal: "For I could wish to be anathema myself from Christ on behalf of my brethren . . ."[5] And we read

---

[1] Augustine, *Solil.*, II, i, 1.
[2] *De Diligendo Deo*, cap. x: "Of the fourth degree of love, when man loves not even himself except for the sake of God."
[3] IIa IIae, q. 26, a. 4.
[4] The problem has been discussed with great acumen by Père Rousselot, S.J., in his *Pour l'Histoire du Problème de l'Amour au Moyen Age* (Münster 1908), and by Père Garrigou-Lagrange, O.P. in his *l'Amour de Dieu et la Croix de Jésus*, tome Ier, ch. 2 (Éditions du Cerf). M. Etienne Gilson suggests some qualification of Père Rousselot's conclusions in an appendix to Chapter XIV of his own *The Spirit of Mediaeval Philosophy* (English translation, pp. 289-303).
[5] Romans ix, 3. As Père M.-J. Lagrange aptly remarks: ". . . c'est un langage de sentiment qu'on ne doit point juger d'après la pure logique." *Épître aux Romains*, loc. cit.

of saints who, in their efforts to be rid of all self-love, have protested their willingness to be lost in hell on condition that they might love God more. What meaning are we to attach to such sentiments as these? Clearly they cannot imply a desire for self-extinction, for that would be against nature, which grace perfects rather than destroys. Perhaps, in the final analysis, the Christian's reluctance to admit the compatibility of any sort of self-love with the perfect love of God rests on the supposition that such an admission reduces our love of God to a desire for Him as fulfilling the needs of our own soul, that is, to a function of self-love. Instead of loving God above all things for His own sake, in point of fact we love ourselves more than God.

St Thomas himself states this difficulty in the light of principles with which we are by now familiar: " Everything that is loved by us is loved as our own good. But that which is the reason for love is more loved than love's own object; as the principles through which we know conclusions are better known than they. From this it follows that man loves himself more than any other good loved by him; he cannot therefore love God more than himself."[1]

This difficulty can be solved by recalling what has been said about our natural love for God. By nature we love God more than ourselves. This primacy of our love for God, far from being opposed to, actually includes rightly-ordered self-love. Correspondingly, true self-love cannot exist without the simultaneous recognition of the paramount claims of God. The spirit within us does not seek for the good which is merely relative but for *absolute* goodness. By nature it was made for something more ultimate than what is simply useful (*bonum utile*) or delightful (*bonum delectabile*); it can be satisfied only with the objective good (*bonum honestum*). Man, as such, loves truth and justice more than the personal advantages to be gained from the pursuit of either.

The bearing of this on our relations with God, the primary object of charity, is not difficult to see; but it throws light also on our connections with our neighbour. There is no radical opposition between the true love of self and the love of the brotherhood. If conflict can arise between individuals

[1] IIaIIae, q. 26, a. 3, obj. 2.

in their attempts to acquire possession, whether for use or pleasure, of those material goods which can only rightfully belong to one, this is not so among those who search after the things of the spirit. The pursuit of truth, virtue, final happiness does not divide one man from another. The collision on the material plane—the strife, for example, between capital and labour—is explained by the fact that matter is itself a principle of individuation. Material goods, by reason of their being individualized and limited, cannot at the same time belong to all. But this law does not apply to the spiritual world. The spirit universalizes and so attains to things immaterial which, in virtue of their universality, can be possessed by all.

Granted that pride be excluded (which is concerned only with the seeming good, *bonum apparens*), spiritual riches unite men rather than divide them. The true good of the spirit is identical with the good in itself, the *bonum honestum*, the value of which, rationally considered, is independent of the peculiar delectation or utility which results from its possession. There is no question of sacrificing this sort of good for some higher end; in loving it and oneself in it, one loves more than oneself the sovereign good which is God. Thus in desiring rightly our own perfection, that is, in loving ourselves as we should, we love God more than ourselves. To be without this desire of self-perfection is to fail in love for God. St Paul who, in his excess of love for the brethren would have foregone the delights of heaven on their account, could never have wished for less than that perfection which corresponded to his heroic charity.[1] The self-hatred to which we are counselled by so many of the saints is a hatred, not of our own best selves, but of everything within us which impedes our union with God.

. . . . .

No one who has followed these reflections up to this point can have failed to grasp how all-embracing is the reality of the love of God. If the approach to God demands a withdrawal from creatures, including even ourselves, it is only to find that these lesser things are restored to us in Him. Nothing noble or of good report has to be finally abandoned

---

[1] See Garrigou-Lagrange, op. ult. cit., p. 147.

for charity's sake. "But what do I love when I love Thee?" asks St Augustine in an unforgettable passage. "Not bodily beauty, nor the splendour of time, nor the brightness of the light, so gladsome to our eyes, nor the sweet melody of varied songs, nor the fragrant smell of flowers, and ointments, and spices, not manna and honey, not limbs pleasant to the embracements of flesh. None of these I love when I love my God; and yet I love a kind of light, and melody, and fragrance, and food, and embracement when I love my God, the light, melody, fragrance, food, embracement of my inner man: where there shines unto my soul what space cannot contain, and there sounds what time snatches not away, where there is a fragrance which no breeze disperses, where there is food which no eating diminishes, and where that clings which no satiety can sunder. This is it which I love when I love my God."[1]

[1] Augustine, *Confessions*, X, vi, 8.

Part II
THE CONDITIONS OF THIS LOVE

I

KNOWLEDGE

"As all things of His divine power which appertain to life and godliness are given us through the knowledge of Him Who has called us by His own proper glory and virtue."—2 *Peter* i, 3.

ALLUSION has already been made to the importance of knowledge in relation to love. It is now time to consider the matter in greater detail. Nothing is loved unless it is first known. This statement has only to be made for its truth to be seen, and yet how often is it ignored in practice! Perhaps most frequently of all is this the case in regard to the greatest of our loves, the love of God. This is no doubt due to the misleading emphasis which is occasionally placed on the service which the individual owes to God, at the expense of the less obvious, though more fundamental, knowledge and love of Him which he is bound to possess. Unhappily religion can sometimes be represented as a legalistic code of observances and prohibitions, as an arbitrary discipline wearisome and oppressive to the spirit, to the all but total exclusion of that progressive enlightenment of the mind and enlarging of the heart which are its real essence.

To love God is more profitable than to know Him: but we should not on that account make the mistake of supposing that we can love Him without knowing Him. Charity, in this life, depends on the knowledge which comes to us through faith. True, it reaches, in a sense, beyond faith, since, as we have seen, the will goes out to its object as it exists in itself whereas the intelligence appropriates its object to its own limited mode of being. We recall that it is for this reason that charity is a nobler virtue than faith, though its dependence upon faith should never be overlooked. In heaven, where faith is superseded by the Beatific Vision, the ontological primacy of knowledge even over love will be restored. *Visio est tota merces.*

In this connection it is of great interest to note how insistent the gospels show Our Lord Himself to be on this factor of knowledge. Unquestionably the greatest of the commandments has to do with the love of God, but its full meaning implies far more than sincerity and subjective good will. For all His compassion and lovingkindness men were to accept Christ on His own terms, not on theirs. He had not come into the world for the purpose of spreading abroad amiable and humanitarian sentiments, but to establish a Kingdom in which God should be worshipped " in spirit and in truth." In explicit terms before Pilate He proclaimed His mission as that of a witness to truth.[1] He was, in the literal and most profound sense, a martyr to truth.[2] It was just this that the Jews, as a whole, were unable to perceive—because they were not " of the truth." Their crime was not, directly and in the first place, a failure in love but a defect in knowledge. The sin was not that of knowingly rejecting the Messiah, but of not knowing Him when He came. When Jesus wept over the doomed city of Jerusalem the burden of His lament was not that His own had refused to surrender to Him their hearts, but that they had not submitted their minds; they had not known the things that were to their peace.[3] The momentous question at Cesarea Philippi had been an enquiry as to whether the truth were known, not an appeal for love. " . . . Whom do men say that the Son of Man is? . . . But whom do you say that I am? "[4] We do well then to give some attention to knowledge.

It is clear that a close relation exists between truth and knowledge. Knowledge, as distinct from opinion and irrational conviction, is, in fact, truth. When the mind is at one with itself and extra-mental reality truth is the resultant. *Veritas est adaequatio rei et intellectus*; truth is the equating of the intelligence and reality. To state what is true is to make an affirmation about something as it really does or can exist. To apprehend truth means that we recognize the conformity of our minds with the facts as they are. Some of the implications of this have already been touched on. The mind is potentially all things; it becomes what it knows. Nor is this process of becoming, intellectually, something other than

---

[1] John xviii, 37.
[2] Vid. M.-J. Lagrange, *The Gospel of Jesus Christ* (from the French), Vol. II, pp. 306-319.
[3] Luke xix, 42.
[4] Matthew xvi, 13, 15.

ourselves to be understood in anything less than its literal meaning. The philosophers speak of the rational creature being, as it were, compensated for its individual limitations by its power of making its own the objects of its knowledge. By our mind we overpass the boundaries of selfhood and are lost in the things we contemplate. Having taken hold of truth we enjoy not only our own lives but the life of the universe around us and all the creatures in it. In knowledge joined with love we have indeed the only lasting riches. Material wealth must always remain something outside ourselves, a mere utility of little intrinsic value; but the treasures of the mind and heart are an eternal possession never to be taken from us.

It is obviously important in this context to point out the distinction between the knowledge here identified with truth and mere erudition or book-learning. A contempt for real knowledge is fundamentally unchristian; not so a distrust of many of our modern academic processes. No mistake could be greater than to identify the vital activity which is knowledge with what Professor Whitehead has called " the intimate timidity of professionalized scholarship which circumscribes reason by reducing its topics to triviality." Knowledge, as distinct from learning, is concerned with things, *res*, and only with words in so far as they symbolize things. Thus it is worth while reflecting that to study a foreign language, that is to say, a new technique of expression, for all the labour spent upon it, brings to the mind an access of truth which is quite negligible. Its value lies in its utility as a training in a certain kind of concentration and as a means of entry into another literature, but in itself it has little to do with knowledge.

These thoughts are not without relevance to our subject. The attainment of ultimate truth, and therefore of the perfect love of God, can be helped or impeded by our normal mental habits. These habits are themselves the product of individual upbringing and environment. In other words our growth in the love of God is conditioned psychologically by all that can be included in the word education. Accordingly it is impossible to pass on without making at least some general observations on the problems involved.

The dissatisfaction expressed by many thinkers, both within and without the Church, at certain aspects of modern education has its roots, as might be expected, in the respective philosophical assumptions of the individual critics. This is borne out by a recently published report on the present state of secondary education. " The history of the traditional curriculum bears witness to the unending struggle between rival philosophies of life and widely divergent theories of education and human development."[1] These words should surely be pondered by all who have the task of helping to bring into being, or to maintain, a specifically *Christian* education in the world as we know it.

It must be plain for all to see that no solution of educational problems can be reached without some general agreement as to the nature and destiny of man. In the absence of definite convictions on these points educationalists are beating the air since they know neither the material they are working upon nor the object for which they are shaping it. In the days when our culture was informed by a common faith learning could be systematized according to universally accepted standards. The arts and sciences were seen to be interrelated and were subordinated one to another in the light of eternal principles. To-day no such thing can be attempted. The priority of place given by a rapidly disappearing tradition to the classics and humane letters is a post-renaissance convention with little justification in the nature of these studies. In place of an ordered progression through the *trivium* and *quadrivium* to metaphysics and theology, the queen of the sciences, we have now to choose between the alternatives of acquiring a more or less vast store of miscellaneous information or intensive specialization within a limited field of research. By metaphysics and theology, without whose guidance all mental activities are left in the void, our contemporaries remain unenlightened.

The limitations of the ancient system are not to be denied and no one would wish to revert to it in its unqualified form, but it is pertinent to inquire how order is to be brought out of our present chaos without a return to the principles on

---

[1] Board of Education; Report of the Consultative Committee on Secondary Education, p. 2. H.M. Stationery Office, 1939.

which it was based. When the world had wiser teachers than those who now control affairs it was realized that there were things which, for some people at least and in certain circumstances, were simply not worth knowing. To conduct education on principles of mass-production would have appeared to such an age an absurdity. Indeed it was precisely the function of the educator to train the mind to discern the things which were worthy of its attention and to neglect the rest. "To delight in and be pained by the things that we ought,"[1] was the Platonic and Aristotelian view of the goal of education; and, if we take it in its ethical as well as its aesthetic import, as including an awareness of moral values, there can be little doubt that it would be endorsed by the great Christian thinkers.

Our modern methods leave no time for the formation of taste, for selectivity. The public-examination mentality, now unhappily fostered from the earliest years, is proof against that capacity for reflection and independent judgment which should mark the educated mind. Teachers and pupils alike are the victims of a closed system which operates in a vicious circle. Standards are set and prizes awarded by university graduates and professional pedagogues, that is to say, by those who are themselves the choicest products of the system they are in honour bound to perpetuate. With the best intention in the world they are only capable of prescribing for others the method of treatment, modified quantitatively in accordance with age, which proved so successful in their own case. As a result the youthful mind, immersed in grammar and philology and the book-learning of scientific and literary opinion, fails to develop along its natural lines. It is obliged to follow the paths laid down for it by those whose gifts, though often considerable within a limited sphere, in comparison with the requirements of life as a whole are shallow and inadequate. Fortunately where teaching is in the hands of those in touch with the origins of our culture the influence of Catholic philosophy can do much to counteract the mischief, but even so the evils are not entirely eliminated.

It must be admitted that there is no lack of good will

[1] Aristotle, *Ethica* 1104b 3, 13.

among the educationalists themselves. They are acutely conscious that mistakes have been made and that something is wrong.[1] The roots of the trouble, however, would seem to lie deeper than they are aware. With their general problems we are not immediately concerned in these pages; but we shall attempt to point out, in very general terms, how, as it seems to us, contemporary education engenders habits of mind which are unfavourable to the reception of revealed religion and therefore to that reverence and love for God which is the object of our discussion. The human mind is by nature philosophical; at least in the sense that it seeks for a rational account of things and to form for itself a unified view of life adequate to its experience. It is true that only a small minority feel at home in the realm of pure metaphysics, but it is no less a fact that men in the mass incline instinctively to common sense—which is itself a rudimentary philosophy. Education accordingly, in so far as it supplies mental training at all, will tend to cast the mind in some sort of philosophical mould. With the majority the underlying philosophy is held unreflectingly, *in actu exercito* rather than *in actu signato* (if we may be permitted the technicalities), but it is there nevertheless working its effect upon our whole mental outlook. Now what is the outlook on the world at large, the intellectual *habitus* modifying everything we apprehend, produced by our normal technique of instruction? Its name in the history of philosophy is Nominalism. The inherently realist tendency of the mind is diverted from its true path and frustrated of its proper object. Instead of being directed towards *things* and to an apprehension of their inner significance it is obliged to rest content with the shadow rather than the substance, with words in place of the realities they signify.

That this is so in the field of literary studies is hardly open to dispute. Experience shows that the energy and concentration necessary for the mastering of foreign languages tend to rob the mind of any genuine perception of the ideas for which they are the medium. Deprived of the deeper

[1] See, for example, p. 257 of the Report mentioned above, where it is admitted that the School Certificate Examination, originally intended to follow the curriculum and not determine it, does now in fact largely determine it.

realities, the student must accept in their place tautologies and verbalism, while facility of expression comes to be regarded as significant in itself and factual memory mistaken for intelligence. Even when, in the study of literature, a stage beyond grammar and philology is reached and works are studied on account of their style and aesthetic appeal the results are scarcely less disappointing. An exquisite sensibility is a poor substitute for intellectual insight and appreciation of meaning. Excessive preoccupation with humane letters and their attendant studies leads to a materialization of the intelligence from which it recovers with difficulty. The mind either loses itself in verbal minutiae or becomes submerged in floods of imagery and metaphor. Signs and symbols are mistaken for the realities themselves. Far from enjoying the power to discern first principles and underlying significance, which it is the business of sound education to develop, the mental energies are dissipated in the activities of phrase-making and the search for the picturesque. In place of the philosopher and poet which, it might have been hoped, would have emerged from such a process, we are presented with the sceptic and elegant dilettante. Wandering between two worlds, cut off at one extreme from the profound simplicities of common sense and at the other from the contemplation of ultimate causes, the mind takes refuge in the dreamland of eclecticism and received opinion. These are the lights, changeful and unsteady, by which the modern man of liberal education is asked to contemplate the Christian revelation. We need feel no surprise that he remains unimpressed with what he sees. Nor is it the vision of the outsider alone that is obscured. Our secular culture can dissolve before the eyes of the believer himself the foundations on which his faith is based. Where positive infidelity is avoided the mind's grip upon objective reality is loosened and the great Christian dogmas, instead of forming an object of intellectual delight, appear of but slight significance and are adhered to, not with conscious intelligence, but by blind tenacity of will.

If the attention at present given to art and letters does little to dispose the mind to the reception of revealed truth, this result is hardly to be expected from a study of the physical sciences. The remarkable practical achievements of modern science should not obscure from view its limitations as an educational discipline. The knowledge it provides, when not directed to a purely utilitarian purpose, is confined to the activities of matter. The formulation of scientific hypotheses and the application of mathematics to physical data undoubtedly give scope to talents of a high order, but, even at its best, the range and extent of mental activity are bounded by the phenomenal world. The scientist wishes to answer the question " What happens? " rather than " Why does it happen? " He is not concerned with causes, as such, but with observing the uniform succession and interrelation of events. So complete is the divorce between contemporary science and what the ancients called natural philosophy that any attempt on the part of the more adventurous among present-day scientists at "philosophizing" their discoveries is discouraged rather than welcomed by their orthodox brethren. An attitude which, it may be remarked, is both consistent with their own premises and abundantly justified by the unhappy performances of one or two celebrated scientists on the stage of metaphysics. The problems before which science rightly professes incompetence are in fact just those with which philosophy is concerned; for example, the origin of movement, the first appearance of life, the apparent finality of nature, the facts of sensation and consciousness, free will.

This essentially non-philosophic character of science[1] is the explanation why a specialized attention to it can have so baneful an influence on the general mental development. Even mathematics—which, as Aristotle observed, prescind from efficient and final causality, and hence from the whole world of extra-mental reality—are not without an unbalancing effect on the mind. It has been pointed out how the mathematical treatment of physical phenomena has led to conclusions which are patently at variance with the witness of common sense. The traditional philosophers have

[1] At the end of a chapter of great interest Professor Whitehead observes: "This antagonism between philosophy and natural science has produced unfortunate limitations of thought on both sides. Philosophy has ceased to claim its proper generality, and natural science is content with the narrow round of its methods."—Whitehead, *The Function of Reason*, p. 49.

had no difficulty in showing that these "paradoxes of modern science" are not quite so disconcerting as they appear and have a very limited validity; nevertheless the practical results they produce and the prominence given to them in the popular press have done much to shake the average man's conviction of his right to pass judgment on matters which are well within his competence and thus led inevitably to the progressive weakening of public intelligence. Where scientific research is unrelieved by the diversion of mathematics the concentration upon material phenomena which it demands deflects the mind even more effectively from the path marked out for it by nature. The spirit is held in bondage to particular facts and is prevented from entering upon those wider fields of general and detached observation which are its due province. There is produced a sort of sclerosis of the understanding, by which it is rendered impervious to any but the experimental impressions with which it is familiar. In consequence it tends to regard the objects of sense-knowledge as ultimate reality and to adopt a view of the universe which is wholly materialistic. Not only do the abiding truths by which our reason lives appear without meaning but all that is immaterial comes in practice to be treated as if it did not exist. The native spirituality of the intellect is deprived of its proper food and loses its vigour. Thus it comes about, through causes in themselves quite natural, that many people of untrained minds and little learning, possess a surer insight into the great human problems than can be claimed by the expert scientist.

Under given conditions, outstanding individual ability and the correctives supplied by peculiarly gifted teachers may well lessen the force of this criticism, but its general truth will surely not be denied. Moreover our unbalanced educational system is but a symptom of the disorganization which affects modern civilization as a whole. In view of the prevailing chaos it is perhaps a matter for congratulation that the methods employed in instructing the young are not more unsatisfactory than is actually the case. The possibilities of true learning are greater than at any other period in history; it is the lack of co-ordination between its many departments, caused in its turn by the absence of any guiding principles derived from a universally accepted philosophy of life, that is here complained of. It is in the high places of the mind that the lights of heaven have been put out. The idealism and nominalism which have dominated philosophical thought for three centuries, despite their apparently opposing viewpoints, lead alike to unrealism and fundamental scepticism. The desertion by Descartes of the realist tradition in philosophy could not fail to bear its evil fruit on the plane of common education. And in the realm of thought we find that a preoccupation with words and ideas has been substituted for the contemplation of things and the vision of the world of being. Nor, for the most part, are the ideas in question those which claimed the attention of Plato and Aristotle and the Christian thinkers; too often they are no more than the impressions gathered from personal introspection, the barren records of our subjective mental processes.

As is well known, the rationalistic attempts to dissolve the objective truth of historic Christianity into myths and the dreams of enthusiastic idealists have their source in the departure from intellectual realism for which Descartes and Kant have been mainly responsible. The moderns have rejected the gospel of Christ, not because they have examined it and found its evidence insufficient, but by reason of an artificially induced attitude of mind which renders them incapable of receiving it. They are without eyes to see and ears to hear. What meaning is to be made of Scripture and Catholic tradition by a mind uncertain whether we can attribute freedom and personality to God? What significance is to be attached to the knowledge of Christ which, according to St John, *is* " eternal life " by one who denies that we can know anything as it is in itself? The spirit, which needs must love the highest when it sees it, is, in fact, prevented from seeing it. That, in a sentence, is the tragedy of the modern mind. Its own deliberate abdication of its rightful place in the natural order has barred its entrance into the higher world of divine truth. It may well be that only by a reawakening of the intelligence to a recognition of its own powers—powers which, paradoxically, depend upon its capacity to submit to realities other than itself—can we hope for a revival of supernatural faith. Not that contemporary agnosticism has even the merit of humility; it is merely man's excuse for turning philosophy into art, a pretext to justify him in fashioning for himself his own universe. The Creator alone is the maker of truth; the creature receives it, if he be wise, humbly upon his knees. Only when the world has relearned this elementary lesson can it hope to be taught of God.

Within the Catholic fold those who are charged with the education of the young have a grave responsibility in our day. Theirs is the task of uniting the heterogeneous elements of secular culture in virtue of principles which it does not acknowledge, a task as worth while as it is likely to prove difficult. There can be no rejection of its positive achievements, no refusal to acknowledge its slightest contribution—that would be to shirk the problem, not solve it—but they must be presented in the light of divine revelation and the Christian philosophy, from which they derive ultimate significance. The pristine purity of the intelligence is to be preserved and nourished with its proper food, so that it develops in its true line and grows to full stature. That the chief glory of man as a rational being is not memory, or imagination, or even a capacity to formulate theories, but the power to understand what is presented to him from without is the simple truth of which the young generation must be convinced. So enlightened, the mind will have opportunity of practising the discrimination, the distinguishing what is essential from what is not, which is the function of intelligence. Bookishness should be encouraged only in those who have a taste for it—and even then with no exaggerated emphasis on its importance; for others it is the high road to intellectual bankruptcy.

By attempting to place education in its natural setting and informing it with the light of divine truth we shall provide an antidote to that learned levity and moral irresponsibility which are the ever-recurring blight of a humanism broken loose from first principles. It will then be possible to present the Christian revelation with some likelihood of its uniqueness, viewed from the merely rational and historical angle, being appreciated. The motives of credibility, from which the reason perpetually demands support, instead of being obscured by a mass of irrelevant historic facts and scientific data, will be seen in their due compelling force. Faith itself will be enlightened; for, notwithstanding its essentially supernatural character, its affirmations are still possessed by the mind in rational concepts. By penetrating to the inner meaning of these concepts—the *fides quaerens intellectum* of Catholic tradition—the faith is strengthened and developed; in the absence of such activity it is in danger of remaining sterile and without effect. But this effort to understand presupposes the recognition of the essentially realist and contemplative nature of the intelligence. To be aware of this truth themselves and to proclaim it to others is surely the first duty of those who are concerned with the spread of God's Kingdom on earth. The bond of union between the members of the Kingdom is assuredly love, but the only way of entry thereto is through truth. And truth comes to us by knowledge.

The knowledge we possess of God comes to us from two sources, reason and faith. We shall consider them in order. It should be noted, however, that when we speak of the knowledge which is attainable by reason we mean that particular sort of understanding which it is possible for man to acquire by his own efforts, but not that the individual has in fact acquired it by reason alone. For the Church teaches a number of revealed truths, the *revelata per accidens*—e.g. the existence of God and the soul's immortality—which are accepted by many as of faith even though, in reality, they can be rationally demonstrated. Teaching of this kind has been divinely revealed so that it may be known by all men easily and without fear of error, which would not be so were the matter left to individual investigation. But it would be a capital mistake to confuse the object of this knowledge with the object of faith properly so called, the *revelata per se*; for this can never be otherwise known by the created reason than through divine revelation. There is no position on which St Thomas is more insistent than this, that a rational truth cannot in itself be an object of supernatural faith and that a truth of faith is completely beyond the reach of reason. The theologian who pressed the claims of the human intellect to their furthest limits had too high an esteem for the exalted dignity of faith ever to allow that its territory could be conquered by the created intelligence.

The importance of this distinction is scarcely in need of emphasis. We have already enunciated the principle that grace perfects nature and shown its application to our love for God: charity, though eminently supernatural, is the perfection of a desire which is rooted in our inmost being. In parallel fashion faith, a grace by which we share in God's own knowledge of Himself, presupposes and makes perfect our natural knowledge of Him. By faith we assent to the content of God's personal self-revelation. It is obvious then that before we can make the act of faith we must have reason's assurance that God exists, that He can reveal Himself to man and that, as a matter of historical fact, He has actually done so. We are not now concerned with tracing the steps which lead up to the act of supernatural belief, but shall confine ourselves to indicating the general scope of faith and reason respectively with reference to revealed truth.

By unaided human reason it can be known that God exists, the Supreme Being and Ruler of the universe. That in Him there must be contained, in a supereminent degree, all that is true and good and beautiful is also a conclusion to which reason apart from faith can attain. On further reflection, our complete dependence on God for everything we are and have is likewise sufficiently evident. From this it is an easy step to the realization of a sense of duty towards Him, the obligation to do His will in so far as it is known to us. Thus St Paul could allow that even " the gentiles, who have not the law, do by nature those things that are of the law."[1] But when this stage has been reached reason begins to falter. If we did not know on other grounds that God has intervened in the course of history and revealed Himself to man, could we deduce that fact, or even the possibility, from merely natural premises? Philosophers have hesitated to do so. Perhaps the most satisfactory way of stating the matter is to say that without the fact of revelation we should not have known its possibility, but, once a revelation has been given us, we can establish the fact before the bar of reason in virtue of the irrefutable evidence which accompanies it.

[1] Romans ii, 14.

The historic revelation of Christianity can be considered from two points of view. We may look at it from without, as a series of facts and truths of peculiar interest, but nevertheless as no more than particular events in the general story of our race. Or, having received the gift of faith, we can study them from within and see that they are concerned with realities of eternal significance. The first of these approaches is the rational investigation of the natural substructure upon which the Faith is based; it has to do with what are called the motives of credibility and should terminate in the recognition of the reasonableness of the act of belief itself. Miracles and prophecies, the authentic signs which accompany and witness to revelation, make their appeal to reason and do not presuppose the faith which it is their object to elicit. What is demanded of us by faith is the acceptance of mysteries the intrinsic truth of which is completely beyond our perception. We adhere to them, not because they are self-evident to us, but on the word of God revealing.

The fact that faith is both eminently rational and, at the same time, essentially supernatural makes a precise description of its nature very difficult. What must be understood is that the antecedent reasoning processes which precede faith, together with the rational substructure which supports it, however close their psychological connection with the act itself may appear to be, are not an essential part of it. Their relation to faith, though of the highest importance, is accidental: *non per se sed per accidens ad fidem pertinent*.[1] Our Lord's miracles, for example, which should have induced his contemporaries to believe in Him, could be recognized for what they were by reason alone and do not form, properly speaking, an object of faith. Confronted by a miracle, or sufficient historical evidence for it, we are obliged to posit some divine intervention; we observe a phenomenon whose extrinsic cause must be supernatural, and the mind awaits,

---

[1] S. Thomas, III *Sent.*, d. 24, a. 2, ad 2am quaest. Cf. *Commentum in Joannem*, cap. IV, lect. v, 2: Inducunt autem nos ad fidem Christi tria. Primo quidem ratio naturalis. . . . Secundo testimonia Legis et Prophetarum. . . . Tertio praedicatio Apostolorum et aliorum. . . . Sed quando per hoc homo manuductus credit, tunc potest dicere quod propter nullum istorum credit: nec propter rationem naturalem, nec propter testimonium Legis, nec propter praedicationem aliorum, sed propter ipsam veritatem tantum.

as it were expectantly, the enlightenment which comes from a revealed truth. Throughout history men have been led to divine faith in this way. The Old Testament prophecies and miracles were the signs that God had spoken and that His word must be accepted. When, in the fulness of time He came in person into the world His coming was accompanied by signs and wonders, that men might have no excuse for rejecting Him. He prepared their minds, supplied them with motives for receiving His message which no one could gainsay, but the message itself was to be accepted unconditionally, on His word alone. Indeed it could not be otherwise; for the secret He was to reveal was not patient of rational proof. It concerned the intimate personality of the Godhead and His plan of salvation for all men. To such knowledge as this, " the mystery hidden from ages and generations,"[1] the creature could only be admitted at the price of submission to God of all his former ways of knowing. Flesh and blood could not reveal it to him, but only the Father Who was in heaven.

Little reflection is needed to see that the distinction between faith and what precedes it is forced upon us by the exigencies of faith itself. The two great Christian mysteries, on which all the others depend, namely, the inner life of the Trinity and the union of the two natures in Christ, can be defended by reason and their credibility established, but they cannot be demonstrated as true or even as antecedently possible. The evidence that they have been revealed can be examined by all, but the inner content of these mysteries, so far as we are concerned, is without evidence. Their evidence is contained in the light of the Godhead on which we shall gaze in the Beatific Vision. In this life we know them by what St Thomas has called the " beatifying knowledge " of faith. They are the objects, not of proof, but of loving contemplation. Faith is the substance of the things we hope for,[2] the first beginnings of the ineffable vision by which we shall be made happy in heaven. Its essential element is not confidence, trust, but knowledge. Yet knowledge of a peculiar kind.

[1] Colossians i, 26.
[2] Hebrews xi, 1.

By knowledge we normally mean our awareness of some fact of sense-experience or principle of reason. We say that we know a thing when we recognize it for what it is and see that it cannot be other than it is. It is thus that we know the objects with which we come in daily contact and the conclusions of our ordinary reasoning processes. Now it is obvious that we do not know the truths of faith in this way. Far from the assent of the intelligence being evoked by the evidence before it, as happens with rational knowledge, it is effected by the intervention of the will in co-operation with grace. Belief is an assent, not on account of intrinsic evidence, but on authority—though, in this case, on an authority which is divine. It is, of course, this lack of evidence which makes the act, the " venture " of faith, our noblest tribute to God; for it implies the submission to Him of our highest faculty, the intelligence, on His word alone. Nevertheless the part played by the will does not affect faith's basically cognitional character. The intellect is specified—has, so to say, over against it—a new order of truth, the truth which is properly the object of God's own intuition of Himself. It is precisely for this reason, because the divine mind alone is proportioned to comprehend the mysteries of faith, that they remain obscure for us in this life. Contemplating them we are like birds of the night gazing upon the sun, blinded by excess of light.

The authority behind faith should not, however, be mistaken for an arbitrary decree in accordance with which the mind submits to certain dogmas, without at the same time acquiring any capacity to understand them. When, for instance, we are introduced to the mystery of the Hypostatic Union, " on the authority of God revealing," it is not meant simply that at a certain point in history God revealed the truth to mankind once and for all and that thereafter we accept the fact on His word. So naïve a conception of the matter is fraught with many difficulties; the chief of these concerns the misgivings that could arise from reflection upon the many centuries which have elapsed between the date of the revelation and the moment of our individual act of assent. Could not error have crept in and the original message become adulterated with the passage of years?

Nor could such doubts be allayed by an appeal to the infallibility of the Church; for that truth is also an object of faith and, in any case, the terms in which supernatural belief is defined exclude such a view. The Church is the divinely appointed means of making known to the world throughout time what God has revealed, but, since this fact is itself an integral part of revelation, it is manifest that she cannot propose herself as the final grounds for our assent. No, the clear teaching of the theologians is that the "authority" in question is nothing less than God Himself presenting the truth to the mind of the believer, while simultaneously infusing the intellectual strength to accept it and eliciting the act of assent. Not only St Peter, but each member of the faithful, confesses Christ to be the Son of the living God because the Father has revealed it to him.

The intimate relations between God and the individual soul suggested by the consideration of divine faith appear to have escaped the notice of some even among the masters in Israel. Excessive apologetic zeal and undue eagerness to prove the reasonableness of what we believe can lead to a materialization of the revealed truths quite inconsistent with their inner nature. The external facts in which God's revelation is embodied derive their entire significance from the point of view, the "light," what the philosophers call the *ratio formalis*, under which they are apprehended. Most of all is this true with reference to what we may call the supreme Christian fact—the Incarnate Word. When the pharisees on the one hand and the disciples on the other looked upon Christ Our Lord, materially speaking, there was no difference in what they saw. But how shall we measure the difference in the essential content of their minds? His enemies were obliged in reason to recognize His incomparable holiness; they could not meet His challenge to convict Him of sin. His claims too were known to them and His miracles were before their eyes. Nevertheless they rejected Him, failing culpably to recognize Him for what He was. Reason itself had indicated that an act of submission was required before an unknown something infinitely beyond reason's grasp. This was the homage they refused to give. In consequence the gift of supernatural faith was denied them, leaving them guilty of the sin of infidelity. They did not know the Christ.

With the believer it is quite otherwise. The light of faith which he receives is not to be understood simply as a grace enabling the mind to adhere to the same truth which the non-believer knew only to repudiate. This would reduce faith to what is at best a supernatural modification of the rational assent demanded by the motives of credibility. Faith, on such a view, would still remain an essentially natural act; for the object specifying the intelligence does not transcend the capacity of reason. On the contrary, with the infusion of faith there is presented to the mind First Truth, *Veritas Prima*, that is to say the order of truth contained in the mind of God Who is Truth itself. This is the background against which the particular articles of our faith are seen. The sublime reality of the Hypostatic Union objectifies the mental gaze, no longer as something to be viewed from without in the wavering light of human reason, but in all its divine intelligibility and consequent mysteriousness (for us) as it is understood by God. By faith we adhere to the truth eternally present in the divine mind, not merely as a fact existing in the world of space and time, as offered to the senses and capable of being apprehended by the natural intelligence: *unde oportet quod fides, quae virtus ponitur, faciat intellectum hominis adhaerere veritati quae in divina cognitione consistit transcendendo proprii intellectus veritatem.*[1]

God revealing Himself, *Veritas Prima in dicendo*, bears in upon the intellect at grips with the dogma proposed by the Church, in accurate though necessarily inadequate language, draws forth its assent and admits it to secret counsels prepared " before the foundation of the world."[2] The mystery remains, for as yet we see " as in a glass darkly,"[3] rejoicing the hearts of individual believers, offering to the Church inexhaustible riches of contemplation for her saints and vast fields of speculation for her theologians. For the Faith does not pause at the words in which its dogmas are pronounced but penetrates to the thing to which they relate: *actus autem credentis non terminatur ad enuntiabile sed ad rem.*[4] How signifi-

[1] S. Thomas, *De Veritate*, q. 14, a. 8.
[2] Ephesians i, 4.
[3] I Corinthians xiii, 12.
[4] IIa IIae, q. 1, a. 2, ad 2.

cant must be a phrase such as this in relation to our belief in the personality of Christ! What the eyes of the disciples saw and what has filled the imagination of succeeding generations was truly the most gracious human figure the world has seen; but no more than that. By faith, and by faith alone, was contact made with the Word which " in the beginning . . . was with God "[1] and which gave to that incomparable humanity its unique personality. Faith does not pass, as it were, from the particular fact proposed to our belief upwards to God; it rather communicates in the first place directly with its divine source, God Himself, and then comes downwards to observe the fact manifesting itself in the world of space and time.[2]

This extremely elevated conception of faith, based on scripture and rooted in Catholic tradition, throws much light on the nature of the supernatural love of God which is charity. It is highly significant that St John, for whom " God is charity,"[3] and who has written of divine love as no one before or since, was also the evangelist of truth and knowledge. The word " truth " comes more frequently from his pen than from all the other New Testament writers together excepting St Paul. Immediately after announcing the Incarnation of the Word he tells us that It was " full of grace and truth."[4] In the knowledge of this truth we shall be made free.[5] Jesus Himself is the truth as well as the way and the life.[6] Most explicitly does our Lord tell His disciples, in what were almost His last words to them, that it is because of their knowledge of Him that they are His friends: " I will not now call you servants: for the servant knoweth not what His lord doth. But I have called you friends; because all things whatsoever I have heard of My Father I have made known to you."[7] In return for their love He will give to His followers an increasing knowledge of Himself: " And he that loveth Me shall be loved of My Father; and I will love him and will manifest myself to him."[8] It is simply this know-

---

[1] John i, 14.
[2] This and the preceding paragraph are reproduced almost verbatim from my article " Faith and the Motives of Credibility," *The Clergy Review*, December, 1938.
[3] 1 John iv, 16.   [4] John i, 14.   [5] John viii, 32.
[6] John xiv, 6.   [7] John xv, 15.   [8] John xiv, 21.

ledge linked with love which is eternal life: "Now this is eternal life: that they may know Thee, the only true God, and Jesus Christ Whom Thou hast sent."[1]

Not for a moment could we suppose that what is here spoken of is merely the detached knowledge of the intelligence. Such an interpretation would be alien to the whole spirit of the Johannine writings. It is a knowledge which issues forth in moral conduct and spiritual desire. By it we are led to "do truth."[2] Nevertheless it is real knowledge that is in question, that is to say, an illumination of the mind. We "walk in the light,"[3] as St John expresses it in his first epistle. He also it is who records how "Jesus spoke to them, saying: I am the light of the world: he that followeth Me walketh not in darkness, but shall have the light of life."[4] Nor is it John alone for whom the new life brought by Christ could be described in terms of light. St Peter speaks of our being "called out of darkness into His marvellous light."[5] St Paul, as might be expected, is no less assured: "For God, Who commanded the light to shine out of darkness, hath shined in our hearts, to give the light of the knowledge of the glory of God in the face of Christ Jesus."[6]

It is unnecessary to bring forward further evidence for what no one would wish to dispute. That the just man lives by faith is a statement often repeated in scripture and an elementary Christian truth. Catholic tradition has affirmed it with no uncertain voice. It seems possible, however, that the religious upheaval of the sixteenth century led certain theologians to a presentation of the Church's teaching on faith which failed to do justice to its profound implications. An atmosphere of embittered controversy is not the one most favourable to good theology. In order to counteract the Lutheran doctrine which denied the necessity of good works and minimized human freedom great emphasis had to be laid on the opposing truths. Not without, in some quarters at least, weighing down the balance too much the other way. The Council of Trent had stated the orthodox doctrine with precision; but the divine safeguards against error

[1] John xvii, 3.
[2] 1 John i, 6. Cf. the Pauline "faith working by charity"; Galatians v, 6.
[3] 1 John i, 7.　　　　　[4] John viii, 12.　　　　　[5] 1 Peter ii, 9.
[6] 2 Corinthians iv, 6.

accorded to a general council do not extend to the works of individual theologians, and these are not without influence on the minds of the simple faithful. Not only did a new attempt to explain the nature of efficacious grace gain a real, though limited, acceptance, while causing consternation in the traditional theological schools and only narrowly escaping official condemnation, but explanations of the act of faith were forthcoming based on the nominalistic philosophy and extreme voluntarism which were then in vogue. As a result the sublime conception of the nature of faith to be found so clearly, for example, in the works of St Thomas was obscured and lost sight of. So complete was the decline that, in place of the essentially supernatural character of faith which he had recognized, theologians were teaching that it was supernatural only in the way in which it was produced (*quoad modum*) and some went so far as to maintain that the assent of faith could be reached at the conclusion of a rational syllogism. It was not surprising that these views were criticized as denying to the act by which the gospel was accepted the dignity ascribed to it by scripture and tradition.

To anyone who has had occasion to study systematically the *Summa Theologica* it will be evident that it presupposes a conception of faith the elevation of which it is impossible to exaggerate. This can be seen from the structure and method of the whole work as well as from St Thomas's explicit teaching on the point. In the first question of all, where the nature of theology (*sacra doctrina*) is discussed, it is made clear that this science must be given the highest place of all, above mathematics and metaphysics, because it derives its principles from the knowledge of the Beatific Vision: *sacra doctrina est scientia quia procedit ex principiis notis lumine superioris scientiae quae scilicet est scientia Dei et beatorum.*[1] In virtue of these principles, which are divinely revealed and accepted by us in the form of the articles of faith, sacred doctrine is a certain impression upon our minds of God's knowledge of Himself: *quaedam impressio divinae scientiae.*[2] Where faith is treated of explicitly, in the *Secunda Secundae*, the same thought recurs: those things properly belong to faith the vision of which we shall enjoy in heaven and by which we are led to

[1] Ia, q. 1, a. 2.   [2] Ia, q. 1, a. 3, ad 2.

eternal life: *illa per se ad fidem pertinent quorum visione in vita aeterna perfruemur et per quae ducemur ad vitam aeternam.*[1] Again, in his article on the description of faith to be found in the eleventh chapter of the epistle to the Hebrews, St Thomas explains that faith can be called " the substance of things to be hoped for " because, by the assent of faith, we possess the first beginnings of things hoped for (i.e. the truths by which we shall be beatified in heaven), since faith virtually contains them: *per hunc modum dicitur fides esse " substantia rerum sperandarum "; quia scilicet prima inchoatio rerum sperandarum in nobis est per assensum fidei, quae virtute continet omnes res sperandas: in hoc enim speramus beatificari, quod videbimus aperta visione veritatem cui per fidem adhaeremus.*[2]

This recognition by St Thomas of the transcendent and mystical quality of faith, which does no more than justice to St John and St Paul, has implications of great interest. It explains the secret of how the apparently detached intellectualism which he had learnt from Aristotle could be combined with a personal religious life of the highest intensity; for this prince of theologians enjoyed that quasi-experimental knowledge of divine things which is the accompaniment of heroic sanctity. It is consistent with his whole theology that mysticism, that is, a knowledge of God by reason of a kinship or affinity with Him (*propter connaturalitatem*), however rare it may be in practice, is in itself but the normal development of the supernatural endowments possessed by every Christian. The gifts of the Holy Spirit, and in particular the gift of wisdom, are the immediate source of the ineffable experience; through them God raises the soul above its ordinary mode of activity to enjoy in anticipation something of the felicity of the life to come. But wisdom itself, chief among the gifts, as high above the wisdom of the philosophers as are the heavens above the earth, presupposes the intellectual virtue of faith. Indeed it is no more than the power to judge truly, through affection and in the light of the highest causes, about the object which faith offers to the mind: *donum sapientiae praesupponit fidem, quia unusquisque bene judicat quae cognoscit.*[3] Or, as he has said elsewhere, the

[1] IIa IIae, q. 1, a. 8.   [2] IIa IIae, q. 4, a. 1.
[3] IIa IIae, q. 45, a. 1, ad 2.

articles of faith are the principles of all Christian wisdom: *principia totius christianae sapientiae*.[1] Faith of itself gives to the mind the highest illumination which it is capable of receiving in this life. Although it is of things unseen—*fides est de non visis*—it introduces us to the abiding realities for which we are made, which alone bring rest to the heart. We need not wonder that the keenest intelligence God has yet given to the Church, obliged while composing his great labour of love to keep his gaze fixed steadfastly upon that First Truth which is the substance and ground of our faith, laid down his pen, dizzy and blinded in ecstasy, unable to finish his task.

It need hardly be said that St Thomas's view of the incalculable dignity of supernatural faith is not peculiar to himself. We have but to consult the pages of the most orthodox among the mystics to find what is essentially the same teaching. The works of St John of the Cross, to whom has recently been accorded the title of Doctor of the Universal Church, despite their difference in purpose and method of approach, are founded upon a conception of faith identical with that of the *Summa Theologica*. Let us quote, for example, the twelfth stanza of the *Spiritual Canticle*:

> O crystalline fount, If on that thy silvered surface
> Thou wouldst of a sudden form the eyes desired Which I bear outlined in my inmost parts!

St John's exposition of this stanza exhibits the characteristic combination of quickening power and theological insight which makes him at once the most inspiring and authoritative of mystical writers.

> As with so great a desire the soul desires union with the Spouse, and sees that in all the creatures there is no means to that end, neither any relief, she speaks again to Faith as to the one who shall give her the most vivid light from her Beloved, and considers her as a means to that end; for indeed there is no other way whereby a soul may come to the true union and spiritual betrothal with God, according as He declares through Hosea, saying: I will betroth Me unto thee in faithfulness (Hosea ii, 20)....
> The propositions and articles which faith sets before us she calls a silvered surface. For the understanding of this and of the

[1] III *Sent.*, d. 35, q. 2, a. 1, sol. 1, ad primum.

other lines it must be known that faith is compared to silver with respect to the propositions it teaches us, and the truths and substance which they contain in themselves are compared to gold; for that same substance which now we believe, clothed and covered with the silver of faith, we shall behold and enjoy in the life to come, fully revealed, with the gold of faith laid bare. . . . But when this faith shall have come to an end, which will be when it is perfected through the clear vision of God, then the substance of the faith will remain, stripped of this veil of silver, and in colour as gold. So that faith gives and communicates to us God Himself, but covered with the silver of faith; but it fails not for that reason to give Him to us in truth, even as one may give a silvered vessel, which is also a vessel of gold, for, though covered with silver, it is none the less a golden vessel that he gives. . . .

Oh that Thou wouldst but give me these truths which Thou teachest me formlessly and darkly, and which are veiled in Thy articles of faith, clearly and formally revealed in them according to the entreaty of my desire![1]

It should be noted that St John of the Cross is not here alluding to any infused ideas or special lights which may be given to individuals to enable them to carry out a particular work for which they have been chosen;[2] he speaks of the faith which is the common possession of all who believe. We need no other light but this to enable us to love God as we should; enjoying only this illumination we shall see the King in His glory.

Perhaps this chapter may fittingly close with the words of St Catherine of Siena, expressing thoughts and desires which should never be far from the minds of every Christian: " Having known the truth through Thy clemency, I have found Thy charity, and the love of my neighbour. What has constrained Thee? Not my virtues, but only Thy charity. May that same charity constrain Thee to illuminate the eye of my intellect with the light of faith, so that I may know and understand the truth which Thou hast manifested to me."[3]

[1] *Spiritual Canticle*, stanza 12: *The Works of St John of the Cross*, Vol. II, p. 245 ff. (This and all other references are to the translation by Professor Allison Peers.)
[2] That is to say, the graces for which the theologians reserve the name of *gratiae gratis datae*.
[3] Dialog., cap. clxvii.

II

DRAWING NEAR TO GOD

"But it is good for me to adhere to my God, to put my hope in the Lord God. . . ."—*Psalm lxxii (lxxiii), 28.*

A TRUTH that spiritual writers are never weary of repeating is that, under the present dispensation, our state before God does not remain fixed. We improve or we deteriorate. If our union with Him is not being progressively intensified then we are falling from our first charity. Life is inseparable from movement; it is an approach towards a goal. If we lose direction and go astray so much the worse for us; but we move nevertheless. Our stability depends upon an unceasing effort to attain an object which is beyond our reach, a pressing towards the mark, as St Paul calls it.[1] This movement towards God—*cui non appropinquatur passibus corporis sed affectibus mentis*[2]—can conveniently be viewed in its twofold aspect, first, as an approach to Him, and secondly, as a withdrawal from all that impedes us on our journey. Accordingly in this chapter we shall deal with the supernatural organism which is the vital source of the divine life within us, and in the next with the control to be imposed on our natural activities in order that they may correspond with this new life. If religion can justly be said to comprise a union of mysticism and asceticism, then what is now to be discussed has to do with the first of these elements while the following chapter will be concerned with the second.

It has been well said that without an adequate notion of the doctrine of grace it is impossible to understand Catholicism. The inner life of the Church, as has also been pointed out, is as mysterious as the processions in the Blessed Trinity. Of that inner life grace is the cause and operative force. It endows the believer at the outset with perfections of an immeasurably higher order than he could hope to achieve by a lifetime of moral endeavour. Grace, the sharing of the intimate life of the Godhead, is not a reward for services

---

[1] Philippians iii, 14.   [2] IIa IIae, q. 24, a. 4.

rendered but a free gift to which we have no title. The life it engenders within us is one whose highest expression goes beyond ritualism and the external services of religion to an inner dedication of mind and heart, the silent gazing of the lover upon the beloved. This last point we shall consider at greater length in our chapter on prayer; about the place of the moral virtues in religion it is necessary to say a word before passing on.

Right conduct, the general conformity of our actions to the cardinal virtues of prudence, justice, fortitude and temperance, is a condition without which the final perfection of a Christian is unattainable, but it is not the essence of Christianity. The moral virtues have reference to the means by which the end is achieved, whereas Christian perfection, that is, the love of God, is concerned with the end itself. We do not desire an eternal union with God in order that we may act justly towards our neighbour and control our baser appetites; we rather do these latter things so that we may be united to God. Christianity transcends as well as includes ethical perfection. The life which Christ came to bring so abundantly is not to be thought of as a means to temperate living, an aid to self-discipline. The pharisaic and pelagian view of religion, whereby righteousness is conceived as a personal achievement in virtue of which we can lay claim to the good things of the gospel, has ever been recognized as the deadliest foe of any true relationship with God. It was resisted by St Paul with terrible ferocity and he has been followed down the centuries by the great minds of Christendom. The life which comes to us with faith and baptism can never be merited and the glory to which it leads is God's crowning of His own first gift. Once this new life-blood has been instilled into our veins we assimilate it, or, more accurately, it revitalizes our natural processes, so that the actions we perform under its influence are our own, but as dependent for their efficacy upon their newly-acquired source of energy as is the ripening harvest upon the sun's rays. Grace itself is the beginning of eternal life; by it we are transplanted to regions not of this world and placed upon the threshold of heaven. All that remains is that we should be faithful to our trust by co-operating with this vital force and allowing it to control each of our activities. Our approach to God is not only wholly initiated by Him; it is entirely subject to His domination throughout its course. In the pages which immediately follow we shall attempt to give some account of the nature of grace, of its outworkings in the theological virtues and the gifts of the Holy Spirit, and of the way in which the supernatural organism so constituted gathers strength and intensifies its life.

In the first chapter of St Peter's second epistle the following words occur: " . . . He hath given us most great and precious promises: that by these you may be made partakers of the divine nature. . . ."[1] The phrase, " partakers of the divine nature," *divinae consortes naturae*, θείας κοινωνοὶ φύσεως, is the scriptural source for the theology of what has come to be called sanctifying grace. It is here that the profound and inspiring mystery of the way in which we are united to God receives its authentic expression. Countenance is given by the Holy Spirit Himself to the use of such words as " divinization " and " deification " which the Fathers of the Church were afterwards to employ in their attempts to explain what takes place within the soul by the infusion of grace. In some way the divine nature itself, the intimate life of the Godhead shared by the three Persons of the Trinity, is communicated to us. Man is raised to the level of a son of God, a co-heir with Christ. At once the inherent dignity of the Christian becomes apparent; on the supernatural as well as on the natural plane it is quality which counts. The marvel of divine grace lies rather in what it makes a man to be than in what it leads him to do. True, our actions reveal our inner worth, they are of a piece with our character and, where grace is present as an habitual state, have themselves a supernatural value. But the fact that their worth is dependent upon the status of the individual who performs them demonstrates their secondary importance. As the redemptive work of Christ Our Lord, the Son of God by nature, draws all its efficacy from what He was, a divine Person, so our own deeds are of eternal moment only because we are in a state of grace and sons of God by adoption.

The controversies which surround the theology of grace

[1] 2 Peter i, 4.

have for the most part centred upon what we may call its operative rather than its qualitative aspect, that is, upon actual, as distinct from habitual, grace. This has had the unfortunate result in many minds of concentrating attention on what is itself of less interest and obscuring from view its primary function. The impression is sometimes given that our chief need for grace is to enable us to get through our daily tasks without falling into sin and to strengthen us in the performance of duty. That this is indeed part of the work of grace is obvious enough, but it is not its main work. We require grace in the first place to unite us to God and confer upon us that participation in the divine nature without which nothing we do is of any avail towards our final salvation. It is true that the first movement towards this state of justification is prompted by actual grace but, until the term of the process has been reached and we have become the adopted sons of God, we are not as yet co-heirs with Christ and can have no part with Him.

From one point of view, after the infusion of the grace of justification, we have reached the goal of our endeavours before we so much as start on our journey; the eternal life promised us by the gospel is already ours. Unhappily we carry our treasure in earthen vessels and can lose it through infidelity—a fact, however, which does not make its possession any less real. What is needed is that our merely human activities should become imbued with the waters of eternal life flowing from the fountain planted by God within the soul. Or, to speak more strictly, that the soul with its twin faculties of intellect and will—the *mens* of the theologians, the seat of divine life, the habitat of grace, the focal point of all personal union with God—, being divinized by the infusion of grace, should dominate the whole man, as is its natural right, shedding the light of heaven upon each of his actions.

The *reality* of grace, the fact that it is not simply a new relation or attitude towards God, cannot be too much emphasized. The reformers, owing to the anthropomorphic psychology with which they endowed the Divinity, could see no more in this gift of God than a pardon analogous to the forgiveness one man extends to another. They thought of justification as something extrinsic to the soul, by which God is pleased to declare the non-imputability of its faults in virtue of the mediation of Christ. Man remained as guilty as ever but God, by His favour, overlooked his sinful state. In this way the concepts of regeneration and the outpouring of grace are emptied of meaning and the whole economy of salvation is reduced to the absurdity of a divine intervention which effects nothing as its term. What had been forgotten was that God, Who is Being Itself, *ens realissimum*, acts in accordance with His nature. In other words, when He operates *ad extra* it must be to produce something within the sphere of being, the result of His action must be an existent reality. As we have seen, the divine love is creative—*creans et infundens bonitatem in rebus*—and realizes itself efficaciously. This was the truth ignored by Luther and his followers.

How far they had departed from traditional Christian thought can be seen from the following passage from St Thomas. He is explaining how grace produces something in the soul, *ponit aliquid in anima*. " A difference is to be noted between the good will (*gratia*) of God and the good will (*gratia*) of man. Because the good of the creature results from the divine will, it follows that from the love of God whereby He wishes some good for the creature a good must result in the creature. Man's will, on the contrary, is moved by the attraction of a good pre-existing in the creature. Consequently man's love does not totally cause the good which exists in a thing but presupposes it either wholly or in part. It is manifest therefore that from the love of God of whatever kind there results the production of a good in the creature, even though this good be realized in time and is not co-eternal with the love which produced it. We are thus led to distinguish in God two sorts of love for creatures corresponding to the different goods He bestows on them: first, a love in general by which He loves everything that exists and from which results the natural being of created things; secondly, a special love by which he draws the rational creature above its natural condition to a participation in the divine goodness. This latter love alone is absolute, for in loving someone in this way, God wishes for him the absolute good which is Himself. Wherefore to say that a man is in the grace of God signifies that there exists in him a supernatural reality issuing from God."[1]

St Thomas's conclusion that grace is a reality inhering in the soul was confirmed by the Council of Trent and is now a part of Catholic teaching. His description of it as a "quality" of the soul has also been incorporated into the Catechism of the same Council. Nothing could make clearer the concrete realism of St Thomas's conception of grace than the arguments by which he establishes this last point: " It is not fitting that God should provide less well for the creatures whom He loves to the extent of giving them a supernatural good than for those to which He gives only a natural good. Now the latter are not simply moved to their activities by God; they receive from Him forms and energies which are for them true principles of action, with the result that they possess an intrinsic inclination to the actions they perform. In virtue of these forms the creatures act, under the motion of God, easily and in a way conformed to their nature, according to the words of Wisdom: ' She (i.e., Divine Wisdom) . . . ordereth all things sweetly.' If He proceeds thus in regard to simple creatures, *a fortiori* ought God to infuse into those who are destined for an eternal good forms and supernatural qualities by means of which they can be moved by Him sweetly and promptly towards the achievement of that eternal good. Therefore the gift of grace is a sort of quality."[2]

The same course of reasoning, from God's providence in the natural order to His still greater solicitude in the supernatural, leads St Thomas to draw a distinction between grace itself and the infused virtues which accompany it. Here again his teaching is echoed in the Council of Vienne and the Catechism of the Council of Trent. Although sanctifying grace and charity go hand in hand they are nevertheless distinct. Nor should a distinction of this kind be dismissed as an over-refinement. It serves to bring out the worth of charity, which is thus an added perfection to the creature already supernaturalized by grace.

Man is by nature endowed with a rational soul from which proceed the faculties of intellect and will. As we have

[1] Ia IIae, q. 110, a. 1. [2] Ia IIae, q. 110, a. 2.

pointed out in an earlier chapter, he achieves his natural perfection by the employment of these faculties upon their proper objects in the activities of knowledge and love. By the infusion of grace the soul is divinized in its essence through a participation in the divine nature and the faculties are correspondingly elevated by receiving the supernatural virtues and gifts; the operations of these last perfect the grace-endowed soul as knowing and loving perfect it on the plane of nature. From this it is easy to see why St Thomas, for whom the harmony between nature and grace is a first principle, should insist on the distinction between grace and the infused virtues, including charity. "And therefore, as the natural light of reason is something over and above the acquired virtues, which are so called because they are governed by reason; in like manner, the light of grace, which is a participation of the divine nature, is something over and above the infused virtues, which both flow out from grace and are directed towards its increase. It is for this reason that St Paul says in the epistle to the Ephesians (v, 8): 'For you were heretofore darkness, but now light in the Lord. Walk then as children of the light.' Now in the same way as the acquired natural virtues perfect a man to enable him to walk according to the light of reason, so do the infused virtues perfect him that he may walk according to the light of grace."[1]

It may be noted in passing that the use of the word "light" should not divert attention from the fact that grace is a *nature*. Though the thought is expressed in scriptural and metaphorical terms, the reality signified is the divine nature as participated by the soul. This is obvious from the context with reference to the rational nature, but it is no less clear in relation to the light of grace which, for St Thomas, is the supernatural counterpart of the light of reason. As Père Gardeil points out,[2] the application of the word "light" to both nature and grace serves to emphasize their spiritual character. But it would be a complete mistake to understand it as an external influx of power instead of an interior habit clothing the inmost substance of the soul. A virtue,

[1] Ia IIae, q. 110, a. 3.
[2] A. Gardeil, *La Structure de l'Ame et l'Expérience Mystique*, Vol. I, p. 366.

whether natural or supernatural, does not exist *in vacuo*, it is the virtue of some being which it perfects. But it can only fulfil this function by perfecting the underlying principle which makes the being in which it inheres to be what it is, that is to say, the nature. A particular nature and its virtues reciprocally complement each other; they must therefore be of the same order. To the acquired virtues, which adorn and make perfect the mind and will in the natural order, there corresponds, as the principle from which they proceed, a rational nature. Likewise to the infused supernatural virtues there corresponds, by analogy, the divine nature as imparted by participation to the rational creature.

These thoughts can scarcely fail to bring home to us how marvellous is the supernatural organism which comprises the divine life of the soul. " The grace of a single soul," says St Thomas, who was not given to extravagant language, " is a greater thing than the natural good of the whole universe," *bonum gratiae unius majus est quam bonum naturae totius universi.*[1] What then are we to say of charity, which perfects and enlarges the life of grace in the same way that good will perfects our normal rational life? This supernatural love of God is, ontologically speaking, the highest endowment of the creature here below and, in all creation, is inferior only to the light of glory which we receive in heaven. It is the soul's most precious possession, a literal participation in the love wherewith the Father loves the Son and they together love the Holy Spirit, a sharing in the affective life of the eternal Trinity. Through charity God and the soul are present to each other in intimate communion: " God is charity: and he that abideth in charity abideth in God, and God in him."[2]

This point becomes clearer if we consider what the theologians mean when they use the word *habit*; for charity, together with faith and hope, the gifts of the Holy Spirit and the moral virtues, is a habit. The common use of the word could mislead us as to its significance in our present context. It does not here signify, as it does perhaps most often in every-day usage, what is the ordinary course of conduct; it should rather be understood in its etymological meaning

[1] Ia IIae, q. 113, a. 9, ad 2.   [2] 1 John iv, 16.

(from the Latin *habitus*, as translating the Greek ἕξις), as a permanent state or disposition. To illustrate by an example: On hearing that a friend has the habit of studying mathematics, we should probably gather no more than that it was his custom to devote himself to that science at regular and frequent intervals. We might conclude that he had acquired some facility therein, but that would not be the first thought aroused by the information. Now it is just this second factor, of ease in performance resulting from an acquired mental disposition and cast of mind, which illustrates the primary and theological meaning of habit. A habit of mathematics so understood does not necessarily imply unremitting application; its possessor, even though he has the " gift," may seldom make use of it in practice. He has the habit because his mind has been modified in a particular way, taken on a certain quality, which enables him to mathematicize easily and naturally.[1] When we speak then of charity and the other virtues being habits[2] it is in this profound and qualitative sense. Similarly, a virtue, which is precisely a *good* habit, does not mean simply right conduct, but an inherent disposition to act virtuously; that is, a fixed inclination to do what is morally right.

It may be remarked in parenthesis that, from the nature of things, this classical conception of virtue can make little impression on the mind of the modern man. And yet without its due appreciation it is impossible to form any true estimate of the riches of Christian spirituality, riches which can only be gauged in terms of quality. The logic of facts demands that a materialistic age should look upon movement and quantity as the great realities, for these are the first accidents of matter. The systematic cultivation of what is superficial depends for its success upon the erection of standards of judgment which are obvious to all. When millions are trained to the belief that wireless-telegraphy and

---

[1] Jowett, in the introduction to his translation of Plato's *Republic* (p. cxlii) remarks as follows: " Neither was he (Plato) aware of the power of habit; the thesis that good actions produce good habits, which is, perhaps, the greatest single principle in education, was first taught mankind, not by Plato, but by Aristotle."

[2] It will be understood that the supernatural habits differ from the natural, not only in their object, but also in the way in which we become possessed of them. They are directly infused by God, since they cannot be acquired by human efforts.

the aeroplane are the high-water mark of human achievement it is not to be expected that they will contemplate life with any sense of proportion, or indeed, that they will contemplate it at all. Not only is the possession of power and wealth taken to be the true measure of successful living but the very nature of man's activity is misunderstood. The value of work is commonly assessed by reference to the speed and efficiency with which it is done rather than in relation to its basic utility and its effect upon the workman. The same shallow and irrelevant tests are applied, often unconsciously and with the best intentions, in the sphere of moral conduct. It is the practical, as distinct from the virtuous, man who comes to be regarded as the model worthy of imitation, the man who gets things done regardless of whether they be worth doing or not. Visible results and quick returns are easier to register, and therefore of greater value, than the moonshine of high motives and noble ideals. In this way the deep significance of the virtues in general, and charity in particular, is lost sight of. Charity is interpreted as a mere serving of tables, a succession of " good turns," instead of being recognized as a vital tendency implanted in the secret depths of the spirit by which it moves, in the light of faith, upwards towards God in passionate longing and outward upon our neighbour in unceasing good will and enlightened activity; such is the ordered charity, the *caritas ordinata*, of the saints.

We ask how much a man has done, but from what degree of virtuous principle he acts, is not so carefully weighed. We enquire whether he has been courageous, handsome, skilful, a good writer, a good singer, or a good labourer; but how poor he is in spirit, how patient and meek, how devout and spiritual, is seldom spoken of. Nature respecteth the outward things of a man. Grace turneth itself to the inward. The one is often disappointed; the other hath her trust in God, and so is not deceived.[1]

Sanctifying grace may be said to represent what is most essential to the Christian life considered as a permanent state, statically; the theological virtues account for its dynamic element, by their activity we grow to our full

[1] *Imitation of Christ*, Bk. III, ch. xxxi, v.

supernatural stature. " Faith, hope and charity," says St Paul with an air of finality, " but the greatest of these is charity."[1] Truly, armed with these, we have substantially all we need. St Thomas has no difficulty in showing how these three virtues are an exhaustive facsimile on the supernatural plane of our natural faculties and gifts.

The theological virtues direct man to supernatural happiness in the same way as by natural inclination man is directed to his connatural end. Now this direction to the end proper to his nature takes place in a double way. First, in respect of the reason or intellect, in so far as it contains the first universal principles which are known to us by the natural light of the intellect, and which are reason's starting point, both in speculative and in practical matters. Secondly, through the rectitude of the will which tends naturally to the good presented to it by the intellect.

But these two fall short of the order of supernatural happiness, according to 1 Corinthians ii, 9: 'Eye hath not seen, nor ear heard, neither hath it entered into the heart of man, what things God hath prepared for them that love Him.' Consequently, in respect of both intellect and will, man needed to receive in addition something supernatural to direct him to a supernatural end. First, as regards the intellect, man receives certain supernatural principles, viz. the revealed truths, which are received by the divine light of faith. Secondly, the will is directed to this end by a double movement: by its stretching forward towards the end as something to be attained, which is hope, and in respect of a certain spiritual union whereby the will is, so to say, transformed into this end, and this is charity.[2]

In concluding the article quoted St Thomas adds, by way of explanation, that the appetite tends naturally towards its connatural end. His meaning clearly is that, through the infusion of charity, our will (the rational appetite or desire) is connaturalized to a union with its supernatural end which is God Himself. This leads us to touch very briefly upon the part played in the supernatural life by the gifts of the Holy Spirit. Through the seven gifts the divine workmanship, by which we are acclimatized to the rarefied atmosphere of the Kingdom of Heaven, is completed.

In St Thomas's view the seven gifts of the Holy Spirit, for which the scriptural source is the eleventh chapter of

---

[1] 1 Corinthians, xiii, 13.   [2] Ia IIae, q. 62, a. 3.

Isaiah, are supernatural habits really distinct from the theological virtues. After seeing the powers conferred on us by these virtues, rooted as they are in sanctifying grace, it might seem that any further divine help was unnecessary. But a little reflection will lead us to correct this view. The *Summa* presents us with a theology of the " gifts " the implications of which have surely not received, at least in England, the attention they deserve. Far from regarding the gifts as in any way superfluous, a sort of spiritual luxury, we must recognize them as necessary for salvation. The virtues of faith, hope and charity connect the intellect and will, as it were, directly with God; they are in themselves more perfect than the gifts and regulate their activity. Nevertheless, although the theological virtues enable the faculties of the soul to act supernaturally, we by no means possess them with the same completeness as we do our natural mental powers. We cannot move in the world of faith and charity with the ease and assurance of which we are conscious when dealing with matters over which the reason has full control. It is in order to make good this deficiency that we are endowed with the gifts of the Holy Spirit. Their function is to render the soul alert and responsive to divine inspiration and make possible the acts of heroic virtue which are demanded of every Christian in the course of a lifetime and for which the theological virtues are insufficient.

The activity which proceeds from the theological virtues, though directed towards God Himself, is still subject to the limitations of rational deliberation. We ourselves, aided by actual grace, can at will elicit an act of faith or charity. What is essential to the act is undoubtedly divine, but its mode of production is human and, to that extent, unworthy of its object. The soul is not yet at home with God. It is like a lover protesting his love in letters and elaborate speeches instead of by a glance and a touch of the hand. When faith is accompanied by the gifts of knowledge and understanding, and charity by wisdom, then all hesitancy disappears and calculation and forethought give place to a heavenly instinct. The Holy Spirit Himself takes charge and we are literally inspired.

Now it is clear that whatever is moved must be adapted to

receive the influence of what moves it. In fact the perfection of anything that is moved, precisely in so far as it is movable, is the disposition whereby it is adapted to be moved easily by its mover. Hence the more exalted the mover the more perfect must be the disposition by which that which is moved is adapted to receive its influence. For example, we observe that a disciple needs a more perfect disposition in order to receive higher teaching from his master. Now it is manifest that human virtues perfect man according as it is natural for him to be moved by his reason in his interior and exterior actions. Consequently man needs yet higher perfections whereby to be disposed to be moved by God. These perfections are called gifts, not only because they are infused by God, but also because by them man is disposed to become amenable to the divine inspiration, according to Isaiah, l, 5: " The Lord hath opened my ear and I do not resist: I have not gone back." This is confirmed by Aristotle's teaching, that those who are moved by divine instinct do not need to deliberate according to human reason but only to follow their inner promptings, since they are moved by a principle higher than human reason. And this is why some hold that the gifts perfect man for acts which are higher than acts of virtue.[1]

In the activities which are ordered to our supernatural end, in which man is directed by reason, informed though it be—partially and imperfectly—by the theological virtues, the guidance of reason does not suffice, unless it be helped out by the prompting and motion of the Holy Spirit. Thus we find in Romans viii, 14, 17: " Whosoever are led by the Spirit of God, they are the sons of God . . . and if sons, heirs also " ; and in Psalm cxlii, 10: " Thy good spirit shall lead me into the right land "—because, as is obvious, no man can receive the inheritance of the blessed unless he be moved and led thither by the Holy Spirit.[2]

It would be a misinterpretation of St Thomas's teaching to confuse the operations of the gifts with a series of actual graces given to a privileged few. Like the theological virtues, the gifts are permanent habits of the grace-endowed soul and form an integral part of the supernatural equipment common to all. It is true that they begin to dominate the individual spiritual life only when a high degree of sanctity has been reached; on lower levels they are for the most part dormant and inactive. The Christian life, like any other, can be led with painstaking industry and it can be led with

---

[1] Ia IIae, q. 68, a. 1.   [2] Ia IIae, q. 68, a. 2.

genius; in the first case we may suspect that the gifts of the Holy Spirit are lying within the soul, an unused treasure, in the second, that their riches are revealed, energizing in light and power. The Thomist theologians have surely been faithful to Catholic tradition in seeing in the work of the gifts, especially that of wisdom, the explanation of the quasi-experimental knowledge of God enjoyed by the mystics. For a mystic is one who has an instinctive knowledge and love of heavenly things, that is, who lives habitually under the guidance of the Holy Spirit. When the gifts are no longer in the imperfect state of habits but are actualized and brought to life by the divine hand they transform the activities of the virtues, imparting to them their own sureness and delicacy of touch. The soul begins to taste and see how sweet the Lord is. Nor, in view of this teaching, can such " tasting knowledge," *sapida cognitio*, be the prerogative of a select and limited circle, a *gratia gratis data*. However rare may be its achievement in practice, it would seem that the title to some such union with God, even here on earth, belongs to every Christian; it is part of the " good news " in which all are meant to rejoice.

Our supernatural life is thus made up of sanctifying (or habitual) grace, by which the substance of the soul receives a participation in the divine nature, and the infused virtues and gifts which inhere in the faculties of intellect and will, enabling them to function on a supernatural plane and correspond in their activity with the Godlike mode of existence to which we have been raised. We must now inquire how this seed of glory, *semen gloriae*, maintains and develops its somewhat precarious existence here below, pending the attainment of full fruition in the light of the Beatific Vision. This takes place in two ways: by the acts of the virtues themselves, especially of charity, and through the instrumentality of the sacraments.

The sacraments are the divinely appointed means by which grace is given to us. They derive their efficacy from Christ's passion, and the Fathers have figuratively described them as so many rivers of grace flowing from the Saviour's side on Calvary. After the Incarnation, itself the supreme embodiment of the sacramental idea, the seven sacraments are God's most gracious gesture to mankind. Though He intends to lead us to a glorious destiny the Creator deals with us as He finds us; and He finds that we are naturally more prone to respond to what we can see and touch than to the things of the spirit. For this reason He draws us to Himself by corporeal and sensible signs; but signs which have the marvellous power of effecting what they signify. Again, it is fitting that we should be healed through the very disorder which caused the disease. In sinning man subjected himself by his affections to things material. Consequently God provides us with a spiritual medicine by means of visible sacraments; for if spiritual food were offered to us unveiled our preoccupation with the material world might lead us to pass it by unnoticed. A third reason suggested by St Thomas shows the greatest condescension of all. Quite apart from sin, our daily duties have mostly to do with material things; in dealing with them we are, as it were, in our native element. Hence we have a natural predisposition to approach religion in a materialistic, matter-of-fact way. If there were nothing to meet this particular need, nothing to exercise ourselves quite naturally upon, there would be danger of our falling into superstitious practices and even harmful and sinful actions. Summarizing his own teaching St Thomas concludes: " It follows therefore that through the institution of the sacraments man, consistently with his nature, is instructed through the things of the senses; he is humbled through having to admit that he is subject to corporeal things, seeing that he receives help from them; and he is even preserved from bodily harm by the salutary frequenting of the sacraments."[1]

In view of what has been said about the completeness of the supernatural equipment provided by the grace of the virtues and the gifts it might seem that no room is left for the reception of further grace through the sacraments. St Thomas in fact proposes to himself this precise difficulty in an article entitled: " Whether sacramental grace adds anything over and above the grace of the virtues and the gifts."[2] He replies by summarizing the doctrine outlined in the foregoing pages and then points out that the sacraments

[1] IIIa, q. 61, a. 1.   [2] IIIa, q. 62, a. 2.

are ordained to certain special effects which are necessary in the Christian life. Baptism, for example, is directed towards a spiritual regeneration by which we die to vice and become members of Christ—an effect over and above that produced by the faculties of the soul under the influence of the virtues and the gifts. And so with the rest of the sacraments; in addition to grace commonly so called, they each bring a particular help from God for obtaining the end for which the sacrament was instituted.

With the sacraments, as with the deep foundations of our supernatural life, the harmony between grace and nature is preserved. Their number can be accounted for by the way in which our spiritual life of grace corresponds with our natural corporeal life. Our natural life comprises two perfections, according as one considers the life of the individual or the life of the society in which he lives. As individuals, our lives are perfected directly and indirectly: directly, in virtue of our being born and thereafter strengthened and nourished in growth; indirectly, by reason of the recovery of health when it has been lost and its complete restoration when the illness has been grave. Likewise in the spiritual life of grace, there is a sacrament by which we are born into that life, namely, Baptism; there is another which makes us strong therein, and this is Confirmation; a third which nourishes us in this life, and this is the Holy Eucharist. If we lose this life through sin it is given back to us in the sacrament of Penance, and such weakness and proneness to evil as remain are removed by Extreme Unction. As to the society in which this life is lived, there are two sacraments which ensure its well-being and continuance: for the spiritual side of the society there is the sacrament of Holy Orders, for its material and corporeal side that of Matrimony.

The Eucharist, it need hardly be said, is the greatest of all the sacraments. Unlike the others it contains Christ substantially, whereas they are but the instruments of His power. In fact the rest of the sacraments are ordered to the first among them in dignity as to their appointed end. We are baptized in order that we may receive the Eucharist and confirmed that we should not be obliged by sin to abstain from it. Holy Orders are conferred for its consecration.

By Penance and Extreme Unction we are prepared to receive the Body of Christ worthily. Matrimony, at least in its signification, touches this sacrament; for it symbolizes the union of Christ with the Church, of which the Eucharist is a figure.

If Baptism is pre-eminently the sacrament of faith the Eucharist is the sacrament of charity and the love of God. Now that Christ's physical presence has been withdrawn from us, the consecrated Host which we receive in communion is the highest visible expression on earth of God's love for the human race. It is only to be expected that the theologian to whom was entrusted the composition of the Corpus Christi liturgy should rejoice in the theology of the Blessed Sacrament. In a moving passage from the *Summa* he states that a reason of itself sufficient for the truth of the Real Presence is simply the charity of Christ. " It accords with Christ's charity, through which He took upon Himself a true human body. Because moreover it belongs to friendship that the friends should live together, as Aristotle observes, He promises us His bodily presence as a reward hereafter.... Yet meanwhile, even in our earthly pilgrimage, He does not deprive us of that same presence. He unites us to Himself through the reality of His body and blood; wherefore He says: 'He that eateth my flesh and drinketh My blood abideth in Me and I in him' (John vi, 57). Hence this sacrament is the sign of the highest charity, and the uplifter of our hope, by reason of so familiar a union of Christ with us "; *unde hoc sacramentum est maximae charitatis signum et nostrae spei sublevamentum ex tam familiari conjunctione Christi ad nos*.[1]

Correspondingly, by the reception of the Eucharist, our own charity is vivified and set on fire. " This sacrament confers grace spiritually together with the virtue of charity. Hence St John Damascene (*De Fide Orthod.*, iv.) compares this sacrament to the burning coal which Isaiah saw (vi, 6): ' For a live ember is not simply wood, but wood united to fire; so also the bread of communion is not simple bread, but bread united to the Godhead.' Moreover, as St Gregory observes in a Homily for Pentecost, ' God's love is never

---

[1] IIIa, q. 75, a. 1.

idle; for, wherever it is, it is powerfully active.' Consequently through this sacrament, so far as concerns its power, not only is the habit of grace and virtue bestowed, but it is furthermore aroused to act, according to 2 Cor. v, 14: 'The charity of Christ presseth us.' Hence it is that the soul is spiritually nourished through the power of this sacrament, by being gladdened in spirit and, as it were, inebriated with the sweetness of the divine goodness, according to what is said in the Canticle, v, 1: 'Eat, O friends, and drink, and be inebriated, my dearly beloved '."[1]

It is because the Eucharist kindles the soul to acts of charity that it is efficacious for the removal of venial sin. The habit of charity—that is, the capacity and disposition to make acts of charity—can co-exist with the state of venial sin; but, wherever venial sin is present, the fervour of our acts is lessened and the inclination to make them diminished. Concupiscence also, that disorder in our affections arising from original sin, hinders the operation of charity. Against these evils this sacrament is the sovereign remedy; it moves the soul to acts of love which, of their own power, blot out venial sin and greatly diminish concupiscence. In a word, the reception of the Eucharist prompts us to those acts which are the most effective of all means to progress in union with God.

In this connection there arises a question of very practical importance. Does every act of this virtue intensify the grace and charity already present in the soul? Or, to put the question in another way: will any act, however perfunctory, provided that it really proceed from charity, draw us closer to God? St Thomas replies to the effect that every act of charity is meritorious, but only those acts produce immediately an increase of the love of God which are of the same, degree of fervour as, or greater than, the charity already present. He suggests that when acts fail to correspond with the intensity of the virtue—*actus remissi*, as the theologians call them—the virtue itself loses strength. In this he is merely repeating in his own way the traditional teaching that not to advance in the supernatural life is to fall back. Not that, by less fervent acts, charity is directly diminished; but its

[1] IIIa, q. 79, a. 1, ad 2.

influence and effectiveness are weakened owing to the obstacles with which its activity is surrounded. A lamp, even though not extinguished, emits increasingly less light if the glass through which its rays pass becomes dulled and stained.

It is noteworthy that, though the virtue of charity is completely lost by mortal sin, it is not directly weakened either by venial sin or by the cessation of its acts. Venial sin is a disorder with reference to the means to the end, but it does not withdraw the will from the last end itself, which is the object of charity. Moreover, as this virtue is infused and not acquired by a repetition of acts (as are normally the natural virtues), it is not, strictly speaking, augmented by such acts or decreased by their discontinuance. Through its acts the virtue is increased by way of merit, *per modum meriti*, but failure to make such acts does not deserve to bring with it the deprivation of the virtue itself. This inactivity, however, diminishes charity indirectly; for it rules out its influence on the other virtues and allows bad habits to take root. These effectively impede its action and, since they are the result of wilful negligence, merit God's withdrawal of the special actual graces without which a serious fall cannot long be avoided. In this way failure to make frequent and fervent acts of the love of God prepares the way for mortal sin and the total destruction of the supernatural life of the soul.

All this serves to make clear the vital importance of not allowing charity to lie dormant within us. It should be constantly active and exercising its proper function of directing the other virtues to their ultimate end. For charity, being first among the virtues, attains to God as He is in Himself and therefore becomes, in a manner, identified with the guiding principle of all morality, the *regula prima*, as St Thomas calls it. Hence charity is the *form* of all other virtues. Not that prudence, justice and the rest are without their respective objects making them virtues in their own right; they are truly such; but, charity being absent, their activity lacks due ordination to its final end. By charity we lay hold of that end, God Himself, and secure it in advance. Without this anchorage we are perforce unable to control and guide our subordinate activities along their proper channels. Thus, deprived of charity, we may be prudent within a limited sphere of reference; we may possess sufficient insight and natural good will—although, in view of our fallen state, this is unlikely—to act in every situation as reason dictates. But this is not enough. In a world redeemed and destined for the vision of God we need higher lights and surer inclinations than those supplied by reason and good will. We have, in every circumstance, to act with a view to eternity and a will fixed steadfastly upon the unchanging Good. And without charity this is impossible.

There could be no more striking commentary on this truth than the confusion and unrest which prevail throughout the modern world. We see men striving to bring about peace and international stability without themselves having the knowledge and dispositions necessary for the task. It is as idle to pay lip-service to justice and altruism, which serve only to cloak hypocrisy and self-interest, as it is to act in open contempt of those virtues. What is wanting is not the "charity" of good intentions and humanitarian sentiment —of that there is no lack—but the supernatural virtue rooted in the depths of the spirit which fixes the desire upon the final Good to which, not a chosen race, but all humanity, is moving. Exclusive nationalism, whether it be labelled fascism, communism or democracy, has arisen on the ruins of faith and charity; it can exist only in a world which has denied the fatherhood of God and the brotherhood of man. Without supernatural faith the nations have no key to the mystery of the universe and no common interpretation of life; they consequently fail to see that they must play subordinate and reciprocal parts in a general scheme, and become instead victims of the illusion that they each have a natural right to world-prestige and undisputed supremacy. Without charity our dealings with others are deprived of direction and driving-force. Prudence rapidly degenerates into astuteness and a capacity to out-manœuvre, and justice into the perception of what is expedient. There can thus be no betterment of our present ills until the theological virtues again take root in the hearts of our contemporaries. Charity is not only a means to personal sanctification; it is a necessity for the restoration of society. No prophetic insight, only an observation of facts, is needed to justify the assertion that without the love of God and of man, as redeemed by Christ, all that preserves our civilization from destruction are the precarious safeguards of unenlightened self-interest and military power.[1]

Charity, we may note in conclusion, carrying all the other virtues in its train, and so perfecting the whole of human activity, should progressively increase in fervour throughout life until it reaches its final term in the possession of the Beatific Vision. The intensification of charity implies a corresponding increase in the other virtues; for all the virtues proportionately gather strength together, much as the fingers of the hand grow simultaneously while preserving relatively the same measurement.[2] Furthermore, in view of Our Lord's injunction: " Be you therefore perfect, as also your heavenly Father is perfect,"[3] the Christian should use every means in his power to increase the charity in his soul. The theologians point out that, when we correspond with grace and place no obstacles in its way, charity grows in intensity with each of its acts. Thus, with every reception of the Blessed Eucharist, our love of God should be always more fervent. Day by day, as life moves on, we should be drawing nearer to God in the only way we can approach Him, *gressibus amoris*, with steps of love, until the moment arrives when faith has given place to vision and hope to possession and charity alone remains.

---

[1] These lines were written before the outbreak of war; they have not been falsified by the event.
[2] Ia IIae, q. 66, a. 2.
[3] Matthew v, 48.

III

UNWORLDLINESS

"Love not the world, nor the things which are in the world. If any man love the world, the charity of the Father is not in him."—*1 John ii, 15.*

We must now descend from the heights and give some attention both to the interior attitude of mind and the outward conduct necessary that man, as a harmonious unity, may conform to the demands made upon him by sanctifying grace. It might be supposed that the endowments we receive from God absolve us from any strenuous effort on our own part towards the attainment of perfection, that we need only remain passively in His hands, allowing Him to work His will in us. This is the reverse of the truth. The same theologian who extols the dignity of grace and its intrinsic efficacy is no less insistent on the truth that God has given to creatures the power of self-action. We co-operate with God in such a way that, even when moved by grace, our actions spring from the vital depths of our own being. Though in a manner which presupposes our complete subordination to the First Cause, we are real causes, and not mere instruments in God's hands, of everything we do. In practice, our correspondence with grace often involves, not passive submission, but a personal struggle which calls forth all the resources at our command.

It must be admitted, however, that this fact appears sometimes to have been overlooked. A superficial acquaintance with the doctrine of grace combined with an application, in a completely wrong context, of the teaching of the mystics on abandonment to God's will can lead to a practical quietism very far removed from the path of Christian perfection. We shall attempt to outline in a later chapter the principles which underlie resignation to God's will; for the moment it is only necessary to guard against misunderstanding them. The reaction, evident in certain quarters, from the uncritical legalism which has notoriously encumbered a particular type of moral theology is in constant danger of falling into the opposite excess. There can result from it a virtual antinomianism far more harmful in its effects than the error it sets out to correct. The authority of St Thomas is invoked in support of a naturalistic ethic, going by the name of humanism, which he himself would have been the first to repudiate. A radical misunderstanding of the principle *gratia perficit naturam*, the way in which grace perfects nature, can very easily lead us to minimise the importance of asceticism in the integral Christian life. In consequence grace, which indeed cannot be rated too highly, is deprived of its natural foundations and robbed of its fairest fruits. The nature which grace (*gratia elevans*) perfects is the vital foundation of our rational being, not the ill-assorted congeries of unregulated dispositions and tendencies which are the product of heredity, environment and education. Grace (*gratia sanans*) no doubt assists the process of drawing order out of chaos by the more natural means of self-discipline and ascetical practice, but it is not a substitute for them. Only when the ground has been well prepared can grace begin its work of perfecting the activities of the whole man.

Man is by nature a rational animal, that is, not a heterogeneous mixture, but an unique substance of which the animal element is in complete subordination to the rational. This is the creature perfected by supernatural grace. Little observation is needed to see that, in the concrete, men are no more than approximations to the ideal state of rational animality; they are not, at least to begin with, the finished product. We achieve that status, or strive to attain it, by a combination of intellectual insight, good will, and sheer physical effort. Unquestionably grace can work through and triumph over temperamental idiosyncrasies and even physical defects, but its perfective work is concerned with something far more fundamental. Grace does not, as we might sometimes be led to imagine, adapt itself to our natural dispositions and character; it rather subjects these to its own higher rule. In order to do this without infringement of our natural rights as beings endowed with personality and freedom, it works upon the ontological foundations of our nature—deeper down than the superstructure of temperament and habit—as they emerge from the omnipotent hand of God. Only secondarily does grace radiate outwards upon activities which, though more evident to us, are but the consequences and not the essence of our nature. Unless these activities have themselves been reduced to conformity with the nature from which they proceed—that is, subjected to reason and right desire—then the movement of grace is frustrated and its effectiveness diminished.

Nor is the perfecting of our nature brought about by grace a mere prolongation, in their own line, of the power and scope of our natural faculties. There is no continuum between the order of nature and the order of grace. Grace, being a participation of the divine nature, is a reality for the reception of which the creature has not even a positive capacity. The soul has no potentiality to be actualized by grace in the way in which it is actualized by the exercise of its faculties of intellect and will upon objects commensurate with their powers. The fact that we receive grace demonstrates that we are able to do so, but the capacity here indicated is no more than the non-contradiction inherent in the nature of the spiritual soul to be raised by God to so high a dignity. The perfection brought to us by grace is not a fulfilment of our natural powers—as if, without it, they would be incomplete—but the result of our being admitted to a share in the life of Him Who is Perfection itself. To suppose that grace adapts itself to nature is to suppose the opposite of the truth. Nature is subordinate to grace, not grace to nature. Because they both proceed from the same all-wise and supremely self-consistent Source we may justifiably argue from the processes of nature—as being better known to us— to gain some kind of analogical knowledge of the operations of grace, on condition that we bear in mind that we are interpreting what is greater in terms of what is immeasurably less. But we must avoid the gross error of expecting the things of supernatural grace and faith to fit neatly into the categories of nature and reason. Grace is a law unto itself and its workings are the proper object not of reason but of divine faith. Unless this is realized the way of the Cross and the self-renunciation of the saints quite naturally remain inexplicable. Moreover we are in danger of allowing our practical conduct to be governed by Aristotelian rather than evangelical principles. St Thomas had too clear an insight into the meaning of Christian perfection ever to make such a mistake; but the same cannot be said of all those who have appealed to him for support.

We have given to this chapter the title of "Unworldliness", as it seems the most suitable heading under which to gather some reflections bearing on the theme of detachment from the things of the world—a detachment which is a condition *sine qua non* of advancement in the love of God. The choice of the word would, however, be unfortunate were it to bring to the reader's mind those suggestions of vagueness and impractical idealism which are often associated with it. The world from which we must be detached is not the sphere of common and every-day duty, but what Mr. Christopher Dawson has described as " secular civilization considered as a closed order which shuts out God from human life and deifies its own power and wealth."[1] Christian otherworldliness is something very different from the attitude of practical acosmism advocated by certain philosophers. It implies not merely the possession of noble ideals but an awareness of how best they can be realized in practice and even the power to recognize circumstances in which such a realization is impossible of achievement. An idealism which is not tempered by the knowledge that what is best in itself is not necessarily the best here and now, and is unwilling to concede that some evils must be tolerated for the sake of a greater good, must develop logically into a ruthless doctrinarianism or degenerate into impractical day-dreaming.

Our Lord Himself is the model of genuine otherworldliness. Far from being uninterested in the world, His mission was to be its saviour and the supreme evidence of the Father's love for it. Most noteworthy is it also that, though personally blameless and inviting all men to moral goodness, Jesus carried out the work of the redemption by what we may justly call an intimate contact with sin. With consummate skill He drew what was good from every situation, and above all from the malevolence which was responsible for His death. The unworldliness embodied by Christ found its expression in His power to see all things in the light of

[1] *Beyond Politics*, p. 113.

heaven and conform each of His actions to the will of the Father, and not in any refusal to have dealings with the society in which He moved.

In order that we may act upon principles of Christian otherworldliness our conduct must be regulated by the infused virtue of prudence. Prudence includes both insight into the relation of the particular duty which is to be done here and now to the final end of life and the operative desire of that end by the will. For its effective working prudence, which we shall analyse in some detail in a later chapter, depends upon that harmony and right disposition in our lower appetites which is called temperance. It is from this last-named virtue, perhaps the most pleasing of all to behold in action, that there results the moral purity, *munditia*, and self-control before all that attracts the senses which form the body's vitally important contribution to true detachment. This detachment arises radically from the nature of the human will but, without temperance, it is unattainable in practice. Accordingly in what immediately follows we shall recall and enlarge upon what has been said about man's freedom and conclude the chapter by considering the virtue of temperance.

Mr. Aldous Huxley, though prevented by what would appear to be a sort of metaphysical monism from understanding the unique element in Christianity, shows his appreciation of the Christian thinkers in pointing to the indispensable condition of true liberty and moral perfection. "The ideal man is the non-attached man. Non-attached to his bodily sensations and lusts. Non-attached to his craving for power and possessions. Non-attached to the objects of these various desires. Non-attached to his anger and hatred; non-attached to his exclusive loves. Non-attached to wealth, fame, social position. Non-attached even to science, art, speculation, philanthropy. Yes, non-attached even to these. For, like patriotism, in Nurse Cavell's phrase, 'they are not enough.' Non-attachment to self and what are called 'the things of the world' has always been associated in the teaching of the philosophers and the founders of religions with attachment to an ultimate reality greater and more significant than self. Greater and more significant than even the best things this world has to offer."[1] About the nature of this "ultimate reality" the writer seems curiously uncertain; but he details with unfailing accuracy the characteristics of non-attachment: " Non-attachment is negative only in name. The practice of non-attachment entails the practice of all the virtues. It entails the practice of charity, for example; for there are no more fatal impediments than anger (even 'righteous indignation') and cold-blooded malice to the identification of the self with the immanent and transcendent more-than-self.[2] It entails the practice of courage; for fear is a painful and obsessive identification of the self with its body. (Fear is negative sensuality, just as sloth is negative malice.) It entails the cultivation of intelligence ; for insensitive stupidity is a main root of all the other vices. It entails the practice of generosity and disinterestedness; for avarice and the love of possessions constrain their victims to equate themselves with mere things. And so on. It is unnecessary any further to labour the point, sufficiently obvious to anyone who chooses to think about the matter, that non-attachment imposes upon those who would practise it the adoption of an intensely positive attitude towards the world." Mr. Huxley lacks the geniality of St Thomas, who could reconcile legitimate fear and even righteous anger with charity and non-attachment, but he is at one with him in subscribing to the truth expressed by Dr. R. R. Marett that " Real progress is progress in charity, all other advances being secondary thereto."

Detachment from all that impedes us on our path towards God must be paid for by effort and self-discipline. It should be noted, however, that the liberty it implies is inherent in our nature. All that is needed is that rational desire—in other words, the will —should take rightful precedence over all our lesser appetites and maintain its grip on the supreme Good by which alone it can be finally satisfied. It is because the desires of the will are boundless, because it can rest in nothing short of infinite goodness, that it can remain indifferent when confronted by each finite good. In the last analysis freedom is simply the indifference of the will before every object not in all respects good—that is, not comprising the

---

[1] *Ends and Means*, pp. 3 and 4. [2] Mr. Huxley's name for God.

totality of goodness—in virtue of which the will is not obliged to make a choice. When we are face to face with Goodness Itself, the Beatific Vision, no violence is done to the will, rather it is perfected in accordance with its nature, but it will be necessitated by its object, it will have no choice but to embrace what it sees.

Strictly speaking the will cannot be said, even by a metaphor, to see. Its power of vision is derived from the intelligence. Indeed it is in this latter faculty that free-will has its roots. Because the intelligence can range over all reality, can see things in their universal context, it endows the will with the power of remaining undetermined in any given situation. We are able to realize that nothing is good enough to draw the will irresistibly; even what is most attractive has, from some other point of view, its drawbacks. Thus liberty arises from the disproportion which exists between the will specified, of its nature, by the universal good and a particular finite object, good under one respect, not good under another, with which it is presented here and now. Freedom essentially consists in the dominating indifference of the will with reference to every object proposed to it by the reason as good from one point of view and not good from another. Even when the choice has been made and the act is being performed the will still retains its dominating indifference over the course of its action. Contrary to popular belief, personal liberty is by no means best demonstrated by "wilfulness" and revolts against habit and social convention; it is shown most clearly by insight into our own motives of action and an awareness that, no matter how "conventional" our conduct, we are never the victims of external constraint.

Awareness of this kind, as we have already pointed out, is easier to talk about in the abstract than to realize in practice. The inner life of the spirit, working itself out through intelligence and rational desire, is by nature other-worldly. Its activities reach immeasurably beyond the limits of space and time. But these activities are conditioned in our present state by the soul's union with the body. Unless it finds at its disposal a rightly-organized sensibility the spirit within is unable to enjoy its proper life, and discord instead of harmony prevails. The senses, unlike the mind, are determined in their reaction to certain stimuli, *determinati ad unum*; they possess no universal range and must respond necessarily to their appropriate objects. If then our sense-life has not been brought under the control of reason it is obvious that habitual liberty of action is out of the question. Freedom lies in the power of deliberation, in our ability to bring considerations to bear other than those to which we are immediately invited by the senses. If there are sights and sounds so intoxicating as to make deliberation impossible, sensations which carry us completely out of ourselves, in the moments we submit to them we are no longer free. Strong emotions are useful servants but bad masters; where life is dominated by them liberty recedes into the background. When reliance is placed upon feeling and imagination rather than on reason and forethought the poise and detachment which are the natural disposition to Christian otherworldliness are inevitably excluded. Clearly until the instrument with which it works has been tuned for its delicate task by the virtue of temperance the soul is unable to offer God the harmonious love-song which is His due.

Without tranquillity of spirit it is impossible to achieve even the beginnings of that conscious union with God in which most of all charity flourishes. Of the many afflictions to which we are subject under the present dispensation, disorder in our lower appetites is at once the commonest and the one best calculated to destroy mental peace. All the virtues have their work to do here, but to temperance belongs the chief task of calming the troubled waters. Accordingly, as St Thomas remarks, "tranquillity of spirit is ascribed to temperance in an eminent degree, although it is a common property of all the virtues."[1] If the concept of beauty is applicable to moral activity it is to the virtue of temperance that it is supremely appropriate. Beauty consists in a certain moderate and fitting proportion which it is the part of temperance to effect in our conduct. Moreover the excesses from which temperance withholds us have their origin in the nature which we share with the lower animals; hence beauty is its foremost attribute.

Repeatedly, when discussing temperance, St Thomas

[1] IIa IIae, q. 141, a. 2, ad 2.

returns to the thought of its beauty. He asserts that honourableness (*honestàs*) is an integral part or condition of the virtue itself, and honourableness he identifies with beauty. "As may be gathered from the words of Dionysius (Div. Nom. iv, 1), beauty or comeliness results from the coming together of clarity and due proportion. For he states that God is said to be beautiful, as being the cause of the harmony and clarity in the universe. Hence the beauty of the body consists in a man having his bodily limbs well-proportioned, together with a certain clarity of colour. In like manner spiritual beauty consists in a man's conduct or actions being well-proportioned in respect of the spiritual clarity of reason. Now this is what is meant by honourableness, which we have stated to be the same as virtue; and it is a virtue which moderates according to reason all that is connected with man. Wherefore honourableness is the same as spiritual beauty. Hence Augustine says, ' By honourableness (*honestum*) I mean intelligible beauty, which we properly designate as spiritual '. . . ."[1]

Temperance may be defined as the virtue which subjects the sensitive appetite to reason so that it is not carried away by pleasure, particularly those pleasures which belong to the sense of touch in the acts which are necessary for the conservation of bodily life. Its function is not to eliminate, or even minimize, sense-pleasure but to keep it within the limits prescribed by reason. Individuals will vary, on account of such factors as heredity and environment, in their natural capacity for acquiring this, as every other, virtue. It is furthermore true that a supernatural temperance, along with the rest of the moral virtues, is infused into the soul together with sanctifying grace; but this must remain ineffective unless it finds at its disposal the corresponding natural virtue acquired by our own efforts. We should note also that temperance is not to be confused with mental sloth and general insensitiveness—which are both vices. Nor on the other hand, is its task necessarily made more difficult by an alert and vivacious sensibility. On the contrary, this last is a favourable disposition to virtue, since it provides material more easily informed by reason.

[1] IIa IIae, q. 145, a. 2.

The body and the senses generally are not designed by nature to be subject to the despotic control of the mind. The relationship is subtler and more delicate. The reason should rule the activities of our sense-life like a wise king presiding over his subjects. The senses work on a lower plane and, lacking reason's swiftness and intuitive power, must lag behind in executing its directions. The first movement of sense-instinct cannot, in fact, be rationalized at all. Only by degrees, and after a period of more or less irksome submission to their influence, does our sensibility become reconciled to the rightful domination of intelligence and will. It is at this point that the acquired moral virtue has become operative. If, after their first immediate and uncontrollable reaction to external stimuli, the desires of our senses are held in check, awaiting the guidance of reason, we have become possessed of the virtue of temperance.

Before passing on to the more specialized activities of temperance it is worthy of note that our normal way of living and habitual social atmosphere greatly affect its fruitfulness, for good or ill. It is doubtless a convention for writers on the present theme to decry the times in which they live as depraved beyond words and readers are, not unnaturally, apt to discount their strictures accordingly. Nevertheless there are surely grounds for the belief that the speed and complexity of modern life are forces strongly opposed to the tranquillizing power of temperance and the rest of the moral virtues. If this is so it is the obvious duty of those concerned with the welfare of society to take account of the fact.

Where the majority of men are without real property, the wage-slaves of others, underpaid or living in constant fear of being thrown out of work, it is unlikely that they will have the time or inclination to reflect upon the things which make for the good life. Not that all men are asked to philosophize, but all are entitled to the freedom and independence without which the practice of even the common virtues calls for a degree of heroism which God alone, since He can give the necessary grace, has the right to demand. Nor are the diversions and escapes from the daily monotony which are now provided for all classes alike calculated to refresh the traveller on his path towards eternity. The sensationalism of the popular news-sheet appeals chiefly to the darker things in human nature. Vicarious emotionalism and opportunities for day-dreaming are perhaps the main attractions of the cinema. The wireless, instead of being used as an instrument for supplying news and occasional entertainment, is in danger of becoming a perpetual and stupefying narcotic. In work and play alike the sensations and nervous energy of the modern man are exercised to a high degree while his intelligence and mental powers lie dormant. In consequence the rational activity, which can never be entirely absent, is exteriorized and debased. At the same time his sensibility, fatigued and over-excited, is unable to respond to the call of the mind and fails to be informed by the moral virtues. In place of unifying and building up human personality the age of industrialism and machines tends with ruthless logic towards its disintegration. A fact which, while stirring them to action, should fill the minds of those who, even though living in that age are in some measure mercifully detached from it, with boundless compassion and charity for its victims.

To examine more closely the work of temperance. The general disorganization affecting our lower appetites, to which temperance brings a remedy, can conveniently be reduced to three sources. First, with reference to what sustains life itself, an excessive concentration upon food and drink. Secondly, in regard to the generation of the human species, an undue absorption in the pleasures attending the act whereby this is effected. Thirdly, as touching our own position in the universe, an inordinate desire for personal excellence, that is to say—pride. There can be little doubt that most of the moral and physical ills to which humanity is subject are traceable to one or other of these three main disorders. Significantly enough they are also the three chief bonds which attach us to the things of this world and prevent us entering into the liberty of the children of God.

The pleasures attending the activities most vital to our existence are an invitation to their use. It is fitting that to do what is natural should occasion delight. It would be monstrous if the operations by which man is sustained and his species propagated should involve pain and discomfort.

We must nevertheless recognize that it is by reason of the pleasures which accompany them that these activities are most of all abused. Eating and drinking are necessities of nature, but they must be regulated by reason. Unfortunately there are few of our actions less amenable to the control of the mind. Only by taking a long view can the thing be done at all. In themselves there is nothing to prevent our eating to the verge of nausea and drinking to the point of satiety. Men have, in fact, thought it worth while to go to these lengths. For the majority medical considerations, as well as the monotony of a familiar diet, would no doubt dictate greater restraint; but these will not suffice to subject our desires for the good things of the table to reason, still less to the law of Christian detachment. For this we need to practise that particular species of the virtue of temperance known as abstinence.

"The regulation of food, in the point of quantity and quality, belongs to the art of medicine as regards the health of the body; but with reference to the internal affections, as touching the good of reason, it belongs to abstinence."[1] And St Thomas reinforces the point with the following observation from St Augustine: "It makes no difference whatever to virtue what or how much food a man takes, so long as he does it with due regard to the people among whom he lives, for his own person, and for the requirements of his health: but it matters how readily and with what tranquillity of mind he does without food when bound by duty or necessity to abstain."

Nor is the reason alone the adequate guide to the right measure of food and drink. The temperance of the Christian is more than rational, it is supernatural and enlightened by faith. "In the consumption of food and drink the mean fixed by human reason is that food should not harm the health of the body nor hinder the use of reason: whereas, according to the divine rule, it behoves a man to chastise his body and bring it into subjection by abstinence in food and drink and the like."[2] It is obviously impossible to legislate for society at large, or even for a small community, upon what are the reasonable limits in this matter, and still more

---

[1] IIa IIae, q. 146, a. 1, ad 2.   [2] Ia IIae, q. 63, a. 4.

so the degree of retrenchment necessary in order to correspond with divine grace. Individuals must make discovery for themselves. A layman earning his livelihood in the world needs and is entitled to more than a monk living in a cloister; a manual labourer more than the student or scholar. A meal which would seem like a rigorous fast for one man is more than normal sufficiency for another. Sedentary and inactive people require less than those who are vigorous and constantly using up energy. And so on. In other words, the golden mean between excess and defect applies proportionately to different cases. It must nevertheless be applied, under pain of playing false to the light of reason and failing to live up to our vocation as children of God.

Frugality in food and drink is not only a first principle of Christian asceticism, it is a necessary condition of leading a life that is truly human. If radiance and beauty are the effects of temperate living it is equally incontestable that an impression of ugliness is created where it is absent. There is something peculiarly offensive to reason in the spectacle of excessive eating and drinking. When it has been occasioned by good fellowship it is easy enough to excuse; but the solitary or habitual practice of it is opposed to all that is best in man. Gluttony is not in itself the worst of sins but it is uniquely degrading. Even more than sexual excess, because with less excuse, over-indulgence at table is a reproach to the native liberty of the human spirit. The things whose purpose is to maintain the body as a responsive instrument to the mind's functioning on its own high plane begin themselves to absorb its attention. The heaviness and torpor which follow upon the immoderate use of food and drink as effectively dissolve our higher aspirations as fasting and abstinence promote them.

With good reason the Church in her Lenten liturgy, and spiritual writers with one voice, praise the efficacy of fasting. " We have recourse to fasting," says St Thomas, " in order that the mind may rise more freely to the contemplation of heavenly things."[1] In this he is a sound psychologist as well as a good Christian. Quite apart from the exercise of penance, it has always been recognized that mental clarity,

[1] IIa IIae, q. 147, a. 1.

without which virtue in its true meaning cannot exist, is greatly assisted by this particular form of asceticism. It is perhaps an unpalatable truth, but the positive advocacy by a St Bernard of a weak state of physical health as a favourable predisposition to contemplation shows a keener insight into the realities involved than is revealed in the humanistic sympathies of some among our more full-blooded contemporaries. Eight hours' sleep and three square meals a day are adequate safeguards of comfortable living, but it may be questioned whether the Kingdom of Heaven suffers any violence by such a régime. We have no reason for supposing that the perfect love of God which casteth out fear is to be bought so cheaply.

The ill effects arising from over-nourishment are, however, less extended in their range than the disorders comprised under the generic name of "impurity." The passions here engaged are more fundamental than even the desire for food and drink. Viewed by human standards, voluptuousness is more excusable than drunkenness and gluttony but it is a greater drain upon the spirit than either. "Sensual delights are more vehement and more oppressive to the reason than the pleasures of the palate : and therefore they are in greater need of chastisement and restraint, since, when they are consented to, the force of concupiscence is increased and the power of the mind weakened. Hence Augustine says (*Solil.* i, 10): ' I consider that nothing so casts down the virile mind from its heights as the blandishments of women, and those bodily contacts which belong to the married state '."[1]

The senses have their part to play in all human affection. Not being angelic spirits, we cannot, nor are we intended to, experience purely intellectual desire. Even man's noblest loves are first awakened by an intimation of the senses and find in them their most natural mode of expression. Friends and lovers rightly desire to be united to each other, a desire which cannot be completely satisfied in the ethereal realm of intelligence and spiritual affection. One has only to read the records of saintly friendships to learn that even for the choicest specimens of mankind

---

[1] IIa IIae, q. 151, a. 3. ad. 2. St Augustine is perhaps excessive here. One may prefer the more delicately expressed Pauline version of the same idea; cf. 1 Corinthians vii, 34.

there was no real substitute for the physical presence of the one beloved. Whatever be the impression gathered from the language used in its discussion, detachment from creatures does not mean that we should feel no pleasure in the company, or sorrow at the absence, of the people we like. There can be no mistaking the implications of the articles in the *Summa* where St Thomas explains the unitive effects of love. He is as uncompromisingly realist in his teaching as the most outspoken of modern psychologists.

In view of all this it may seem difficult to account for the hesitancy and misgivings of many holy and unsophisticated people when confronted by what is commonly called the problem of sex. In reality it is not so. There exist in the sex-instinct, which we share with the lower animals, deep-rooted elements of what is irrational and uncontrollable. This is proved not only by physical evidence but by the extreme difficulty of assessing degrees of moral responsibility in actions where this instinct is involved. The conjugal act has in fact a high spiritual significance as symbolizing the union between man and wife; although it seems possible that some writers, in an access of romanticism, have allowed themselves to exaggerate its extent. The love which it expresses and the issue to which it leads clearly fall within the supernatural scheme of the redemption, but the act itself and the orgasm in which it culminates are only remotely controllable by reason, as weakened through the fall, and cannot so easily be sanctified by grace. There are involved a submergence of the spirit and an abandonment to a powerful but merely natural instinct which, though human and therefore good, cannot be said to represent man at his noblest and best.

The Church has always defended the moral legitimacy of the marital act. It is unthinkable that the means ordained by God for the propagation of the race could be in any way blameworthy. Nevertheless, despite our proneness to what is naturally pleasurable, Christian tradition has always maintained that intimate union between man and woman is permissible only within the state of matrimony. In that context it has its only justification. Although it is possible for individuals to attain through marriage greater sanctity than many who are vowed to chastity,[1] there can be no question that, as states of life favourable to growth in holiness, the second is higher than the first. "Sexual intercourse casts down the mind not from virtue, but from the height, i.e., the perfection, of virtue. Hence Augustine says (De Bono Conjug. viii): 'Just as that was good which Martha did when busy about serving holy men, yet better still that which Mary did in hearing the word of God; so too, we praise the good of Susanna's conjugal chastity, yet we prefer the good of the widow Anna, and much more that of the Virgin Mary'."[2]

There is no more convincing proof that what is essential to Christianity is not of this world than the Church's teaching and practice in matters of moral purity. Not only does she defend marriage against exploitation by our animal nature, but maintains that to seek substitutes and compensations for it outside the state itself is gravely sinful. Even where it can enlist every temporal interest in its support the most imperious of all human passions is checked and humbled before an ideal which can be realized only beyond time. "The kingdom of this world and each ornament thereof have I scorned for the love of Jesus Christ, my Lord, Whom I have seen, and have loved, in Whom I have believed, Who is my love's choice."[3]

The dedication implied in life-long and deliberately chosen chastity has always been held in the highest honour by the Church. Not that insensibility in such matters is to be regarded as a virtue, nor that any importance is to be attached to celibacy for its own sake; it is its voluntary character and its high purpose which give to such a life its immense significance. So far as concerns mundane pleasures self-abnegation could not be more complete. Moreover the increase of intellectual and physical power resulting from continence is, or should be, directed wholly to God's service. But perhaps only the saints have been entirely successful in canalizing the energies liberated and placed at their disposal by the vow of chastity. The "sublimated eroticism"

[1] Vid. IIa IIae, q. 152, a. 4, ad 2.
[2] IIa IIae, q. 153, a. 2, ad 1.
[3] Prayer attributed to St Agnes, sung by consecrated virgins at their profession.

attributed to them by the psychologists is a phrase not without meaning. The forces which would otherwise have found their natural outlet are consumed in the intense activity of the spirit. Their austerities are no inhuman denial of all that is best in life, they are witnesses to a love in comparison with which all earthly passions pale into insignificance. It has long been recognized that the immanent operations of knowledge and love, when they become habitual, impose a strain on the merely physical resources of the body. Contemplation and the love of God are not of themselves conducive to a robust state of health. It is chastity which supplies the fuel to the flames of divine charity. When it does not fulfil this function it may well be a source of danger and disillusionment.

Although chastity, in the strictest sense, is for the few its benefits accrue to society as a whole. Its obligations are not of a sort to commend themselves to men in the mass. But, in virtue of the solidarity of mankind and of the Church, Christ's members, the self-restraint of individuals is of advantage to all. The many, who are responsible for the procreation of the race, and the minority, who are called to the celibate state, mutually complement each other and together contribute to the well-being of the whole community. " Wherefore sufficient provision is made for the multitude, if some betake themselves to carnal procreation while others, abstaining from this, betake themselves to the contemplation of divine things, for the beauty and welfare of the whole human race. Just as in an army, some take sentry duty, others are standard-bearers, and others fight with the sword: yet all these things are necessary for the multitude, though they cannot be done by one person."[1]

It would, however, be a deplorable mistake to conclude that the state of matrimony is incompatible with that detachment from the things of the world with which this chapter is concerned. The fact that marriage has been raised to the dignity of a sacrament is of itself sufficient to refute the suggestion. The union from which issues the Christian family is something essentially sacred. Furthermore the trials and difficulties inseparable from married life—with

[1] IIa IIae, q. 152, a. 2, ad 1.

which many who are vowed to chastity, being unfamiliar, are perhaps not sufficiently sympathetic—can often prove a far more effective purgation of the spirit than is effected by virginity. While the bringing up of children not seldom entails heroic sacrifices in comparison with which the life of the average religious is a régime of self-indulgence. Again married people are able to enjoy the benefits of chastity; for this virtue, like every other, is essentially a thing of the spirit. Spiritual chastity, the adherence of the mind to the things of God, is in no way dependent on merely physical integrity. " For if the human mind delight in the spiritual union with that to which it behoves it to be united, namely, God, and refrains from delighting in union with other things against the requirements of the order established by God, this may be called spiritual chastity, according to what is said in 2 Cor. xi, 2: ' I have espoused you to one husband that I may present you a chaste virgin to Christ '. . . . The essence of chastity consists principally in charity and the other theological virtues, whereby the human mind is united to God."[1]

By abstinence and chastity we are freed from bondage to the external necessities of life and our own strongest instincts. But there is another source of disorder, taking its rise not in the body but in the depths of the spirit, and therefore all the more insidious in its effects. It has issue in that exaggerated estimate of our own worth and the general importance of what we do—pride, in a word—for which the only antidote is humility. St Thomas, from whose thought these pages draw their inspiration, has sometimes been criticized for his apparent neglect of the virtue of humility. What has been the main theme of many of the masters of the spiritual life he treats of quite briefly, in a single question of the *Summa*, as a potential part of the moral virtue of temperance. The truth is that here, as elsewhere, he is of one mind with the whole of Christian tradition; the practical importance of humility is paramount—without it there can be no approach to God; nevertheless, when analysed precisely as a virtue, as a deliberately cultivated attitude of mind and heart, its contribution to the supernatural life of the soul is not so vital as that of the theological virtues and the gifts of the Holy

[1] IIa IIae, q. 151, a. 2.

Spirit. This statement may occasion surprise and must not be misunderstood.

Humility, the general attitude of complete submissiveness before God, arises from self-knowledge. St Bernard had in fact defined humility in these terms a century before St Thomas. *Humilitas est virtus, qua homo verissima sui agnitione sibi ipsi vilescit.*[1] If the knowledge of God and of ourselves given us by revelation, instead of remaining theoretical and sterile, truly determined our actions and outlook on life we could not fail to be humble. It has been pointed out that humility is a specifically Christian virtue, of which the pagans seem to have had little idea. For them " humble," ταπεινός, was synonymous with " low," " vile," " abject," " servile," and " ignoble." The revealed dogmas of creation *ex nihilo* and of the necessity of divine grace for every salutary act provide, so to say, the ontological foundations for humility. That we were produced from nothing by God; that He preserves us at every moment, by His positive act of conservation, from falling back into the original nothingness from which we came; that further we cannot make the slightest movement towards our salvation without His efficacious help are facts so all-embracing in their significance as not to fall within the category of any virtue. These are the truths which dominate the *Summa Theologica*; so that Thomism—whatever may be said of the shortcomings of the Thomists—might fairly be described as the theology of humility.

There are, moreover, certain advantages in setting humility in its wider context and then considering it in particular as a function of temperance. It is obvious enough that the virtue cannot be acquired without some measure of personal realization of our comparative insignificance in the whole scheme of things. There result from this knowledge the sense of balance and proportion, good humour, an absence of fussiness and self-importance which are often surer signs of genuine humility than downcast eyes and studious self-effacement. The humble man will unconsciously reveal the virtue in his actions, but as an effect of an inner conviction, not of seeking after the appropriate attitude. In this connec-

---

[1] *De gradibus humilitatis et superbiae*, cap. i, 2; P. L. 182, c. 942.

tion it seems possible that to approach humility, convinced of its absolute necessity and yet without insight into its relation to the theological virtues, is to run the risk of a certain unreality and pharisaism in the spiritual life. Indulgence in elaborate depreciation of self and all forms of mock-modesty merely bring discredit on the virtue they counterfeit; and yet such pitfalls are not always avoided even by those whose intentions are of the best. It is worth recalling that St Thomas had no difficulty in reconciling magnanimity, the desire to do great deeds which does not exclude the public recognition of them, with the possession of humility. " Humility restrains the appetite from aiming at great things against right reason: while magnanimity urges the mind to great things in accord with right reason. Hence it is clear that magnanimity is not opposed to humility, indeed they concur in this, that each is according to right reason."[1]

It may fairly be said that humility which is not based on right reason—that is, truth—is not far removed from hypocrisy. This is why St Teresa of Avila, and so many of her kind, learnt that humility is to be found more surely in the unself-regarding contemplation of the great truths of the Faith than by an introspective analysis of their own wretchedness. In so doing they can claim support from theology. Considering the question whether humility is the foundation of all virtue, St Thomas allows that indirectly this is true, since it expels pride and opens up the soul to the influx of grace; nevertheless, directly and principally, it is not humility but faith which holds first place. " A thing is first among the virtues directly because it is the first step towards God. Now the first step towards God is by faith, according to Heb. xi, 6: ' He that cometh to God must believe.' In this sense faith is the foundation of the spiritual life in a more excellent way than humility."[2]

We must, however, beware of over-simplification. Humility is the most difficult of all virtues to acquire, yet without it there can be no intimate union with God. It is the virtue which makes us repress whatever touches our own worth, in such wise that we do not seek more than accords with our

[1] IIa IIae, q. 161, a. 1, ad 3.   [2] IIa IIae, q. 161, a. 5, ad 2.

degree of excellence as fixed in the divine plan. Experience teaches us that the mere beginnings of this state of mind are only acquired at the price of unremitting effort. A preliminary acknowledgment of our complete dependence upon God is not sufficient to extinguish the seeds of pride within us. Co-operating with grace, we have continually to control that spiritual intemperance by which we tend to get above ourselves. The signs of the disease are painfully obvious to ourselves—and others. Complacency in our own achievements or in those of a society to which we belong (the corporate pride, for example, of a religious community at what it may consider its successes must be answered for proportionately by each of its members), impatience under criticism or rebuke, readiness to take offence and to be " hurt," anxiety that our efforts should be appreciated, the disparagement of others who excel in what we may conceive to be our own peculiar province, and the innumerable pettinesses which can disfigure daily life and effectively render the soul proof against the inspirations of grace. And then the deadlier forms: the habit of self-justification to the disregard of truth, intellectual arrogance and contempt for the stupid and unlearned, and all the multitudinous varieties of snobbery. There can scarcely be a more injurious food with which to minister to self-esteem than this last. Not only is it unsubstantial and without nourishment, it is a more or less thinly-diluted poison. In less figurative language, it is not merely opposed to that truth in our relations with God and our fellow men which is the basis of humility, but it tends to destroy charity, " the bond of perfection," by which we are united to them.

Charity, like faith, unites us more closely to God than humility; but unless the soul is humble charity can find no place there. This was the lesson Our Lord strove to teach us by so many examples: " The reason why Christ chiefly proposed humility to us was because it especially removes the obstacle to our spiritual welfare, which consists in our aiming at heavenly and spiritual things. And in this we are hindered by striving to become great in earthly things. Hence Our Lord, in order to remove an obstacle to our spiritual welfare, showed by giving an example of humility, that outward exaltation is to be despised. Thus humility is, as it were, a disposition to our untramelled access to spiritual and divine goods. Accordingly, as a perfection is greater than a disposition to receive a perfection, so charity and the other virtues whereby we approach God directly, are greater than humility."[1]

The expulsion of pride is the precondition of our growth in charity. Nor should a pretended regard for truth blind us to the depths of our inherent insufficiency. Our need for God's help is far more essential to our being than any of the gifts with which He may have endowed us. How true this is only the saints have realized. Nothing we have said above would justify us in ascribing to exaggeration their professions of personal worthlessness or to anything but sincerity their acts of self-abasement. Commenting on St Benedict's degrees of humility St Thomas declares: " It is possible without falsehood to deem and avow oneself the most despicable of men, as regards the hidden faults which we acknowledge in ourselves and the hidden gifts of God which others have. Hence Augustine says (De Virgin. 52): ' Bethink you that some persons are in some hidden way better than you, although outwardly you are better than they.' Again without falsehood one may avow and believe oneself in all ways unprofitable and useless in respect of one's own capability, so as to refer all one's sufficiency to God, according to 2 Cor. iii, ' Not that we are sufficient to think anything of ourselves, as of ourselves, but our sufficiency is from God '."[2]

It need hardly be said that, after Christ Himself, the Mother of God is the great model of this spiritual temperance we call humility. On realizing what was the Father's will, she did not hesitate to accept the highest office ever given to a mere creature; she could prophesy also that thereafter all generations would call her blessed. And yet the lowliness of her part in the public life of her Son, so far as externals go, could scarcely have been more complete. She kept His words in her heart.[3] Only with the passing of centuries has it come home by degrees to the faithful how tremendous were the implications of that keeping faith. Not without her

[1] IIa IIae, q. 161, a. 5, ad 4.   [2] IIa IIae, q. 161, a. 6, ad 1.
[3] Luke ii, 51.

pleading shall human pride be humbled and we find a place " In the heaven of humility, where Mary is."[1]

We may conclude this chapter with a summary of what has been said. In order that the life of grace should become effective in us it is necessary that we co-operate therewith. Grace can only perfect nature if nature itself is playing its due part. We have to assert our natural right to liberty and achieve in action detachment from the things of this world. The chief means by which this is attained is in the practice of the virtue of temperance. This in its turn involves a warfare on three fronts: retrenchment in the use of the things by which life is materially sustained, that is, food and drink; moderating the passions and instincts which centre round the generation of the human species, entailing chastity of spirit; a curbing of those tendencies to presumption and self-sufficiency, the thirst for independence, so completely alien to that poverty of spirit for which alone the Kingdom of Heaven is reserved.

In other words union with God in this world can be enjoyed only in an atmosphere of the evangelical counsels and the vows of religion. The literal fulfilment of these is necessarily for the few, but what is essential to them must be reflected in every Christian life. No one can hold himself absolved from striving after at least some measure of indifference to what are commonly called the necessities of life—and the vow of poverty is merely a fixing of the will on this particular objective. Without moral purity, fostered especially by the vow of chastity, we cannot hope to draw near to Him before Whom the angels themselves are not pure. Humility, in the last analysis, implies nothing more nor less than the submission of our own desires to God, that is, our conformity to the divine will. Only by obedience to God, or His representatives, can we appreciate the meaning of humility—a lesson taught no doubt more effectively in the cloister than in the world, but a lesson which all must learn whatever be their way of life. In charity our perfection essentially consists; but poverty, chastity and obedience are its most effective instruments. By living in their spirit we attain to the glorious liberty of the sons of God.

[1] Dante, *Vita Nuova*, 34, 7.

Part III
THE EXPRESSION OF THIS LOVE

I

PRAYER

"Pray without ceasing."—1 *Thessalonians* v, 17.

IN treating of prayer as the expression of man's love for God it is not suggested that this is the only point of view from which it might be discussed. It is by no means always from the fulness of our hearts that we speak to God. More often it is to voice some need, to ask that some request may be granted. Not seldom our prayers are dictated by self-interest; and even at their best they are perhaps more generally an expression of worship than of love. This is why St Thomas, with characteristic insight, treats of prayer rather as a part of the virtue of religion—itself a part of justice—than as related to charity. Nevertheless if prayer be understood in its widest sense, as a raising of mind and heart to God, it is the result of at least an initial love and desire for Him. Although we shall attempt in this chapter to consider its chief elements, it is this quite general meaning of prayer we have in mind when speaking of it as the outcome of charity.

The useful, though somewhat unfortunate, grouping together of such various activities as petition, meditation, liturgical worship and mystical contemplation under the simple notion of prayer has occasioned not a little confusion which might possibly have been avoided. Here, as elsewhere, before a synthesis can profitably be attempted it is of the first importance that we should analyse the elements which it is proposed to unite. And this is necessary, not only in the interests of speculative truth, but in order to avoid serious errors of judgment in the practical order. What, for example, is the right relation between vocal and mental prayer? Is communal always to be preferred to individual prayer? What is the relative importance of meditation and the public recitation of divine office? What place is to be assigned to fixed formularies of prayer when the contemplative state has been reached and the spirit feels itself constrained thereby? No one who has given any thought to such matters will deny that these are real problems. With the correct answers to be given to them we are not here directly concerned; nevertheless it is possible that the pages which follow may throw some incidental light on how they are to be solved. Little presumption is implied in such a suggestion, since whatever wisdom is to be found there has its source in the relevant questions of the *Summa Theologica*.

Prayer, according to St Thomas's analysis, is an activity of the virtue of religion. Religion itself is a perfection of the will disposing us to acknowledge dutifully our absolute dependence on God, Who is our first beginning and last end. It constitutes the bond *par excellence* uniting man to the source whence all his good proceeds. After the theological virtues the virtue of religion is the noblest of all, for it orders our activities to God more directly than any other. Prudence, fortitude, temperance and the rest direct man either in regard to his private conduct or in his dealings with his fellows, but religion directs him towards God. Its effect is to make him look to God, recognizing His sovereign majesty, serving and honouring Him by his acts as one Whose excellence infinitely surpasses every created thing. But the subordination of religion to the theological virtues, and particularly to charity, should be carefully noted. By charity we are raised to a friendship with God on terms of equality, we approach Him, not with reverential awe, but as the lover of our souls; by religion we pay homage to Him as the Creator and Lord to Whom everything is owed. Both these attitudes towards God are integral parts of the Christian life but the first takes precedence of the second; we have the divine assurance that we are not so much His servants as His friends. Religion is natural to man; reason of itself informs us that we must worship God and pray to Him. Charity is supernatural and of a higher order. It goes without saying that, in the Christian, religion should be elevated and transformed by charity so that it becomes a service of love. So understood, religion can be identified with sanctity, for it effects the detachment from the things of the world and the fixity of our intention upon God wherein sanctity or holiness consists.

Religion finds its expression in devotion and prayer. Devotion is a tendency of the will giving itself and all that it controls to the service of God with holy zeal. After devotion our first act in the worship of God is prayer. To this we must now give our attention. St Thomas is at pains to make clear that by prayer he does not mean some vague aspiration towards God. Prayer is an activity of the practical intellect consisting essentially in petition. It is the reason expressing itself in speech; this much, according to Cassiodorus, we can learn from the etymology of the word: *oratio* signifies *oris ratio*. Prayer is not an affair of feeling and sensibility, it is the work of the reason. The brute creation, being without reason, cannot pray. Now the reason has a twofold function: first it apprehends and co-ordinates its ideas for the sole purpose of knowing truth; secondly, it orders the knowledge so acquired to some practical end: it employs truth for the purpose of action. This second activity, unlike the first, is productive of effects; it is causative. It is true that in order to execute its design it must have recourse to the will; but this executive function of the will subtracts nothing from the causality exercised by the practical intelligence. It is the latter which is the real cause of the ordered effects which result, as the architect's plans are the cause of the building which emerges from the hands of the workmen.

A further distinction is necessary if we are to understand the manner in which prayer operates. The practical intelligence exercises its causality in two ways. It can command those things which are totally subject to it, as the will directs the lower members of the body or a king his subjects. Or it can lead up to its effect by so arranging matters that the desired result is brought about by an agent not directly subject to the will. In other words it can exercise a *dispositive* causality, by revealing such an attitude of mind and desire that it can truly be said to be instrumental in bringing about the successful issue. It is in this sense that prayer is said to be causative. Prayer is a beseeching or petition, an exposing of our needs before God that He may fulfil them.

"If, when we wish to make any request to men in power, we presume not to do so except with humility and reverence," says St Benedict, "how much more ought we with all lowliness and purity of devotion to offer our supplication to the Lord God of all things?"[1] St Thomas's theology of prayer is contained implicitly in these words of the Benedictine Rule. Nor is it out of place to draw attention to the nobility of the activity involved. Prayer is not an exercise of the imagination, an outlet for excessive emotionalism. It is the human reason unveiling itself before God, an act of homage whereby it reveals to Him—what indeed He knows already—the plan which it desires to see executed, while recognizing that on Him alone its execution depends. This is the profound implication behind every request we make of God. The highest power with which man has been endowed acknowledges its relative impotence before the Author of all and asks His help. A truth which suggests to us that only for worthy and excellent things should the reason have recourse to prayer; towards ordinary and inferior things its attitude should be one of command. We should only pray for the things we are unable to acquire by our own efforts.

When we speak of prayer being answered we mean that the wished for result has come about through the instrumentality of our prayer. If we had not prayed we should not have received the benefit asked for. Prayer has been truly productive of its proper effects. How is this to be understood? Are we to infer that the eternal plan in God's mind has been in some way altered in consequence of a creature's prayer? The answer to this problem throws further light on the sort of causality here in question. Far from changing God's designs, our prayers are the instruments by which from all eternity He has decreed to carry them out. "Divine providence disposes not only what effects shall take place, but also from what causes and in what order these effects shall proceed. Now among other causes human acts are the causes of certain effects. Wherefore it must be that men do certain actions, not that thereby they may change the divine disposition, but that by those actions they may achieve certain effects according to the order of the divine disposition, as happens in natural causes. And so it is with prayer. For we pray, not that we may change the divine disposition, but that we may impetrate

[1] St Benedict, *Regula*, cap. xx.

that which God has disposed to be fulfilled by our prayer: in other words, ' That by asking, men may deserve to receive what Almighty God from eternity has disposed to give,' as Gregory says."[1]

This answer leads to no fatalistic conclusion; for God moves us to pray while preserving intact the natural freedom of the will. But we have here the explanation why one of the conditions of the efficacy of prayer is that it should be in conformity with the divine good pleasure. Also it becomes clear how prayer is an instrument wherewith God carries out His government of the world and the particular decrees of His providence with reference to ourselves. He wishes that we should co-operate with Him causatively and pray for the good things He intends to give us. From this it is easy to see not only the necessity of prayer, but that no inspiration to pray should ever be neglected, and, consolingly, that such inspiration may well be a sign that this is the means whereby God proposes to fulfil our desires. The prayer of petition, that is, prayer in its essence, is at once a tribute of worship and a pledge that what we ask for will be granted. How significant is the light shed on the Church's liturgy by this truth! The liturgical prayers are almost invariably petitions, a beseeching of divine favour and solicitude for mankind. The official prayer of the Church is thus the world's supreme act of homage before its Creator and our best assurance of God's perpetual lovingkindness towards ourselves.

It might seem from this that our prayer should always take the most general form of a request that the will of God be fulfilled. Socrates did in fact hold the view that man should ask the immortal gods for nothing more explicit than that they should grant him good things; for they at least know what is good for us, whereas we, when we pray, often ask for things we should be better without. St. Thomas admits that this principle is sound as applied to things which may have an evil result and such as we may easily abuse—as riches, honours, power and the like. But there are certain goods to which no such disadvantages are attached: those, namely, which appertain to our eternal happiness. Things of this sort cannot be ill-used and for them we may ask unconditionally

[1] IIa IIae, q. 83, a. 2.

when we pray. For example, we can pray absolutely in the words of the Psalmist: " Show, O Lord, Thy ways to me, and teach me Thy paths."[1]

It is useless to pray without resignation to the divine will, for there can be no homage to the Creator and no efficacy in such a prayer. We do not pray in order to wrest from God what He is loth to give us, but to provide Him with an instrument wherewith He may fulfil His design in our regard. When this is understood our prayers can have as their object not only the things of eternity but our temporal necessities as well. Our Lord indicates as much in reminding us that if we ask we shall receive and in teaching us the Our Father. We have then a divine invitation to make detailed and definite requests in our prayers. Unfortunately, owing to our weakness and clouded vision, we do not always know the things that are good for us. Happily God Himself comes to our aid and orders our prayer aright: " Likewise, the Spirit also helpeth our infirmity. For we know not what we should pray for as we ought: but the Spirit Himself asketh for us with unspeakable groanings."[2]

But even when this much is admitted we may still feel that our own interests must be sacrificed in prayer, that we are no more than the playthings of divine fate. To avoid this conclusion we must recall what is the first principle which underlies all our relations with God: that He desires our well-being more earnestly than we desire it ourselves and—what is of no less moment—that He knows wherein it consists far more certainly than we. It is true that He views the matter from His own point of view rather than from ours. Living and acting in accordance with an eternal plan, His regard for us is measured in terms of imperishable things. In this respect He identifies our interests with His own. Judged by ultimate standards, no prayer whose object represents in the eyes of divine wisdom a true good is ever lost. As Père Gardeil has pointed out, " We receive payment now in what seems to us the coinage of our prayer, now in the coinage of immortality. All depends on the wise goodness of God; for His thoughts are not our thoughts nor His ways our ways. As the heaven is exalted above the earth so are His ways

[1] Psalm xxiv, 4.   [2] Romans viii, 26.

exalted above our ways and His thoughts above our thoughts."[1] And he continues: " Those who understand this will not leave off asking in their prayers for determined things. The mere fact that we pray with uprightness and confidence in God is the sign that God's power is being revealed in our prayer, that His divine providence is at work. The mere fact that we are inspired to pray for a particular object with piety and perseverance ought to give us the hope that this object is part of the eternal plan. Such a coincidence is frequent. It was from seeing St Monica praying in this fashion that St Ambrose had the intuition of the future victory of her maternal prayer. How many saints have experienced in this way the triumph of prayer, and later, recognizing the result, have said, paraphrasing the words of the disciples on the road to Emmaus: 'Had we not the certitude of that which has come to pass when we were inspired to pray thus?'"

The gospel urges us to seek in the first place the Kingdom of God, but it does not forbid us to ask afterwards for our temporal needs. St Thomas appeals to Augustine to state the principle which governs this second kind of prayer: "'It is lawful to pray for what it is lawful to desire.' Now it is lawful to desire temporal things, not indeed principally, by placing our end therein, but as helps whereby we are assisted in tending towards beatitude, in so far, namely, as they are the means of supporting the life of the body and are of service to us as instruments in performing acts of virtue.... As Augustine says: 'It is not unbecoming for anyone to desire enough for a livelihood, and no more: for this sufficiency is desired not for its own sake, but for the welfare of the body, or that we should desire to be clothed in a way befitting our station, so as not to be out of keeping with those with whom we have to live. Accordingly we ought to pray that we may keep these things if we have them, and if we have them not, that we may gain-possession of them'."[2] What is forbidden us by the gospel is an exaggerated solicitude for material goods, a preoccupation with them at the expense of our eternal interests. Such carefulness cannot

[1] A. Gardeil, *La Vraie Vie Chrétienne*, pp. 303, 304. The whole of the present chapter owes much to this admirable work.
[2] IIa IIae, q. 83, a. 6.

fail to distract us from our true love. But, when temporal things are viewed in relation to our final end, our hearts can even be uplifted by them. "When our mind is intent on temporal things in order that it may rest in them, it remains immersed therein; but when it is intent on them in relation to the acquisition of beatitude, it is not lowered by them, but rather raised above."[1]

These words show both the true nature of Christian otherworldliness and the profound act of homage implied in the request for merely earthly goods. Far from regarding our temporal necessities as of little importance in God's eyes we can use them as means of raising our hearts to Him. We look to Him for material as well as spiritual benefits. In this way the petitions for our daily needs assume the dignity of an act of religion. Through the medium of things apparently unrelated to the eternal scheme we acknowledge our dependence on God and thereby draw nearer to Him.

It is possible to summarize the whole doctrine of prayer by reflecting on the most admirable of all petitions made to God, the Our Father. St Thomas need exercise little ingenuity in showing that this is the best of prayers:

The Lord's Prayer is most perfect because, as Augustine says to Proba: "If we pray rightly and fittingly we can say nothing else but what is contained in this prayer of Our Lord." For since prayer interprets our desire, as it were, before God, then only is it right to ask for something in our prayers when it is right that we should desire it. Now when we say the Lord's Prayer we both ask for the things we may rightly desire and in the order wherein we ought to desire them; so that this prayer not only teaches us to ask, but also directs all our affections, *informativa totius nostri affectus*.

Clearly the first object of our desire is our final end, and only in the second place do we wish for the means by which this is attained. Possessed of the pure love of God, which is charity, we have as our end His glory simply for its own sake. This is what we pray for in the petition: *Hallowed be Thy name*. But the last end implies also our own possession of God's glory, our participation therein. Hence we pray: *Thy Kingdom come*, that is, to us.

The means to this end are of two kinds. The first of these

[1] IIa IIae, q. 83, a. 6, ad 3.

consists in those things whose whole *raison d'être* is to lead us to the end; of which the principal is that our life should be such that, by submission to the will of God, we merit our beatitude. For this we ask in the words: *Thy will be done on earth as it is in heaven.* In addition to this fundamental means there is another which is indispensable as a condition of our merit: life itself. Accordingly we ask God to *Give us this day our daily bread*—both that of the Eucharist, the sacramental food of our souls, and the corporeal bread by which our natural life is sustained. Thus in this petition there is contained a request for all that is necessary for soul and body.

Moreover on our path towards God we meet with many obstacles to our progress. In addition to the all-important petitions just enumerated we must ask protection against the many accidents which can befall us. *Forgive us our trespasses as we forgive them that trespass against us*: against those sins which directly exclude us from the Kingdom. *Lead us not into temptation*: that we may not be allowed to yield to temptation. *Deliver us from evil* : to be spared the extreme calamities of our present penal state which deprive us of the necessities of life.[1]

The Our Father, as might have been expected, is the noblest appeal for divine help that ever fell from human lips. It indicates what should be the interior state of the truly Christian soul: one of filial relationship to God and utter dependence on Him. Entreaty is made not to an earthly father, who, for all his affection, is limited alike in his realization of our necessities and in his power to minister to them, but to a Father " Who is in heaven." Our heavenly Father is not only well-disposed towards us to a degree of which we can form no conception but is possessed of omnipotence wherewith to make His love effective. We could have no surer grounds for confidence. It has been pointed out that the whole prayer takes its point and direction from the opening words: " Our Father." What we ask for in effect is the right ordering of our love for the Father; *ordinavit in me charitatem*. The initial salutation gives its character to all that follows. It manifests the essentially *religious* nature of each of our petitions. Again Père Gardeil is to the point: " The prayer of petition is not what it seems at first sight, by reason of the self-interest it expresses, the furthest removed

---

[1] IIa IIae, q. 83, a. 9 (somewhat paraphrased).

from the intention of the virtue of religion—the virtue which most of all resembles the theological virtues, and charity in particular because of its object: God Himself loved above all things for His own sake. When we say the Pater we need have no fear of the pettinesses of the prayer of petition. Each of its supplications is related to the glory of God and all converge in perfect order upon what is the whole end of religion, the honour of God. And it is the supreme praise of this sublime prayer, to have brought such unpromising material into the service of the virtue of religion; to have transformed the expression of our bodily and spiritual needs into religious aspirations towards the divine excellence, towards the Father Who is ' in heaven '."[1]

The plural form in which the Our Father is expressed suggests to us that there is an excellence attaching to prayers offered in common which cannot be claimed for the petitions of isolated individuals. Where two or more are gathered together, Our Lord has promised us, there is He in the midst. It would, however, be a mistake to press such a text too far. For the gospel also warns us against " much speaking "—the *multiloquium* of the heathens who imagined that they would not otherwise be heard[2]—and we are further invited to retire from the crowds and pray to the Father in secret. Nevertheless the Church, comprising the members of Christ's Body, has certainly interpreted the mind of the Master aright in giving preference to communal prayer. We pray to our Father in recognition of that paternity by which we all as brethren are His adopted sons. Even when we approach God silently and in solitude it is as members of the Church that we pray. We can never be " alone with the Alone " to the exclusion of the brotherhood. The Church's own prayers, which should be our models, are not personal requests but supplications for the whole Christian Society.

Now it would seem that the only effective means of giving expression to this corporate act of prayer is by means of the voice; for such is the normal method of ensuring a union of intention between the presiding minister and those who are assembled. Purely mental prayer, both on account of its

---

[1] Gardeil, op. ult. cit.; pp. 315, 316.
[2] Matthew vi, 6-7.

individualism and the fact that it leaves one of the noblest of man's faculties—that of speech—unengaged, is not so complete an act of worship as vocal prayer. Petitions uttered aloud and, still more, the use of the chant, are surely the means best adapted for impressing us with the significance of what we are about and awakening devotion. One may recall, in this context, St Augustine's emotion on listening to the Ambrosian music at Milan: " How did I weep, in Thy hymns and canticles, touched to the quick by the melodies of Thy sweet-attuned Church! The melodies flowed into mine ears, and the Truth distilled into my heart, whence the affections of my devotion overflowed, and tears ran down, and happy was I therein."[1]

It happens sometimes that what is best in itself is not the best in a given set of circumstances. This principle has no doubt justified the substitution by some of the modern religious congregations of more or less lengthy intervals of mental prayer in place of the traditional recitation of the Divine Office in choir. The exigencies of the active apostolate have demanded a new technique, a fact which the Church has so far recognized as to prescribe even for members of the older orders certain periods of this form of prayer. Religious activity has had to be concentrated and canalized in order to meet the necessities of modern life. Where formerly the choral recitation of Office and the Church's liturgy could work their influence undisturbed, fostering peace and disposing to contemplation, other more forceful means have had to be devised to counteract distractions. Point by point meditation, mental prayer, the Spiritual Exercises have been the chosen substitutes and it would be ungracious and, in view of authoritative approval, presumptuous to criticize them. The work and influence of the Society of Jesus are sufficient testimony to the value of such methods. Nevertheless the present liturgical revival and the desire of so many of the faithful to pray with the Church's own voice are signs that her worship corresponds to a deep-felt human need which cannot be otherwise answered. When all concessions are made to the efficacy of mental prayer it still remains that the official prayer of the Church,

[1] *Confessions*, IX, vi.

vocal prayer, is in itself the better and worthier form of divine worship.

Considered strictly and absolutely, we believe that this conclusion is not open to discussion. And, since conduct is ultimately governed by absolute standards, it is a conclusion of no little moment. In practice, however, matters become rather more complicated. It is obvious, for example, that to pronounce words which do not really reflect our mental state is less valuable than purely mental prayer. Such an activity is not in fact prayer at all, since prayer is, by definition, an exposing to God of the desires of our mind. Moreover, though by words and signs people normally find it easier to raise their thoughts to God, there are some who are sufficiently devout to be able to dispense with them. With reference to private prayer St Thomas observes: " We should only use words and suchlike signs when they help to excite the mind internally. But if they distract or in any way impede the mind we should abstain from them; and this happens chiefly to those whose minds are sufficiently prepared for devotion without having recourse to those signs."[1] On the other hand it is possible for words to be the very medium in which devotion finds its expression: " We have recourse to vocal prayer, through a certain overflow from the soul into the body, through excess of feeling, according to Psalm xv, 9: ' My heart hath been glad and my tongue hath rejoiced '."

Moreover there are certain movements of the mind towards God which are in themselves nobler and more meritorious than vocal prayer. An act of charity or of infused contemplation are cases in point. In order to avoid confusion and the appearance of going back on what has just been said it is necessary to recall the distinction already insisted upon between the theological virtues and the virtue of religion. It is from the point of view of the last named that we have been discussing prayer. On the terrain of religion, of the worship and service of God, vocal prayer holds primacy of place. Through religion we pay to God the debt of justice we owe Him as His creatures. To Him is due the service of our bodies as well as of our minds. For this reason: " The

[1] IIa IIae, q. 83, a. 12.

voice is used in praying as though to pay a debt, so that man may serve God with all that He has from God, that is to say, not only with his mind but also with his body."[1] In the light of this it is easy to see why the liturgy, and in particular the Mass, is the perfect form of worship. It engages the whole man, all that he has and is, and is the divinely appointed means whereby we acknowledge that we owe everything to God and are prepared to return everything to Him. But, as has been remarked on a previous page, our relationship to God is not only one of servitude; we are His friends as well as His servants. Our friendship with God brings us into the realm of His own peculiar dominion of the soul, the activity of the theological virtues and the gifts of the Holy Spirit.

There appears some justification for thinking that the interrelation between the theological virtues and the virtue of religion has not been given sufficient attention by some among the more enthusiastic supporters of the liturgical movement. Not without prejudice to their own cause and to even more vital interests. To confine the varied activities of the supernaturalized soul within the limits of liturgy, of the divine *cultus*, is a simplification which is open to many objections. It is true that the liturgy is claimed to be so all-embracing as to include every aspect of the Christian life, and indeed its apologists are only too anxious to insist upon its comprehensiveness. Unfortunately they seem only to succeed in doing so by sacrificing the manifold richness and variety they wish to safeguard. Names and definitions have of course a wide as well as a strict application and it would be pedantic to expect that they should always be used in their exact sense. But names and definitions are indicative of things and when they are used to signify anything and everything they are apt to lose any real meaning. Such ideas as " Liturgy," " Mystical Body," " Christ-Life " and the rest have a profound theological content; and precisely for this reason it is necessary that they should be submitted to calm analysis before being laid down as the principles of all-sufficing, if somewhat incoherent, philosophies of life. Syntheses of this sort bear witness to the personal vision and

[1] IIa IIae, q. 83, a. 12.

zeal of their authors but, to more prosaic minds, they have sometimes the appearance of leaving the chief problems of man's relations with God more involved than they find them.

The truth surely is that when the attempt is made to co-ordinate the many different elements of the spiritual life before they have been subordinated to each other confusion can hardly fail to result. "Co-ordination presupposes subordination," say the philosophers; and it is a golden rule. Likewise, and no less to the point, synthesis presupposes analysis; before bringing them together we must examine individually the various things we propose to unite and so determine their interrelation. Otherwise the union which results will be no more than a juxtaposition of heterogeneous elements upon which a collective name has been more or less arbitrarily imposed. Now the great realities with which the liturgists are so genuinely concerned have long since been submitted to the most scrupulous analysis by the theologians. While it is true that the liturgy can profitably be discussed from other than the theological viewpoint, when the liturgists claim to have discovered the solution to the chief problems of life, the panacea of all our ills, they implicitly take their stand on the ground of theology. And on that ground their showing is not always impressive. The centuries of thought which have gone to the formation of the theology of grace, of the theological and moral virtues and the gifts of the Holy Spirit, have accumulated a treasure which the apostles of the liturgy cannot afford to disregard.

It is difficult to see that any good purpose is served by using the Papal condemnations of nineteenth century individualism as a stick with which to beat the backs of those who prefer mysticism to religious ceremonial. There could be no surer way of playing into the hands of the enemy than by exalting social worship at the expense of the personal element in religion. For it is precisely this charge which is levelled against the Church by her more cultivated, and therefore more deadly, opponents. It is the glory of Catholic orthodoxy to meet the needs of man both as a social animal, asking to worship the Creator with his fellows, and as a *person* eternally alone with his God. No doubt we tend temperamentally to over-stress one of these aspects and neglect the other, but it is the obvious duty of those who wish to give instruction on such matters to aim at stating the case rather than pleading a cause. Little profit can be gained by labelling whole epochs as "individualist" because their outstanding religious personalities seem to have taken the liturgical life of the Church more or less for granted. Even in the last century it was not the masses who were guilty of the crime of "individualism" but the comparatively few in control of affairs who exploited the rest for their own selfish ends. The majority had little chance of practising any such iniquity, since they were deprived of all influence as well as of the respect due to personality. So long as human nature remains what it is men will tend to egoism and self-centredness, but the large-scale social evil which now confronts us is not individualism but its opposite, communism and all forms of totalitarianism. It is the person, *id quod est perfectissimum in tota natura*, which is now the object of attack and in urgent need of defence.

Nor is it by appealing to abstractions like "humanity" and "man" that the balance is most likely to be restored. What is needed is a recognition of the value of personality, a reverence for this particular man. It is easy enough to cherish sentiments of justice and charity towards mankind at large, but we shall be judged by our conduct to the human race as individuals. Even the doctrine of the Mystical Body remains unfruitful and in the vague if unenlivened by an appreciation of the uniqueness of each of its members. The individualism to which the reality of the Mystical Body is so valuable a corrective should not be confused with the "personalism" which is at the heart of all vital Christianity. Those who see in the doctrine of private judgment the chief cause of our modern chaos do not carry their diagnosis far enough. It is because the world has lost the true conception of God and the creature's value in His eyes that it has become "individualistic." In other words, it is the destruction or weakening of faith and charity which lies at the root of our preoccupation with ourselves. Lives of devoted public service and philanthropic endeavour are happily not lacking in our day. What is absent is the recognition of man's relationship to His Redeemer—the view of each individual as the "brother for whom Christ died," of the race collectively as forming His "Body." We should note, however, that through faith alone does this vision come to us; only with such enlightenment can we look upon the world as it really is. Moreover, while it is true that our external acts of devotion tend to increase faith and charity, it should not be forgotten that these two virtues are themselves the primary foundation of all Christian worship.

We might perhaps be reminded more often than we are of the principal danger inherent in all forms of ritualism—the danger of external worship becoming a substitute for, instead of an expression of, inward dedication of spirit. This was the burden of the denunciation of the prophets through many centuries of Israel's history; and Our Lord Himself, recalling the very words of Isaiah, spoke in no milder terms: "This people honoureth me with their lips, but their heart is far from me."[1] There could be no greater presumption than for us as Catholics to suppose that the awful warning implied in that message has no possible application to our own case. The Church's worship, in so far as it is Christ's, is perfect and all-pleasing to the Father, but no individual can claim as much for his own participation therein; that is to be gauged only by the measure of his charity. The Mass, considered in itself, is the one adequate act of worship ever paid to God, since it is Calvary reproduced on our altars; after the Mass there is nothing more to add: *consummatum est*. But neither the priest through whose instrumentality this marvel is effected nor the faithful who are present at it can appropriate its infinite worth to themselves. They cannot even say how much of it is theirs; for that depends on charity and the divine good pleasure. If the sacraments, effecting by their own power, *ex opere operato*, the graces they signify, are abused when made to do duty for the moral virtues and personal integrity, how much more so must this be true when liturgical worship is treated in this way. The Mass is not—still less are the other liturgical offices—sacraments in this distinctive sense. The increase of grace we derive from them depends upon the virility of the theological virtues and the

[1] Mark vii, 6.

virtue of religion operative within the soul. It is by the activity of these virtues that we " take part " in the liturgy. A taste for plain chant and ecclesiastical antiquity is to little purpose when not so vitalized from within. And further, this inward vitality can often find outlet along channels other than the ones marked out for it by those whose sense of liturgical propriety is above criticism. In the rosary, in Benediction, in popular hymns, equally well with Vespers and Compline. The crucial test is not enthusiasm for the liturgy but the degree of our personal love for God.

These remarks are admittedly no more than the commonplaces of Catholic piety and the liturgists would doubtless be the first to subscribe to them. It may be suggested, however, that there are heights and depths of the devotional life of the Church with which they do not seem sufficiently sympathetic. Nor is this lack of sympathy, not to say familiarity, concealed by their unquestionably sincere efforts to be large-minded and comprehensive. It is distressing, for example, to find an explanation of the liturgy which appears openly to attack the principles of Christian detachment—that is to say, the teaching contained in such classics of spirituality as the *Imitation* and the *Ascent of Mount Carmel*—with the object, it would seem, of establishing more firmly the humanism of liturgy and corporate worship. Naïveté of this kind need not be taken very seriously and the best of movements have to suffer from the indiscretions of their over-zealous supporters; but the results can be unfortunate. Not only is perplexity caused to the faithful themselves but the way is opened unnecessarily to the attacks of unbelievers; the *irrisiones infidelium* are seemingly justified and the Faith is discredited.

As is well known, modern psychologists are prepared to explain mass-worship and popular religion as manifestations of sub-human emotionalism. Communal prayer and hymn-singing, if not quite an " opium of the people," are at least a species of intoxication. By ritualism and corporate worship, they tell us, we take a holiday from ourselves and enter the lower world of unrestrained feeling and uncriticized belief. The substratum of truth underlying all this is obvious enough. Nor do the less-guarded apologists of the liturgy make the task of meeting the implied attack upon Catholic practice any easier. It is not by emphasizing what is palpable to all, viz., that liturgy corresponds to a very human need, that we are likely to bring home to the uninitiated the uniqueness of our worship. It is rather by pointing to the inner realities which inform the outward ceremonial, of which the latter is but the imperfect expression, that this will best be done. What distinguishes Catholicism from all other religions is not its material and human elements, with which liturgy is bound up, but sanctifying grace and the presence of the Holy Spirit by which it lives.

It may possibly be urged that the liturgists, having no apologetic aim, address themselves to the faithful, not to the world at large. But in any case they should surely remember that the Church of the liturgical revival is also the Church of St Augustine and St Francis, of Pascal and Newman. The Catholic system and individualism are admittedly incompatibles, but there is no incompatibility between the most rigid orthodoxy and the lonely and intensely personal union with God which is the stuff of mysticism. The *beata solitudo* of the Charterhouse offers at least as genuine a Christian atmosphere as that of a Eucharistic Congress. At the Reformation it was not so much individualism, as embodied in Martin Luther, that triumphed, as stupidity and licentiousness. The intensity of Luther's personal religion, despite its perverted subjectivism, was perhaps the best thing about him; had it been allowed its true development he might have been of the company of St Bernard and St Francis of Sales.

A living participation in liturgical worship must of necessity foster personal devotion. But it is no accident that the liturgy has not been a conspicuous preoccupation of some of the noblest religious minds. The reason is that, despite appearance, liturgical worship, strictly considered, is not so immediately concerned with God as the theological virtues of faith and charity and the gifts of the Holy Spirit. From these proceed that experimental knowledge and love for which the liturgy is a preparation or a means of expression. It is true that the liturgy provides opportunity for the exercise of these virtues, but it also offers scope for others not so patently supernatural. Musicianship, an appropriate sense of the antique, an eye for colour, delicate sensibility and all those qualities which go to form what is called the artistic temperament are admirable gifts to place at God's service, but it is possible for them to co-exist with defects which make them on the whole very mixed blessings. Nor do they form in themselves the most valuable natural asset, considered as a ground-work for the activity of grace. They are not so valuable as sheer intelligence, as prudence, justice, fortitude and temperance. Where these last are lacking, in any marked degree—and the artistic virtues can, and notoriously do, exist without them—it is possible for the liturgy to become an object of unconscious exploitation in the interests of aestheticism. The only safeguards against this danger, which is perhaps inherent in so variegated and manifold a complexus as the liturgy, is a study of the theology on which it is based and, above all, the development within the soul of the virtues of faith and charity.

We have seen that the prayer which expresses itself in speech and corporate worship is an activity of the virtue of religion. A virtue takes its worth from the object, or subject matter, with which it has to do together with the end to which it is directed. Thus religion is the highest of all the moral virtues because its object, though something created and often material (e.g. bread or wine or speech itself), is offered directly to God. Religion is always concerned with God, but *indirectly*, that is, through the medium of something else. The theological virtues and the gifts, on the other hand, are concerned with God *directly*, without any created medium. An act of faith, or of love, is not a directing or offering of something to God, whether it be the expression of a need or the dedication of some material object, but a direct aspiration towards Him of the intellect or will. In practice, of course, religion and the theological virtues mutually interact: acts of religion will normally be influenced by faith and charity and these will find their external expression in prayer and worship and the other activities of religion. Notwithstanding this they are different virtues and the distinction between them has practical implications of some importance. Different types of holiness are ultimately to be accounted for, not indeed by the operation of some virtues to the exclusion of the rest, but by the predominance of certain among them —with the result that the individual's spiritual life becomes, as it were, characterized by their activity. Thus the virtue most clearly revealed in the life of St Benedict was religion, in that of St Thomas Aquinas faith joined with wisdom, in St Ignatius's perhaps supernatural prudence.

Furthermore religion, being a moral virtue and therefore concerned with the means to the end, must to this extent be regulated by prudence. It must observe the golden rule, *ne quid nimis*, nothing in excess. Our strictly religious activities must be performed with due regard to time and place and circumstances and the claims of the other virtues. Curiously as it may sound, it is possible to be too religious. It is to no purpose to be praying in church when duty demands that we should be elsewhere. It is vanity and illusion to be devout, which is sometimes a luxury, when what is required of us is that we should behave justly towards our neighbour.

But the theological virtues know no such embarrassments as these. Having God for their object, they are not limited by the restrictions of time and place and the exigencies of the material world. They regulate prudence and the moral virtues and are not ruled by them. Accordingly the golden rule does not apply to the theological virtues; they cannot exceed a rule which is itself infinite; we can never have too much faith or hope or charity:

> Quantum potes tantum aude:
> quia major omni laude,
> nec laudare sufficis.

Or, in Crashaw's lovely rendering:

> Stretch all thy powres; call if you can
> Harpes of heaun to hands of man.
> This soueraign subject sitts aboue
> The best ambition of thy loue.

Again, unlike the virtue of religion, the theological virtues are in no way dependent on matter. Without speech we cannot pray in common, without bread and wine we cannot celebrate Mass, without favourable times and places we cannot engage in the liturgy; but without any of these things we can place ourselves in God's presence through faith and love Him through charity. And thus we are led to speak of contemplation.

Infused contemplation, the theologians teach, is not an activity of the virtue of religion and is not therefore prayer in the sense described above; it is rather an actualization of the virtues of faith and charity with the co-operation of the gift of wisdom. So considered, it is a higher and nobler operation of the individual soul than prayer, even than the common prayer of the liturgy. In practice contemplation normally issues from preceding meditation. A passage from scripture, a verse of the psalms, or some consideration of the life of Christ is the point of departure. Thence the soul moves upwards towards God in acts of faith, hope and love, the gifts of the Holy Spirit at the same time conferring some kind of experimental knowledge of divine things, and, with contemplation proper, the whole supernatural organism becomes dynamically alive. Contemplation is caused by charity and in its turn promotes charity's increase. For the will, in its desire for God, directs towards Him the intelligence in loving regard, and the intelligence, enlightened by an ineffable knowledge, leads on the will.

That contemplation and the affective movements of the soul which normally accompany it are distinct activities from prayer, particularly vocal and public prayer, is obvious to anyone who cares to give thought to the matter. These acts of religion can foster contemplation, although it must be acknowledged that on occasions they may seem to hinder it. Thus the feeling of incongruity about engaging in the Divine Office, or any set forms of vocal prayer, immediately after Communion has *prima facie* a certain theological justification. Communion is not only an act of religion, it is also the sacrament of charity, and the instinct which suggests that the moments which follow on its reception should be given over, not merely to acts of religion, but to acts of intimate love is very sound. It seems inappropriate that we should play the part of servants when we are being invited to behave as friends. But if these alternatives present themselves to us as a practical difficulty it is because we have still to achieve the balanced harmony between our outward actions and inner spirit. There can be no real opposition between the virtue of religion and the theological virtues. Liturgical worship, St Thomas reminds us, should be but an expression of that interior devotion which consists in faith, hope and charity: *exterior autem cultus proportionari debet interiori cultui, qui consistit in fide, spe et charitate.*[1] Thus the priest or religious would clearly be wrong, and foredoomed to failure, who attempted to cultivate a personal relationship with God at the expense of his duty to Him as a representative of the Church as a whole. And it is in this latter capacity that he takes part in the Divine Office, the " work of God " *par excellence*. When, in practice, the claims of charity and religion appear to be in conflict we may conclude either that our religious worship is as yet insufficiently motivated by love, or else that our charity is not strong enough to express itself outwardly in acts of worship. We are still far from the state of Christian perfection.

While it is necessary, in order to avoid a *simpliste* view of the spiritual life, that we distinguish the theological virtues from religion, contemplation from prayer, it is of equal importance that we should not erect an unreal dichotomy between them. A departmentalized spirituality is no less a misfortune than one that is over-simplified. Charity is not religion and religion is not charity, but charity can be religious and religion can be informed with charity. Contemplation and liturgical worship are not the same things but they can, and obviously should, exist harmoniously together. St Thomas tacitly admits that this is so when he speaks of the attention needful for prayer.[2] He declares that the mind's absorption in God, while at prayer, can sometimes be so great, as to make it oblivious of all else. Moreover it is just this kind of attention, of our thoughts to God, that is most necessary. Attention to pronunciation of the words or to their meaning is of secondary importance compared with the fixity of our minds on Him to Whom we pray. And this attention is possible for all, even the simple and unlearned, the *idiotae*. An unlettered nun, reciting words she does not understand, can be more closely united to God at Divine

---

[1] Ia IIae, q. 103, a. 3.   [2] IIa IIae, q. 83, a. 13.

Office than the scholar and linguist well aware of the significance of all that he utters.

Again, in the light of these principles, it is possible to understand how modern methods of " mental prayer" can compensate for the absence of the full liturgical life. The meditative atmosphere and elevation of spirit engendered in the monastic orders by the chant and the Office in choir can be fostered by other means. The Exercises of St Ignatius have led so many to sanctity that, even apart from the weight of authoritative approval, their efficaciousness is proved beyond dispute. They must have stirred into activity many hundreds of souls whom the calmer, less picturesque intimations of the *opus Dei* would have left untouched. Nor can it be doubted that they dispose the mind to receive the gift of contemplation. Mental prayer, as we have seen, considered strictly as prayer, as petition, is not so worthy a service of God as the Divine Office, but the Exercises imply far more than mental prayer. Once the stage is reached where the imaginative setting can be more or less set aside and strenuous personal efforts give place to a divine influence, the way is open to contemplation and the closest union with God. Contemplation is indeed the lamp of the spiritual life; without it the soul walks only in twilight. The lives of St Francis Xavier, of St Alonso Rodriguez, or of St Ignatius himself, are as inexplicable without it as are those of St Bruno and St John of the Cross.

Of the relation of contemplation to action we shall say something in a succeeding chapter. Here it is only necessary to recall that contemplation is not an accomplishment acquired by our own efforts, but a gift of God. Nevertheless, according to the teaching of the masters, it is a gift He is willing to bestow on all who co-operate with Him, in other words, on all who are prepared to pay the price. What that price is we have indicated from one point of view in the last chapter and shall return to it again in the next. Contemplation is not precisely the love of God but it is the indispensable condition of any intensity of love. For love presupposes knowledge, and the knowledge given us through faith must be quickened by contemplation before we truly know in Whom we have believed.

Without contemplation we shall never make much progress in virtue, and shall never be fitted to make others advance therein. We shall never entirely rid ourselves of our weaknesses and imperfections. We shall remain always bound down to earth, and shall never rise much above mere natural feelings. We shall never be able to render to God a perfect service. But with it we shall effect more, both for ourselves and for others, in a month, than without it we shall accomplish in ten years. It produces acts of great perfection, and such as are altogether pure from the alloy of nature; most sublime acts of the love of God, which we perform but very rarely without this gift; and, in fine, it perfects faith and all virtues, elevating them to the highest degree to which they are capable of rising.[1]

[1] Father Louis Lallemant, S.J., *Spiritual Teaching*, 7th Principle, IV, article 4.

II

SELF-ABNEGATION

" If any man will come after Me, let him deny himself and take up his cross and follow Me."—*Matthew xvi*, 24.

In view of a point which has already been made, namely, that charity is in no way opposed to rightly ordered self-love, the title of the present chapter may appear somewhat out of place. We have seen that the love of God is inseparable from the desire for our own perfection; for without the latter that love cannot attain its realization. We feel conscious that whatever meaning is to be attached to self-denial and the giving up of our own will they cannot imply any diminution of personality or ultimate frustration. The self which we abandon for God's sake is not the self that is to enjoy the Beatific Vision. Nevertheless the soul's movement towards God involves a purification, an adjustment of its powers to the lofty heights of the supernatural order, so painful in its effects that spiritual writers have not hesitated to describe it in terms of self-destruction. The natural movements of the mind and body must be brought into harmony with the law of grace, a process which cannot be achieved without suffering. We have to be transformed into the sons of God; or rather, the transformation produced in the depths of the soul by the first infusion of grace must work itself out in all our activities. Where grace is allowed its true development it does not remain hidden within the soul but bears fruit in every human action.

It is this co-operation with grace, not the initial possession of it, which is so afflicting to nature. And yet it is only by entering upon this path, the royal road of the Cross, that we can be said effectively to love God. Charity draws us onwards and itself gains strength by our fidelity; it sweetens suffering, but it does not make it less real or less necessary. The love of God is more delightful to the spirit than all else besides, but, lest the happiness beguile us, it is ever accompanied in this life by sacrifice and pain. That charity finds its inevitable expression in these ways is a truth we can learn, not only from the lives of each of the saints, but also, and preeminently, from Our Lord Himself. " O foolish and slow of heart to believe in all things which the prophets have spoken. Ought not Christ to have suffered these things and so to enter into His glory? "[1]

We have touched also in a previous chapter on the necessity of detachment and unworldliness. We saw that these are achieved chiefly through the virtue of temperance. What we shall now have to say can be considered as an elaboration of principles there laid down but from a rather different point of view. A measure of asceticism is a condition without which the supernatural life, and even normal rational existence, is impossible. Self-discipline is simply a law of our being the infringement of which carries with it its own penalties. Without systematic retrenchment of some sort it is morally impossible to avoid mortal sin, let alone advance in charity. We are not now concerned, however, with what we may call the subsistence level of grace and charity, but with their growth and development. What was formerly accepted by the soul as a more or less irksome necessity is now used by it as a means for expressing its love. It is from this viewpoint that we shall here venture some reflections on suffering and self-abnegation and their place in the Christian life.

Suffering essentially consists in the endurance of something distasteful. That it implies passivity rather than action is noteworthy. The virtue of fortitude, by which it is met, is more surely demonstrated by the power to endure than by aggressiveness.[2] And in practice our trials come to us, for the most part, from without, from circumstances beyond our control. It is true that the saints have been led by their charity deliberately to seek pain; yet, even with them, it is by their docility to divine inspiration and the passive purification of the senses and the spirit that they have been united most closely to God. Their " follies " are rather a response to a grace which urges them to conformity with Christ than calculated self-laceration. The Passion itself is the prototype of suffering passively endured. " He was led as a sheep to the slaughter: and like a lamb without voice before his shearer."[3] Though deliberately accepting them and even

---

[1] Luke xxiv, 25-26.   [2] IIa IIae, q. 123, a. 6.   [1] Acts viii, 32.

rejoicing therein, as the instrument of our redemption, Our Lord submitted to the torments of Calvary as we submit to our own sufferings—against His every instinct and as conflicting with His natural human will. Not the least consoling incident in that incomparable life is the dark hour in the garden of Gethsemane, wherein our Divine Master is prostrated in fear and horror at what lies before Him. From that moment until the end He Who was most of all qualified to do so wrestled with the problem of evil and the mystery of iniquity—the two questions before which the philosophers prove so unhelpful—and brought them to triumphant solution.

The self-abnegation of Christ in His sufferings was the complete and perfect expression of His charity. "Greater love than this no man hath, that a man lay down his life for his friends."[1] The mystery of the Hypostatic Union forbids any close scrutiny of what that agony involved, but theology can take us a certain distance. While the flesh shrunk before its tormentors the spirit within turned everything to profit. On its outer surface (if we may so speak), in its immediate connections with the body, the spirit also felt the stress of conflict; but far in the depths, at the well-springs of the intelligence and will, there was peace. Our Lord did not allow, as He might have done, the consolations of the Beatific Vision to overflow into the sensibility assuaging its pain, but He controlled all in the light of knowledge and the strength of love. He saw the purpose of each of His afflictions, recognized at once their eternal value and partial futility, knew them as something fixed in the divine plan before the ages, and, as such, accepted them. What His mind saw so clearly His will embraced, not indeed as desirable for its own sake—suffering can never be that—but as the means whereby we were to be restored to life.

Christ was in no need of being detached or purified from the things of the world; but of Him alone among the sons of men could that be said. He underwent the process vicariously, to make the thing possible for us and to show us in what way it was to be done. The purpose of suffering is to teach us that, in the last resort, we have nothing to hope for

[1] John xv, 13.

apart from God, to force us to place all our desires in Him. When pain is prolonged beyond the point at which nothing can distract us from it, becomes so intense that our whole attention is absorbed, then we must lose consciousness or go temporarily mad or master it by charity. Our Lord's method was the last. His whole sensibility outraged, deserted by His friends and deprived of all earthly consolation, He sent forth His spirit in longing towards the Father in the supreme act of love whereby we are redeemed. " Father, into Thy hands I commend My spirit."[1] This was the heart of the redemption, of the sacrifice of the Cross. Not pain, not individual suffering offered up to God as a sort of gift—as if we could give anything to God which is not already His, or as if (which is equally unthinkable) He could take pleasure in human anguish. The blood and wounds of Calvary are tokens of an immortal love. Through them Christ demonstrated to the world how close was His union with the Father.[2] In this way He proposed Himself as the model, and gave countenance to the universal and only significant meaning of sacrifice to God: inner dedication of spirit. " Whatever is offered to God in order to raise man's spirit to Him may be called a sacrifice." *Omne illud quod Deo exhibetur, ad hoc quod spiritus hominis feratur in Deum, potest dici sacrificium.*[3]

That we may better understand what is implied by self-abnegation we must attempt to formulate some clear ideas about the nature of evil and suffering. From the early days of philosophy men have concerned themselves with the problems to which these darker realities give rise. But only in the light of Christian revelation have conclusions been reached which can be regarded as satisfactory. After the creation God looked upon His handiwork and saw that it was good. Man has not always shared that view. Convinced that all was not well, some have wished to identify matter with evil and allowed goodness only to the spiritual world. Material life was for them, in Shelley's phrase, " a dome of many-coloured glass staining the white radiance of eternity." If we would overcome evil, they tell us, we must shun all contact with matter and aspire to the life of disembodied spirits. Others, more crudely, have tried to account for the

---

[1] Luke xxiii, 46.   [2] Cf. John xiv, 31.   [3] IIIa, q. 22, a. 2.

chaos of the world by some great principle, evil of its nature, from which all disorders proceed. According to this view, we have God on the one side, the origin of all good, and over against Him a malignant power, as real and positive, in its way, as the good principle, which is to be credited with the production of evil.

It should be noted that suffering and pain, considered in themselves, are unquestionably species of evil. Or, to be more accurate, they denote that absence of goodness wherein evil essentially consists. Some few, even among Christians, have wanted to deny this, thinking that the divine benevolence and omnipotence are thereby compromised. They take refuge from the unpleasant facts of life either in an attitude of brutal optimism and *sang froid* or by a refusal to acknowledge their existence. Outside Christianity evil as a practical difficulty, as suffering, has been met, broadly speaking, in two ways. By blind submission to a relentless destiny, the " will of Allah," the kismet of Islam. Or, with even more ruthless logic, by the attempt to achieve a state of ataraxy, a mastering of evil by yielding to no emotion before it, which was the aim of Stoicism. Neither of these solutions has commended itself without qualification to the Christian thinkers. The first ignores human freedom and minimises unduly our power to co-operate with God in controlling events and overcoming unfavourable environment. The second confuses fortitude with insensibility and substitutes a patronizing condescension for genuine sympathy with the misfortunes of others.

Evil, as we have remarked above, lies in the absence of goodness. It is not something positive—we shall speak of the *positive* aspect of pain in a moment—something really existing, but the privation of what seemingly ought to be present. Thus it is no mere negation, that would be to empty it of meaning, but the lack of what should rightfully be there. It is no evil that a man should be without wings and therefore unable to fly, but it is an evil that he should be blind, for the power of sight is his by nature. Strictly speaking there is nothing *essentially* evil, since evil is not a substance and cannot exist suspended in a vacuum; it is always a parasite, a blemish on what is good. To take a homely example. A tooth-ache is caused, we may presume, by some foreign substance coming into contact with the ivory of the tooth. In consequence disintegration and decay set in, unwonted pressure follows on the free nerve-endings within the tooth, and pain results. On analysis none of the elements which have combined to produce the pain turns out to be anything but good. A morsel of food has lodged between two of our teeth. Being affected by the saliva in the mouth, it is modified in such a way that it ceases to be a healthy piece of food and becomes a substance reacting unfavourably on its environment. It is still good in its way with, no doubt, valuable properties all of its own. The evil comes about through its being juxtaposed at this particular moment with a substance with which it cannot agree. The chemical action which is going on is a perfectly normal one and could be reproduced without any unpleasant results in the laboratory. As to the pressure on the nerve-endings which immediately causes the pain: the substance which presses is good enough in its way, though it is not good precisely as tooth-stuff. The nerve too is good; it is just because it is good that it protests so violently, for that is its function. But the evil is a reality. In what does it consist? Surely in this, that the tooth is not enjoying its ordinary healthy life. It has been deprived of this by the presence of an alien factor: the chemical reaction set up by dissolving food. All that is positive in the affair, from the dissolving food to the vibrating nerve, is good. The evil and pain are genuine enough; their explanation, however, is to be sought, not in something positive, but in the absence of what should rightfully be there, viz., the highly organized and intricate working-together of everything which contributes to sound tooth-life.

The principles just applied to the every-day example of tooth-ache are universal in their range and hold good for all disorders in the physical world. Christian philosophers are agreed in ascribing evil to lack of harmony. Diverse elements, good of themselves, are juxtaposed in an unnatural situation. Factors, harmless in isolation, are brought together out of their context. This is true also of moral evil, sin, though we have here the added and more fundamental discord of malice and ill-will. The physical concomitants of sin can be analysed in the way already indicated and even the malevolence wherein it essentially consists can be reduced to a failure of the will in its movement towards goodness; in other words, to an absence of what should be there. Thus, in a case of murder by stabbing, the physical evil lies in this, that the normal balanced arrangement of veins and arteries and tissues has given place to an instrument of violence, a knife-blade—an admirable and useful product of human ingenuity in its due place. The ill-will from which the crime originated was injustice, a failure to recognize in practice the rights of another. For this failure the will itself, in virtue of its freedom, was responsible. We are accountable for our own lack of good-will. It should be noted, however, that it is the lack of what ought to be there, not the presence of something positively evil. Moral perversity is indeed the chief source of chaos and human misery, but it is a witness to creaturely deficiency, not to the presence of a creative principle of evil at work behind the universe.

As suffering inevitably arises from some kind of disorder, and as suffering is also bound up with life as we know it, the question cannot fail to suggest itself: What is God's responsibility for the evil whereby it is occasioned? "Thy hands have made me and fashioned me wholly round about. And dost Thou thus cast me down headlong on a sudden? Remember, I beseech Thee, that Thou hast made me as clay and Thou wilt bring me into dust again."[1] Was Job justified in thus making complaint to God? It is surely of high significance that one of the divinely inspired books presents us in dramatic form with the spectacle of man standing over against his Creator, questioning Him as to the meaning of the calamity which befalls him. God would not allow us to deceive ourselves; He desires us to enter into the mystery of pain. Without this initiation we can hold no intimate communion with Him. The gospel, the good news, began with sacrifice and that word is writ large across the pages of Christian history. Through sacrifice we gain entrance into the world of the spirit and remission from impurity. "And without the shedding of blood there is no remission."[2]

Let it be acknowledged that God wishes us to suffer. The

[1] Job x, 8-9. [2] Hebrews ix, 22.

treatment meted out to His Sole-Begotten Son and to the noblest and best among His friends cannot but be a law of His dealings with men. Not that He wills pain for its own sake. Such a conclusion is repugnant to the attribute of divine mercy and is refuted by the ministry of Our Lord Himself who worked His miracles, the very proofs of His Godhead, for the relief of human distress. In view of this example we have every authority for overcoming evil by good and employing all available means for counteracting pain and making life as a whole easier and pleasanter. Suffering has not of itself a purifying power—that depends upon the insight and moral worth of the sufferer—and it is perhaps as well for many of us that we are not called upon to endure any great privations. Misfortune is productive of patience and heroic fortitude, but also of bitterness and cynicism. As St Augustine remarks: "For as in one fire gold gleams and chaff smokes, and as under one flail the straw is bruised and the ear cleansed ... so likewise one and the same violence of affliction proves, purifies, and melts the good, and condemns, wastes and banishes the bad. Thus, in one and the same distress, the wicked offend God by detestation and the good glorify Him by praise and prayer. So great is the difference when we consider not what misfortune a man suffers but how he suffers it."[1]

Short of an inspiration of the Holy Spirit to the contrary, and provided charity be not infringed, we are justified in making every effort to better our temporal lot. But any attempt to make of this life a paradise on earth is foredoomed to failure. Those who look for indefinite human progress, until the world is peopled only by supermen enjoying every conceivable amenity, base their hopes on the shallowest philosophy. History lends little support to such a view. God might have made a universe from which sorrow and pain were excluded but the evidence is before us that He did not choose to do so. Under the present dispensation trials and difficulties can be escaped by none. It is true that had Adam persevered in grace we should have known few of our present discontents; but such felicity would have had its source, not in nature, but in original justice—a supernatural gift.

[1] *De Civitate Dei* I, vii.

Philosophers have little difficulty in accounting for evil and pain by the natural constitution of the world and of man as we known them. Wherever there is change, generation and corruption, decay and death—and by these signs of radical instability we are surrounded—there must inevitably be present that privation of good which is the essence of physical evil. Wherever there is perception, whether on the plane of the senses or intelligence, an awareness that things are not what they should be, there must always be pain. Evil and pain thus fall within the scheme of divine providence; through them, in mysterious fashion, we are meant to draw nearer to God. Even sins, *etiam peccata*, despite the sinner's folly, can serve God's ends in showing forth His mercy and justice.

It is scarcely necessary to point out that God is in no way the cause of sin, neither directly nor indirectly. When spiritual writers tell us that all our good comes from God, all evil from ourselves, they are not merely following the dictates of piety but stating a conclusion demonstrable from premises of reason alone. As has been pointed out above, the essence of sin consists in the falling away of the will from its proper object, the good. Now it is impossible, because contrary to the divine nature, for God to cause in the created will a defection from good. God cannot act save for His own goodness; the divine will is rooted in that infinite goodness which is His very being. When He moves our wills it is by reason of that goodness; that is to say, He is drawing us to Himself, the quintessence of the good. If the human will fails to concur in this process, as it can do by reason of its freedom, clearly its defection lies with itself, not with God. God can no more cause the will to fail in its movement towards the good than a rushing torrent can cause the straws which float upon it to move against the stream. Assuredly He knows that men will sin, and there would have been no sin had He chosen to prevent it. That He has allowed it, says St Augustine, is because He wishes to draw a greater good therefrom. " God writes straight with crooked lines," a modern poet has well observed. The blood and tyranny which built up the Roman Empire were to contribute to the spread of the Catholic Church. The sins of their persecutors serve but to enhance the glory of the martyrs. Even original sin, the root of all our ills, was, from one point of view, a blessing; for it was the occasion of the Incarnation. *O certe necessarium Adae peccatum,* sings the Church on Holy Saturday, *quod Christi morte deletum est! O felix culpa, quae talem ac tantum meruit habere Redemptorem!* " O truly necessary was Adam's sin that was blotted out by the death of Christ! O happy fault that merited such and so great a Redeemer! "

But if sin is in no sense the result of God's activity the same cannot be said of physical evil. This, as was shown above, consists in the disharmony arising from an unnatural union of incompatible elements which are good in themselves. It is obvious that the omnipotent Creator of the universe must be in some way responsible for bringing them together. St Thomas teaches that God is the cause of physical evil as it were incidentally, *quasi per accidens.*[1] That some have wished to resist this conclusion is due to their not taking a sufficiently large view of the question. Criticizing those who attempted to posit a causative principle of physical evil other than God, St Thomas points out that they fell into this error " because they did not give thought to the universal cause of all being, but only to particular causes of particular effects. Accordingly, if they found that one thing had of its nature a harmful effect on another, they considered it to be essentially evil. As if one were to say that fire is essentially evil because it burnt the house of a poor man." And he goes on to give judgment with characteristic finality: " But the goodness of anything is not to be assessed by its reference to any particular thing, but in itself, and with respect to its position in the whole universe, wherein every part has its perfectly ordered place," *in quo quaelibet res suum locum ordinatissime tenet.*[2]

If, in the face of evil and suffering, we are to see life steadily and see it whole we must realize what sort of a universe it is that God has created. Nor are we in any way committed to the view that this is the best of all possible worlds. It is the world which perfectly suits God's purpose, but He could have made a million others different from,

[1] Ia, q. 49, a. 2.   [2] Ia, q. 49, a. 3.

and, in human eyes at least, perhaps better than the one we know. As we have remarked, in the present scheme of things, change and transformation, generation and corruption, are the order of the day. "The generation of one thing," says Aristotle, "involves the corruption of another." The growth of the oak-tree means the destruction of an acorn. The gazelle must die to satisfy the lion's hunger. Our daily food ends the life of innumerable animals. If we pause here, as many have paused, we may feel baffled by the seeming ruthlessness of nature's working, "red in tooth and claw." But this is a short-sighted view, confined to the relations between " a particular cause and a particular effect." We must raise our eyes to the universal order of things.

From this angle it is possible to see, even apart from divine revelation, evidences of a superintending providence both wise and good. True, there is much waste difficult to explain, but the reality of a certain " dexterous and starlight order " is not to be denied. The realm of inanimate matter, the mineral world, is in some way subordinate to the world of vegetation. This in its turn serves the needs of the animal kingdom. The animals again are subject to man. Only on the narrowest view is it an evil that the soil should be robbed of its fertility to give life to the harvest. Few feel it to be unjust that the fresh grass should be destroyed for the benefit of the pasturing herd, that grapes should have the life crushed from them to provide us with wine. Even the slaughter of animals for the sake of man's food offends the moral sense of none but an eccentric minority. The evils which affect us more closely, death and disease and human sorrow, are not so inexplicable when seen as part of the general plan, as the prelude to eternal happiness and the hour when God shall wipe away all tears.

It is of practical importance that we should understand how suffering both implies the presence of physical evil and contributes to the sufferer's ultimate well-being. So enlightened, we are spared the impossible task of attempting to welcome pain for its own sake, while we can at the same time recognize the finger of God in the afflictions that come our way. In consequence we are able to accept them with the resignation and joy proportionate to our charity. That material and bodily discomforts are caused by the deprivation of what should normally be there is not difficult to appreciate. The generic term by which they are described—destitution, poverty, ill-health—are sufficiently indicative of this. But it is no less true, though more profoundly, of mental suffering as well. The anxieties and troubles that perplex us, remorse over the past and fears for the future, alike indicate some cleavage between what is and what we know should be. It is the same with all anguish of spirit. We sorrow over the death of those dear to us because the world seems empty without them. We feel the parting from our friends, or their desertion of us, as a partial frustration of a love which is noble and good. Our sense of justice is outraged at our own or another's wrongs because we perceive a failure to render what is due. Even the petty difficulties of every-day have as their explanation a sense of futility and incompleteness. The disappointing of our hopes; the clash of temperaments; the obligation to be polite, to be kindly, when we are tempted to be violent and overriding; the effort it costs us to accept reversals with nothing more heroic than calmness and good humour, are so many means of informing us that life is not just what we should like it to be.

Opposition to our desire, whether of the intelligence or the sensitive appetite, is then the constitutive principle, the *ratio*, of suffering and pain. Our distress is caused by the disparity between what we wish for and the situation as it actually confronts us. Herein lie the potentialities of suffering as a purifying force. The mind of man, refusing to capitulate before it, can, by its inherent power, mount upwards into its own ideal world and, clad in the impenetrable armour of the spirit, do battle with adversity. It may readily be acknowledged—for here, as elsewhere, grace builds upon nature—that men have met suffering in this way for ideals that are no more than natural. The great dramatists have recognized that this is the very stuff of tragedy. The hero " learns by suffering." His triumphant emergence from the conflict, a triumph enhanced rather than diminished by his death, his tenacity of purpose in the face of all opposition, his mastery of suffering by intellectual or moral force are the factors which make high tragedy so exhilarating an experience. We feel, and rightly, that in such circumstances man is lord of the material universe. Be it noted that the ideals in question need not be morally praiseworthy; for good art and good morals do not always coincide. It is their capacity to detach the hero from what is mean and small, to purify him (within limits, at least) and lead him, for whatever motive, to engage in human action on the grand scale that gives tragedy, as a spectacle, its peculiar power.

The purification effected by suffering will be proportionate in its depth and extent to the objective worth of the ideals for which it is endured. The more ultimate the ideal the more radical the purification. In fact only when detachment from what is base and trivial has as its counterpart the fixing of our desires upon final Truth and Goodness is it wholly a blessing. The tragic hero and the great men of history are not without their limitations; only the saints are wholly children of light. They walk in the beauty of holiness, unattached because truly free, happy because moved by love, suffering because far from home.

Self-abnegation is more surely revealed by our attitude towards the painful realities of life which come our way unasked than by self-imposed privations. The element of selectiveness, of self-will, in the latter can easily diminish their purifying effect. We are often not unwilling to do penance if only we may choose the sort we feel best suits our temperament. It is possible to indulge in the more spectacular mortifications while habitually failing to meet everyday reversals with patience and lightness of heart. Not that for this reason we are absolved from the effort of self-discipline; but its spirit should rather be that of an answer to an impulse of grace than of an asceticism deliberately thought out. We may surely suppose that many of the austerities of the saints were so inspired. They were the response to the call of charity. For love tends of its nature to conform the lover to the likeness of the one beloved. When an Ignatius of Antioch or a St Francis longed for suffering it was not as a means of controlling their lower appetites, but in order that they might be united with the Crucified. The *aut pati aut mori* of St Teresa is the cry of heartfelt recognition that, since Calvary, pain is the truest emblem of charity.

Christ's passion was, by the very meaning of the word, something passive; it was indeed accepted with active good will, but it was submitted to, endured, not sought after as an instrument of self-torment. So it is that the most searching and unitive of purifications are those which God, in His providence, brings to pass in the senses and the spirit. There are impediments to union with Him which our sight is too feeble to discern and our good will powerless to remove. Only if we submit to the treatment of the divine physician can we be healed and grow strong in His love.

In order that our charity may develop it is necessary that we be purged of disordered self-love. We have seen that there is a legitimate love of self: when we love ourselves according to our value in God's eyes. But, owing to mental blindness and the weakness of our wills, we tend always to desire our own good inordinately. We may be enabled, through grace, to avoid serious sin; but this is only a condition *sine qua non* of the perfection of charity, it is by no means the perfection itself. When there is habitually present within us an enfeebled will and ill-disposed sensibility we are apt to judge everything that is in conformity with these inclinations to be, in practice, good. In other words, even when we refrain from actual sin, we are continuously prone to pride and sensuality. It is this proneness to evil, *pronitas ad malum*—too deep-seated to be removed by our own efforts—that God Himself must uproot before we can enter into the full liberty of the children of God.

The divine purifications, first of the senses and then of the spirit, have been described in varying terminology by spiritual writers; but there is complete unanimity as to the essential doctrine. St Thomas views our spiritual progress, in Aristotelian fashion, as having a beginning, a middle and an end. This corresponds to what is perhaps the best known classification, that of the " three ways ": of purgation, the stage of beginners; of illumination, that of the proficients; of union, that of the perfect. Others, like St Catherine of Siena and Father Lallemant, employ the word " conversion ": after the first turning to God, a second conversion leads to a closer union with Him, and a third to the most intimate union of all. But perhaps the most satisfactory treatment, both by reason of its psychological insight and theological accuracy, is to be found in the works of St John of the Cross. He speaks of the purification in terms of " darkness "—a " night " of the senses and of the spirit—through which the soul is led to the loving contemplation of God. " This night, which, as we say, is contemplation, produces in spiritual persons two kinds of darkness or purgation, corresponding to the two parts of man's nature—namely, the sensual and the spiritual. And thus the one night of purgation will be sensual, wherein the soul is purged according to sense, which is subdued to the spirit; and the other is a night or purgation which is spiritual; wherein the soul is purged and stripped according to the spirit, and subdued and made ready for the union of love with God."[1] And he adds that the night of the sense is common and comes to many, but the night of the spirit is the portion of very few.

Two points are noteworthy in our present context about the teaching of St John of the Cross. First, its extreme severity, and secondly, the emphasis which he places on contemplation—the dark night is, precisely, contemplation. Despite their theological foundation, his writings have about them a highly personal quality which must be allowed for before the universal validity of his teaching can be rightly understood. That teaching, as has been pointed out, is of a piece with the doctrine of St Thomas Aquinas. If St Thomas can be appealed to for his humanism while St John is ignored on account of his uncompromising austerity, it is by reason of the form in which their thought finds expression, not because of any disagreement between them. The calm detachment of the speculative theologian is replaced by the dramatic intensity of a passionate soul exhibiting in his own person the message he has to deliver. What St Thomas regards as the stage wherein man " principally strives to adhere to God," St John speaks of in these terms:

Oh, night that guided me, Oh, night more lovely than the dawn,
Oh, night that joined Beloved with lover, Lover transformed in the Beloved!

St John was a Carmelite friar writing, in the main, for his

[1] *Dark Night of the Soul*; bk. I, ch. viii, p. 371 (Works, vol. i)

brethren. Moreover much of his work was produced under the stress of persecution and indescribable suffering. His genius, both as poet and psychologist, has been recognized by all who are competent to judge. It is nevertheless possible that the historical setting of the saint's life, the stark realism of his own practice, the note of lyrical rapture which pervades his writings, while exciting admiration, may combine to weaken the force of his teaching in the mind of normal Christians. And yet, from an examination of the processes involved, it is impossible to escape the conclusion that, whether in this world or the next, before the perfection of charity is reached, every man must pass, in one form or another, through the two "nights" described in such detail by the great Spanish mystic.

The place assigned by St John of the Cross to contemplation is of great significance. We saw, at the end of our last chapter, that until prayer becomes in some way contemplative the spiritual life is without depth. On the other hand contemplative prayer, while being incompatible with the state of beginners,[1] does not demand that perfection should have already been reached. Contemplation begins at the entrance into the *dark night of sense*, the illuminative way; it becomes purer and more intense through the *night of the spirit*, the unitive way, but it is established within the soul before that more drastic purification takes place. It seems probable that, with the majority, this second purgation does not come about in the present life; it is left to the fires of purgatory to produce its effects. Few pass through it, says St John; not that God would not cleanse us in this world were we willing to submit, but normally we are not sufficiently responsive to His call. The night of the sense, however, is the lot of many. That is to say contemplation, at least in an intermittent form, is given to those who are as yet far from heroic sanctity. The purgation which leads up to it can be endured, and its reward achieved, by all who strive earnestly towards the perfection of charity.

St John's association of the degrees of prayer (to use the

---

[1] In the technical sense, *incipientes*; that is, those whose spiritual life exhibits the characteristics of the "purgative way." Obviously—and the saints themselves would be the last to deny it—man never ceases, in the present life, to be a "beginner" in the ways of God.

word in its widest meaning) with moral purification has implications of great importance, though often overlooked. Contemplative prayer is sometimes discussed as if it were an intellectual exercise, dependent for its success on concentration and our power to control the imagination. Surely prayer of this sort cannot be considered apart from the measure of personal holiness of the one who prays. It is a gift of God proportioned to our love. Accordingly if we are in serious difficulties about prayer, the root of the trouble is probably not in our failure to find the suitable "technique." We pray best, says St Anthony of Egypt, when we know not how we pray. The prayer of contemplation is rooted and grounded in charity; it is to this last that we must look if we wish to give an account to ourselves of our state of prayer.

The catalogue of faults (of beginners) from which the night of sense is calculated to deliver us is extensive enough. Luxuriating in sensible devotion and the selecting of our own forms of penance. The subtler forms of pride: self-complacency over our good works, the desire to edify, a certain pharisaism towards those we consider less virtuous than ourselves, reluctance to praise others while wishing for their praises. Another class of imperfections is given the name of *spiritual avarice*: for example, seeking after consolations and undue attachment to particular articles of piety. The remaining capital sins—luxury, gluttony, envy, sloth—each have their counterpart in a whole series of disordered inclinations too numerous for individual mention. They are ruthlessly exposed in the first seven chapters of the *Dark Night of the Soul*.

When treating of the signs whereby it may be known whether a soul is undergoing the purgation of the senses St John shows some anxiety to distinguish them from the normal indications, superficially similar, of lukewarmness and bodily ill-health. He gives as the first sign an absence of pleasure or consolation in the things of God; but, since this can arise from causes by no means supernatural, he adds that neither is pleasure to be found in the things of this world. In order to make clearer the distinction between the genuine aridity and mere apathy or indifference he gives a second sign by which we may judge: namely, that the memory be centred on God with painful solicitude, thinking that it is backsliding rather than serving Him. By this means the sensual part of the soul is brought low while the spirit soars aloft. The most conclusive sign of all is revealed in the individual's state of prayer.

The third sign whereby this purgation of sense may be recognized is that the soul can no longer meditate or reflect in its sense of the imagination, as it was wont, however much it may of itself endeavour to do so. For God now begins to communicate Himself to it, no longer through sense, as He did aforetime, by means of reflections which joined and sundered its knowledge, but by pure spirit, into which consecutive reflection enters not; but He communicates Himself to it by an act of simple contemplation, to which neither the exterior nor the interior senses of the lower part of the soul can attain. From this time forward, therefore, imagination and fancy can find no support in any meditation, and can gain no foothold by means thereof. [1]

As the chief effect of the night of the sense is to lead the soul to contemplation it will not be out of place to summarize St John's teaching on the point. Following the traditional doctrine, he holds that, before the first purification, that is, while the soul's behaviour is characteristic of the " purgative way," mental prayer does not habitually rise above meditation and discursive acts. These are the necessary preliminaries, but no more than that. Since they are bound up with sense and imagination they can be but indirect means of uniting the soul with God. Only by its purely spiritual faculties can it enjoy direct communion with Him. For this it must pass into the night of contemplation. Nevertheless it is of the first importance that this step should not be premature. Contemplation, as distinct from the state of acquired recollection (the natural pre-disposition to contemplation proper), is infused and not achieved by our own efforts. Hence, while we may humbly desire that our prayer should become contemplative—for that, under grace, is its true line of development—it is simple presumption to affect the prayer of contemplation before we receive God's call. Mysticism, the contemplative knowledge of God, is not something to be cultivated by those who feel they have a

[1] *Dark Night*; bk. I, ch. ix, p. 377 (Works, Vol. I.)

taste for it; it comes as a free gift from on high to such as dispose themselves for its reception by asceticism and meditation. Contemplation without preceding meditation, says St Bernard, is miraculous. And we are not justified in looking for the performance of such a miracle in our own favour. There are three signs which indicate when the point of transition has been reached.

The first sign is his (the spiritual person's) realization that he can no longer meditate or reason with his imagination, neither can take pleasure therein as he was wont to do aforetime; he rather finds aridity in that which aforetime was wont to attract his senses and to bring him sweetness. But, for as long as he finds sweetness in meditation, and is able to reason, he should not abandon this, save when his soul is led into the peace and quietness which is described under the third head.

The second sign is a realization that he has no desire to fix his meditation or his sense upon other particular objects, exterior or interior. I do not mean that the imagination neither comes nor goes (for it is wont to move freely even at times of great recollection), but that the soul has no pleasure in fixing it of set purpose upon other objects.

The third and surest sign is that the soul takes pleasure in being alone, and waits with loving attentiveness upon God, without making any particular meditation, in inward peace and quietness and rest, and without acts and exercises of the faculties— memory, understanding and will—at least, without discursive acts, that is, without passing from one thing to another; the soul is alone, with an attentiveness and a knowledge, general and loving, as we said, but without any particular understanding, and adverting not to what it is contemplating.

These three signs, at least, the spiritual person must see in himself, all together, before he can venture with security to abandon the state of meditation and sense, and to enter that of contemplation and spirit.[1]

The stripping from the soul of all that is alien to its supernatural life is negative in name only. It is the losing of life that we may find it. Our apparent loss is in reality all gain. What we abandon in the order of nature is given back to us a hundredfold in the order of grace. No one is more explicit on this point than St John of the Cross.

For the cause of this aridity is that God transfers to the spirit

[1] *Ascent of Mount Carmel*, bk. II, ch. xiii, pp. 115-116 (Works, Vol. I.)

the good things and the strength of the senses, which, since the soul's natural strength and senses are incapable of using them, remain barren, dry and empty. . . . But the spirit, which all the time is being fed, goes forward in strength, and with more alertness and solicitude than before, in its anxiety not to fail God; and if it is not immediately conscious of spiritual sweetness and delight, but only of aridity and lack of sweetness, the reason for this is the strangeness of the exchange; for its palate has been accustomed to those other sensual pleasures upon which its eyes are still fixed, and, since the spiritual palate is not made ready or purged for such subtle pleasure, until it finds itself becoming prepared for it by means of this arid and dark night, it cannot experience spiritual pleasure and good, but only aridity and lack of sweetness, since it misses the pleasure which aforetime it enjoyed so readily.[1]

Again, " the senses remain in a state of aridity, inasmuch as their treasure is transformed into spirit, and no longer falls within the capacity of sense."[2] But the treasure is there, never to be lost.

Having passed through the night of sense and entered the illuminative way, the soul, while enjoying the beginnings of contemplation, is still far from the perfection of charity. If the sensibility has been in large measure purged from its cruder faults—spiritual sensuality, inertia, jealousy, impatience—there still remain in the spiritual part of the soul what St John calls the " stains of the old man." Until these be removed by the purgation of the night of the spirit the soul cannot attain to the purity of the divine union. Even at the stage so far reached the Christian is still too much attached to the things of the world. Among the signs of this condition are excessive distraction at prayer, insensibility to the things of God, mental sluggishness, dissipation of spirit, movements of roughness and impatience, natural affections in which charity plays little part. People at this stage, having advanced some way in the life of grace, are liable to fall victims of arrogance and vanity. They become convinced of the rightness of their own point of view on spiritual matters and wish to be regarded as authorities to whom due deference should be shown.

---

[1] *Dark Night*, bk. I, ch. ix, pp. 374-375 (Works, Vol. I.)
[2] *Living Flame*, stanza iii, 30; p. 76 (Works, Vol. III.)

Thus they become bold with God, and lose holy fear, which is the key and the custodian of all the virtues; and in some of these souls so many falsehoods and deceits are apt to be multiplied, and so persistent do they become, that it is very doubtful if such souls will return to the pure road of virtue and true spirituality. Into these miseries they fall because they are beginning to give themselves over to spiritual feelings and apprehensions with too great security, when they were beginning to make some progress on the way.[1]

The night of the spirit is, of its nature, a far more radical purification than the night of sense. The soul has already been purified with reference to its activity in the sphere of the senses and imagination, but not yet in regard to its peculiarly spiritual operations.[2] For this the only sufficient means is that it should be deprived of all human consolation and move towards its goal in the obscurity of faith. In order that we may draw near to the infinite majesty and purity of God, transcending all human conception, it is needful that we rely on that knowledge which alone can unite us to Him. Reason, no matter how acute, cannot join us to God, nor sensible devotion, nor yet spiritual consolation: even the delights of contemplation, because desirable for their own sake, can make the love of God less absolute.

Wherefore, in order to come to this union, the soul must needs enter into the second night of the spirit, wherein it must strip sense and spirit perfectly from all these apprehensions and from all sweetness, and be made to walk in dark and pure faith, which is the proper and adequate means whereby the soul is united to God, according as Hosea says, in these words: I will betroth thee—that is, I will unite thee—with me through faith (Hosea ii, 20).[3]

It is unnecessary to reproduce here St John's description

---

[1] *Dark Night*, bk. II, ch. ii, p. 401 (Works, Vol. I.)

[2] It should be borne in mind that, when spiritual writers speak of the "sensitive" and "spiritual" *parts* of the soul, their language is not to be taken quite literally. They refer to the soul's powers, or faculties, as determined by their different operations. The soul, being an immaterial substance, has no parts; but within the simplicity of its own essence it contains *virtualiter*, as an effect within its cause, the principles from which its diverse activities proceed. So, in our present context, the grace-endowed faculties of intelligence and will, as directed to the senses and imagination, form the soul's "sensitive part"; considered in themselves, as the instruments of a supra-sensitive knowledge and love, they form its spiritual part.

[3] *Dark Night*, bk. II, ch. ii, p. 402 (Works, Vol. I.)

of the nature of the sufferings whereby this purgation is brought about. His language is intense and dramatic, but the lives of those who have reached heroic sanctity are there to prove that he does not exaggerate. One has but to recall the last days of St Teresa of Lisieux, an agony of blankness, to realize its truth. Before the soul can know experimentally its own nothingness, and so achieve true humility, and how lovable is God, and so reach the perfection of faith and charity, it must pass through the valley of the shadow of death. It is no more than fitting that there should come a moment in the life of every Christian when, like his Master, he is forced to cry out: " My God, my God, why hast Thou forsaken me?"

We shall speak later of the effects produced by that perfect love of God to which the soul attains after passing through the night of the spirit and reaching the unitive way. Suffice it to say that the spirit, even in this life, is on the brink of heaven and has acquired riches in comparison with which the good things of this world are as dust.

Mine are the heavens and mine is the earth; mine are the people, the righteous are mine and mine are the sinners; the angels are mine and the Mother of God, and all things are mine; and God Himself is mine and for me, for Christ is mine and all for me. What, then, dost thou ask for and seek, my soul? Thine is all this, and it is all for thee. Despise not thyself nor give thou heed to the crumbs which fall from thy Father's table. Go thou forth and do thou glory in thy glory. Hide thee therein and rejoice and thou shalt have the desires of thy heart.[1]

[1] St John of the Cross, *Prayer of the Soul enkindled with Love*; (Works, Vol. III, p. 244.)

III

ACTION

"He that hath My commandments and keepeth them; he it is that loveth Me."—*John xiv, 21.*

CHARITY, a virtue hidden in the soul, shows itself to the world in action. By their fruits you shall know them, said Our Lord—thereby giving us the right to make external activity a test of the genuineness of our love for God. It was the test appointed by Himself. "Not everyone that saith to Me, Lord, Lord, shall enter into the kingdom of heaven; but he that doth the will of My Father Who is in heaven, he shall enter into the kingdom of heaven."[1] "If you love Me keep My commandments."[2] His followers must imitate Him in carrying out the will of the Father. He "went about doing good."[3] When John the Baptist sent to inquire of Him whether He was of a truth the Messiah He replied by appealing to His deeds. "Go and relate to John what you have heard and seen. The blind see, the lame walk, the lepers are cleansed, the deaf hear, the dead rise again, the poor have the gospel preached to them."[4] The later insistence by St James upon the necessity of good works and positive well-doing is thus as much a part of original Christianity as the Pauline teaching on faith.

The emphasis laid by Christ, in the Sermon on the Mount and elsewhere, upon ethical goodness, together with the perfect exemplification of it in His own life, have led many to maintain that morality and good conduct were the essential part of His message. In so doing they mistake the means for the end, the outward expression of charity for the love of God itself. Accordingly they have supposed that the priority of place given by the Church to contemplation over action has been a departure from the primitive gospel. Greek intellectualism has tempered the ardour of first discipleship and humanitarian zeal has been replaced by the θεωρία of Plato and Aristotle.

[1] Matthew vii, 21. [2] Jol xiv, 15.
[3] Acts x, 38. [4] Matthew xi, 4-5.

The truth is that the application of philosophy to revelation by the Fathers and mediaeval thinkers was for the purpose of laying bare its inner content, not of synthesizing it with conclusions drawn from created reason. Although the language of the New Testament is in appearance far removed from that of later theology, the latter is but a more developed expression of what is contained in the former. To examine the gospels in the light of the highest human thought, far from adulterating its purity, serves to bring out its true inwardness. It is clear, for example, that the knowledge of Christ, His personality and divine sonship, is the key to the understanding of all that He did. But without some ultimate notions about the meaning of nature and person, that is, without philosophical insight into their implications, this knowledge can be no more than rudimentary. Similarly if the conduct to which the gospel invites us has an eternal significance, this can only be in the light of some vision, an everlasting possession which is one day to be ours. Our actions, as we have seen, have their value from the end for which they are performed, in other words, from the thoughts and intentions which direct them. " For where thy treasure is, there is thy heart also."[1] It is for this reason that contemplation is, in itself, worthier and more meritorious than external activity; for it is that loving knowledge of God and His will in our regard of which Christian morality should be the outward expression. To find this teaching we need not turn to the Greek philosophers but to the gospel itself. In the commandment to love God and our neighbour is summed up the whole law and the prophets.[2] This love depends in its turn on that knowledge of God which is eternal life.[3] All our good works must proceed from the knowledge and love of God, that is, from faith and charity. And these are the twin sources of divine contemplation.

It has been pointed out that " The formula of the two lives, the active and the contemplative, derives from Greek philosophy and according to its original Greek conception does not fit exactly on to the Christian life."[4] Unless the implied antithesis between them is rightly understood there must

[1] Matthew vi, 21. [2] Matthew xxii, 37-40. [3] John xvii, 3.
[4] Dom Justin McCann, *Saint Benedict*, p. 179.

result an oversimplified view of the multifarious ways of serving God which fails to take account of their diversity. St Augustine, in his exegesis of the scriptural story of Martha and Mary,[1] and St Thomas, dividing human activity into an exercise of either the speculative or practical intellect, were well aware that the complexities of every-day life cannot always be fitted into such a neatly tabulated scheme. In practice man is as incapable of perpetual contemplation as he is of unremitting activity. His life is contemplative when, as a whole, it is directed towards the contemplation of divine things; it is active when, as a whole, it is directed towards the performance of external works. But it is an error to regard action and contemplation as mutually exclusive. It is unfortunately true, as St Thomas points out,[2] that our external activities lessen the purity of contemplation; the reason being that the senses, which are necessarily engaged in each of our actions, tend to distract the mind from its direct preoccupation with God. This is why contemplatives enter upon activity with a certain reluctance. Nevertheless their charity, which cannot be idle, together with the natural tendency—never suppressed by mortification—of man's sensitive life to express itself outwardly prompt them to action. "The love of truth seeks a holy leisure, the demands of charity undertake an honest toil." *Otium sanctum quaerit charitas veritatis: negotium justum suscipit necessitas charitatis.*[3]

Action, it has been well said, is the ritual of contemplation. If this truth has been well understood by the best minds in the western Church, where orthodoxy has been preserved, it has not always been so with the Christianity of the east. There an exaggerated Platonism, with its distrust of the senses, has at times induced a quietistic attitude highly critical of the religious activism of the west. No doubt the devotional aberrations of individuals have, in some measure, justified this criticism, but an impartial observer could

---

[1] It is surely noteworthy that St Augustine and St Thomas, in following the Latin version, are led to emphasize the excellence of Mary's part, to the prejudice of Martha, in a way that the original hardly justifies. Unquestionably Our Lord implied that Mary's action was to be preferred but, with characteristic courtesy, He does not appear to have said so explicitly. He did not say "Mary hath chosen the 'best' (or even the 'better')—but, simply, the 'good'—part." Cf. Lagrange's *Commentary* and the *Westminster Version*, Luke x, 42.
[2] Ia, q. 112, a. 1, ad 3.
[3] IIa IIae, q. 182, a. 1, ad 3 (from Augustine's *De Civ. Dei*, 19, 19.)

scarcely dispute the fact that Latin Catholicism, in its manifold forms of expression, has shown a surer insight into the religious needs of mankind as a whole than the impractical otherworldliness of the oriental churches. St Augustine, St Gregory and St Bernard are among the greatest Christian contemplatives,[1] but each of these men combined with their contemplation a life of prodigious activity. They were not dreamers absorbed in heavenly things while ignoring opportunities for well-doing round about them. Like Christ Himself they were ever at the service of men, and just as His unceasing contemplation did not diminish His activity, so could they enter upon the active life without losing the fruits of the contemplative. They did not lead the " mixed life," if by that is meant the disconnected and haphazard alternation of periodic prayer with external good works. Their activity was of the sort in which they remained at home while they were abroad. Their lives, simplified and reduced to unity by love, were fulfilled in works of charity. They were true disciples of Christ in that their contemplation led them inevitably to become apostles. The life which Christ Himself led, St Thomas teaches,[2] was better than the life which is merely contemplative, for it flowed from the abundance of contemplation. With reason then we may conclude that, apart from the direct worship of God, the work of teaching and preaching divine truth, when it proceeds from the superabundance of contemplation, *ex superabundantia contemplationis*, is that by which most of all we are conformed to the likeness of Christ.[3]

[1] Cf. Abbot Butler's *Western Mysticism*.
[2] IIIa, q. 40, a. 1, ad 2.
[3] It is of great importance in this connection to distinguish between the abstract doctrine of the relation between the " two lives " and the way in which action and contemplation are interrelated in the concrete. St Thomas's conclusion that contemplation which expresses itself in action is nobler and more meritorious than contemplation by itself cannot, on his premises, be disputed. It would be grossly unjust to regard it as a piece of special pleading for the work of his own Order. Nevertheless the achievement in practice of this ideal must necessarily be rare. Contemplation is itself *de facto* exceptional enough; how much more so an activity which proceeds from it, not as a dissipation of spirit, but *per modum additionis*. The intensity of charity which this implies must presuppose all but heroic sanctity. Whatever be the case theoretically, in practice, the life of the contemplative orders is rightly held, by the spiritual masters and the faithful alike, to imply greater self-renunciation and conditions more favourable for close union with God than that of the active orders.

Before passing on to discuss the nature of external activity it will not be out of place to indicate the fundamental reason why contemplation is in itself superior to action. St Thomas states the underlying principle in the fewest possible words: " In the operations of the soul, especially of the sensitive and the intellectual soul, it must be noted that, since they do not pass into external matter, they are acts or perfections of the agent, e.g., to understand, to feel, to will and the like: because actions which pass into external matter are rather actions and perfections of the matter transformed; for ' movement is the act produced by the mover in the thing moved' (Phys. iii, 3)."[1] In other words, contemplation is an *immanent* movement or activity of the soul, whereby it perfects itself through its faculties of intelligence and will, whereas action is a *transitive* movement or activity perfecting rather the material with which the action has to do. Contemplation, though implying quiescence in respect of things sensible and material, is itself the highest form of activity, *actus perfecti*. The repose and absence of discursive thought which the mystics emphasize in their experiences should not be confused with a state of mental inertia. In the night of contemplation the soul receives, darkly and all but unconsciously, an access of truth, *simplex intuitus veritatis*, to which it could never otherwise be admitted. Sharing the divine secrets, the contemplative reproduces on the creaturely level something of the immobility of God Himself gazing eternally into His own essence. Not, as we have already seen, an immobility of potentiality, of having perfections yet to acquire, but the immobility of act, of being in a state to which there is nothing to add.

From the very fact that contemplation is superior to action it implies more, not less, actuality than is involved in movement. " It is true that contemplation enjoys rest from external movements. Nevertheless to contemplate is itself a movement of the intellect, in so far as every operation is described as a movement; in which sense the Philosopher says that sensation and understanding are movements of a kind, in so far as the act of a perfect thing is a movement."[2]

[1] Ia IIae, q. 31, a. 5.
[2] IIa IIae, q. 179, a. 1, ad 3.

But we must descend to the level of action as it is commonly understood, that is, the *transitive* movement or activity through which our regard for others and our attitude towards the external world find expression. Just as by faith and charity we know and love the things of God, so by fidelity to grace in action do we help to the realization of the livine plan in space and time and thus prove the genuineness of our love. There is nothing in this world more divine, declares the Pseudo-Denis, than to become a co-operator with God. We carry out this function when our deeds are in conformity with the charity in our hearts, and when charity is accompanied by that sensitive awareness which dictates the appropriate moment for action. It should be noted that if precipitancy and over-eagerness can mar the effects of charity so also can apathy and indifference. These last are the common failings, not indeed of true contemplatives, but of thinkers and intellectuals, who feel themselves naturally better disposed for contemplation than action.

For human action to be good, and therefore a means of expressing charity, it must be prudent. We have already touched upon the importance of the virtue of prudence and we shall return to it again presently. Here we must allude to a form of human activity which, strictly speaking, is independent of prudence. We speak of art. The word " art," in modern usage, is commonly restricted to what are called the fine arts—poetry, music, painting and the rest— but its application is immeasurably wider. Works of art are the product of an artist, that is, a man who possesses an art. From this point of view art is an intellectual virtue or habit in accordance with which we make or do something. St Thomas defines it as the *recta ratio factibilium*, the " right rule of the things to be made." To associate art solely with beauty and aesthetics is to limit unjustifiably its field. Mr Eric Gill and others have pointed out the disadvantages of this restricted view-point. It unnaturally dissociates the artist from the life of society as a whole, encourages the belief that he is a being to whom the ordinary laws of morality do not apply, and places a premium on the ornate and merely decorative to the detriment of what is functional. When the fine arts were less of a luxury than they are to-day the carpenter was as truly an artist as the poet, the stone-mason as the musician. Words and music are obviously worthier media of expression than wood and stone and the arts concerned with them correspondingly higher, but the business of the artist in relation to his selected medium is the same in each case: to embody in matter the plan or idea formed in his mind, the *recta ratio factibilis*. According to his capacity to do this is he to be judged as an artist. The worth of a poem or a symphony will be assessed in the transcendental terms of beauty and truth, that of a table or a house by reference to function and usefulness.

Art has nothing to do with morality. *Ars vero non pertinet ad scientiam moralem.*[1] The excellence or otherwise of a work of art does not depend on the virtuousness or depravity of the artist. The private lives of the great poets and musicians have not always been conspicuously above reproach; while, on the other hand, personal integrity is no guarantee of sound aesthetic taste. Those who have the interests of religion at heart are often embarrassed by this fact and occasionally refuse to admit it. If they are obliged to allow that all the saints were not good artists they maintain strenuously that the truly great artist must also be a good man. When the evidence against an individual is too strong they feel it necessary to question his claim to distinction as an artist. This is a mistake. Such an attitude must logically vitiate all aesthetic criticism and demands of artists what it is no part of their task to provide—moral edification. No doubt the Byrons and Wagners of this world might have been better artists had they been better men, but it is irrelevant to pass judgment on their work on account of their personal shortcomings.

This raises the point of the interrelation between art and prudence.[2] Art, as such, is independent of prudence. But the artist is not; he, like every other man, must act prudently. At times this is only possible for him at the cost of immense effort. In practice it is in the fine arts that this difficulty, the duty of the artist to conform to the moral law,

[1] Prologue to the *Secunda Secundae*.
[2] M. Jacques Maritain's *Art et Scolastique* (Eng. tr. *Art and Scholasticism*) is by now a classic on the moral problem involved in art. Its value as a contribution to the subject can hardly be over-estimated.

is most keenly felt. And the reason is not far to seek. The manual arts make little demands upon the resources of personality, they can be approached with a certain detachment. It is comparatively easy for artistic activity of this sort to be subordinated to prudence. Not so those arts wherein the intelligence and imagination are working at their highest pitch and the energies of the whole man called into play.

Prudence, unlike art, presupposes the rectitude of our will in regard to the ultimate end of life; its task is to reduce all our subordinate activities to conformity with that end. It does not prescribe to the arts the rules which govern them—these are derived from their respective essences—but it requires that the artist shall behave, even when engaged in his art, as a responsible moral agent. He must act with a view to the end for which he was made. This in no way demands that his work should be religious or morally edifying, only that it be done with an eye to its effect on himself as a man and on the community at large.

The pursuit of beauty which is implied in the fine arts is not easily controlled by prudence. The inspiration and intense imaginative excitement which precede and accompany the composition of a great poem cannot consciously be subordinated to anything more ultimate than themselves. One does not write *King Lear* in a spirit of detachment. To deliberate in the moment of creative activity is to spoil one's art. What is needed is that the artist should have acquired the habit of prudence. He can then, when the moment arrives, abandon himself to his muse with no fear as to the result. On subsequent reflection he may chasten and polish his work while its basic inspiration remains. He will also calculate its effect upon those for whom it is intended. Here it is possible for conflict to arise between his instinct as an artist and the dictates of moral conscience, that is, of prudence. The proneness to sensuality of fallen human nature may sometimes be unduly affected by works of art aesthetically faultless. The artist, as a member of society with obligations to his fellow men, must take account of this. Nor will his art suffer in the long run by such discipline. The form which he has projected into matter will shine out with added splendour for being stripped of all extraneous adornment.

Prudence must also govern our approach to works of art as objects to be appreciated or enjoyed. In the enjoyment of what is beautiful, no less than in the active expression of it, the situation, from the moral standpoint, is often difficult to handle. From the nature of the case it could scarcely be otherwise. Experience shows that to be struck with beauty is not to receive an impulse towards moral goodness.[1] Beauty, objectively considered, is the perfection of a thing arising from the harmony of its parts precisely as apprehended, *id quod visum placet*, whether by the senses (not necessarily only by that of sight) or by the mind. The impression of the beautiful does not compel us to a judgment, either speculative or practical, about the object which conveys the impression; hence there is no urge to action. We remain inert, in contemplation that is not love.

The perception of beauty depends upon sensibility, upon the responsiveness of the senses and the mind; and the measure of a creative artist's greatness is his capacity to work upon our powers of receptivity, both mental and sensuous, in such a way that the very operation causes delight. Artistic sensibility can and should, when controlled by prudence, lend grace and attractiveness to the moral life. But it frequently happens that the allurements of beauty prove so strong that the response to them tends to degenerate into mere aesthetic indulgence. The lover of beauty is concerned above all else with the joyous experience of what is pleasing; when unchecked by other considerations he seeks logically an ecstatic existence of perpetual intoxication, through eye and ear and mind, with beautiful objects. Beauty, in isolation from truth and goodness—and, precisely as the object of aesthetic experience, it is always so isolated—makes no demands upon the will. This last point is of capital importance and often unhappily overlooked. The moral life—for the Christian, the life of active charity—aims at possessing what is good and achieving for itself a permanent state of

[1] This statement may be regarded by some as highly disputable. Wordsworth, for example, and those who think with him, would assert the opposite. But Wordsworth was not in the habit of distinguishing beauty from goodness. A distinction of great importance in our present context.

well-being. To this end the will goes out in desire and gives effective direction towards its realization: *amor meus pondus meum.* But the appreciation of beauty postulates no such striving. The worshipper at this shrine does not wish to possess, he is content simply to " stand and stare." The

> . . . daffodils
> That come before the swallow dares, and take
> The winds of March with beauty . . .

have not to be snatched at. All their charm lies in being seen. So it is with all beautiful things; they give to the beholder a repose which borders closely upon enervation. The state of passivity is dangerously complete.

It would be a mistake to interpret the foregoing remarks as a disparagement of the value and importance of the arts. The moral dangers implicit in aesthetic experience can be outweighed by other factors. Although that experience itself prescinds from the knowledge and love which motivate virtuous conduct, the objects which evoke it can provide, together with a perception of the beautiful, food for thought and incentives to action. Allusion has been made in the last chapter to the exhilarating effect of great tragedy, and the drama is but one instance of the artist's power to elevate the mind. " Fine art," Mr Bernard Shaw somewhere remarks, " is the subtlest, the most seductive, the most effective means of propaganda in the world, excepting the example of. of personal conduct." And the reason for this is that the artist is dealing with ideas, by which alone the mind lives, in the most attractive of all forms, that of beauty. When the idea, the form, which the work of art embodies is worthy, " something more philosophic and of graver import than history," then the artist is the unconscious teacher of truth; he uplifts the mind into the world of spirit and invites us, though again undesignedly (for it is no part of his task to moralize), to noble conduct.

Hence the Christian cannot afford to be indifferent to the arts. The practical problems raised by art are to-day more acute than at the time when our culture was Christian. In the middle ages the subject-matter of poetry, painting and sculpture was almost exclusively religious. Artists took for their theme scenes from the Bible and the lives of the saints.

Accordingly it was easy for them, even when their aim was something more than moral edification, to keep within the bounds of prudence. Since the renaissance and the rise of modern humanism, however, the scope of artistic expression has been vastly enlarged. Whether art has profited by its emancipation from service to the Church is perhaps a moot point. Certainly no one would wish to deny the artists' right to claim the whole field of human interest for their province. But the philosophy of art for art's sake and the enthronement of the goddess of beauty in the place of the saints were unlikely to prove of much help either in their work as artists or in the business of saving their souls.

It would be beyond the purpose of these pages, which aim at keeping as closely as possible to first principles, to enter into the particularities of aesthetic criticism. But if the foregoing remarks are true, it is not difficult to conclude from them what should be the general mental attitude of the Christian artist, both in the execution of his own work and the evaluation of that of others. He may refuse to accept the too facile antithesis between classicism and romanticism, but he should incline towards simplicity and restraint rather than to their opposites. The loose impressionism which characterizes so much of present-day art and literature is one of the many signs of the materialism in which we are immersed. Be it remembered that the arts, though demanding a cultivated taste for their appreciation, are not to be finally judged by individual preference. Their criteria are not relative but absolute. Given a harmony of spirit and matter, of content and the mode of its expression, one work of art will be better than another in proportion as the idea which it embodies, its inner significance, is nobler and more profound.

It is here that the Christian moral code helps rather than impedes good art. The mind, enlightened by faith and charity, seeks instinctively for the essential, for the *form*, revealing itself in matter. To an intelligence quickened by grace the merely sensuous has a very limited appeal. The Christian artist must not expect art to fulfil the function of religion, but he has the right to demand that it should be pure as art. His theme may be the reverse of what is morally edifying, but his handling of it will be free from what is superfluous and gross. His work should have about it a certain radiance, the "splendour of form," wherein the ancients discovered the essence of beauty. Thus the exigencies of his own art as well as the virtue of prudence invite him to practise restraint, to shun the florid and overdone. The artist whose heart is filled with the love of God has an unique opportunity of working for the restoration of Christian society. He need not, like Fra Angelico, be himself vowed to religion, or choose for his subject-matter a religious theme; if he but remain true to his craft and to the rule of prudence—which, in the modern world, is asking him to practice heroism—he will accomplish his task. The purification of the intelligence and sensibility, effected through great art, is an admirable predisposition to the work of grace. In this way, on the plane of nature which must itself be perfected before the supernatural life can come to fruition, the artists and poets can contribute to the spread of God's Kingdom on earth.

As has been stated above, all human activity must be regulated by prudence. On an earlier page the importance of this virtue has been pointed out. It is now time to consider the matter in greater detail. We should note in the first place that it is not the task of prudence to discover the end of human life. Before we can act prudently we must already know the end to which we are moving and have our desires fixed upon it. Prudence has to do with the means whereby we reach the goal to which our intention has been directed from the beginning. The man who is prudent, by ultimate standards, orders his conduct in the light of the truths of the Faith and takes as his point of departure the vital inspirations of charity within his heart. He strives to control the details of his life by these master motives. Thus the first act of self-government which prudence implies is to see clearly the ends proposed to us by charity and to adhere to them by desire. As St Augustine repeatedly teaches, virtuous action (which depends on prudence) is impossible without right desire. For him prudence is nothing else but our love for God discerning rightly what we ought to do, *amor bene discernens*. And St Thomas does not disagree:

As stated above the will moves all the faculties to their acts. Now the first act of the appetitive faculty is love; accordingly prudence is said to be love, not indeed essentially, but in so far as love moves to the act of prudence. Wherefore Augustine goes on to say that "prudence is love discerning aright that which helps from that which hinders us in tending to God." Now love is said to discern because it moves the reason to discern.[1]

As a consequence of this the foundation of prudence is not moral science but, precisely, love. It is true that prudence is formally an intellectual virtue and presupposes, not merely good will, but the direct perception of what is the right thing to be done here and now. The judgment of prudence, which initiates action, must record the situation as it is, it must be true; but the truth in question is of the practical, not of the speculative, order. Reflection is needed in order to see the importance of this distinction. A moral philosopher or theologian can determine the general principles of right conduct, he may be able to solve cases of conscience with insight and ability, but neither of these things necessarily implies the possession of the virtue of prudence. Although he is dealing with matters which are, at least remotely, practical, his viewpoint is speculative, he is considering impersonally and with detachment what should be done in a given case. All that is needed here for him to discover truth are perception and good judgment; good will is not indispensable, since his personal desires are not involved but only objective truth. What this demands is simply a conformity of the intelligence with extra-mental reality: *verum intellectus speculativi accipitur per conformitatem intellectus ad rem.*[2]

But the truth of the practical intellect, the basis of the prudential judgment, is on another plane. It must be arrived at in the moment of action. The decision to be made is not abstract and universal, but concrete and particular. We have not to elucidate a general case but to resolve, it may be on the instant, what is to be done in a situation in which we ourselves are vitally concerned. Nor can we expect absolute certainty; we have sometimes to be content with the assurance that our course of action is right on the whole, *ut in pluribus.* Human acts, unlike abstract speculation, have to

[1] IIa IIae, q. 47, a. 1, ad 1.   [2] Ia IIae, q. 57, a. 5, ad 3.

do with minutiae and particular facts—the *singularia* of which there can be no science. The remote principles which underlie the science of ethics are an insufficient guide when immediate action is called for. It is notorious that philosophers, though aware of the general laws which govern behaviour, can themselves hesitate and fail when engaged in practical matters. On the other hand, it is possible for people ignorant of any ethical system, who could perhaps give no rational account of their conduct, to behave with practical wisdom in the most complicated situation. The chaste man, as Aristotle observes, judges how to act chastely by a certain natural instinct or sympathy for chastity. This is but a particular instance of the function of the virtue of prudence. When our desires are rightly ordered, when, as it were by nature, we wish to do what ought to be done, we are in possession of that virtue. We are in the way of acquiring, on each occasion, that dynamic truth which regulates good action. As a result we tend almost unreflectingly to act as we should. This truth comes to us, not by the intelligence alone, but through the will, by reason of its right desires. " The truth of the practical intellect depends on conformity with right appetite "; *verum autem intellectus practici accipitur per conformitatem ad appetitum rectum.*[1]

Human action, when it is truly prudent, is always an expression of the love of God. The fixity of our will on the last end, on God Himself, is the rock-foundation of prudence. The prudent man chooses, deliberates, commands only by reference to this fundamental principle; it is the source from which each of his acts proceeds, its vivifying power, the immobile axis of his whole moral life. Little thought is needed to perceive that the all-embracing point of view from which the prudential government of ourselves and others must be considered is that of charity, the love of God for His own sake and above all things.

It is by this unceasing dependence *vis-à-vis* the divine life of grace that the prudence of the children of God is utterly distinct from the various kinds of false prudence which claim to control us. It repudiates the prudence of the flesh, the enemy of God, as St Paul says, which places man's end in base enjoyment; it

[1] Ia IIae, q. 57, a. 5, ad 3.

rejects all compromise with the prudence of the world, which substitutes the goods of this world for the true end of life, namely, God and His love; it surpasses all varieties of human prudence, however praiseworthy, whose objects are secondary, particular and temporal; it transcends moral prudence itself which, even though it envisages man's complete good, nevertheless views it with the limitations of human nature and from the standpoint of reason—while these, notwithstanding their nobility, are still part of ourselves, bound up with our own imperfect ways of conceiving and desiring God Himself.[1]

Prudence implies the possession of the "right rule," or underlying principle, of what is to be done, the *recta ratio agibilium*. As distinguished from art, it is not concerned merely with something to be made, a *factibile*, whose only laws are those inherent in its own nature, but with each of man's activities set in the framework of life as a whole. The arts presuppose capacity in the handling of a restricted subject-matter, without it being necessary that the will be fixed on our final end, but prudence has for its material the entire field of human action and draws all its strength from the desire of our will to be united to the supreme good for which we were made. It should be noted that the perfection of prudence presupposes the possession of the other virtues while, reciprocally, completing and uniting them. We cannot be prudent unless we are also temperate and just, for the absence of these virtues means that our appetites are disordered; on the other hand, the possession of temperance and justice indicates the presence, in some measure at least, of prudence.

On analysis we can discover three distinct moments in the prudent act. In the first place, having previously settled upon the end, we consider the different means by which it may be realized. We take counsel, *consilium*, passing in review the various ways whereby we may attain our object. We next judge which of these means is the most suitable. In making this judgment, *judicium*, we are still weighing the situation with detachment. It is at the all-important third point that the act of prudence properly so called takes place. This is the decision to employ the means, the *imperium*. The moment has arrived for the practical intellect to come into

[1] Gardeil, *La Vraie Vie Chrétienne*, p. 118.

play, dictating to the will what here and now is to be its choice. Everything for good or ill depends on our dispositions at this juncture; for the practical intellect judges rather by its own inclinations than by the standards of objective truth. " As a man is so does his end appear to him to be "; *qualis unusquisque est talis videtur finis ei.* We needs must love the highest when we see it, says the poet, and utters only a half-truth. If it were wholly true why do we so frequently fail to act upon it? The answer is that, when the call to action comes, our eyes are prevented from seeing what is the highest, unless we have long since held it in our hearts by love.

Among the elements which go to make the prudent man St Thomas places memory in the first place. We cannot act wisely simply on *a priori* principles. We need experience—and memory is the store-house of experience. Often it is necessary to argue from similar cases in the past in order to know how to act in the present. Principles are insufficient; they are too general and, when taken as the sole guide to conduct, produce rigidity and intransigence in action. The incalculable variety of circumstances in which we have to act calls for suppleness and adaptability. The evils of mere expediency are best avoided, not by an uncompromising adherence to the principles of abstract morality, but by a knowledge of the numberless ways in which they can be realized in the concrete. And these we learn through experience and retain by memory.

To employ experience rightly we need understanding, insight. Without this memory is of little value. Unless we can interpret aright our accumulated knowledge of the past we are in danger of falling into a moral empiricism which has little to do with prudence or any other virtue. We must have always before our mind's eye the " vision of the principle." Now each human act works out as a sort of dynamic syllogism, comparable to the reasoning process by which we arrive at truth in speculative matters. First we have in our practical intelligence some general principle, the major premise; for example, " One should do evil to no man." But we must also be able to discern in every instance what would be a case of doing evil to some man. It is to provide us with this information, the minor premiss of our practical syllogism, that understanding (*intellectus*) is needed. Before we can deduce the conclusion which dictates action: " Do this " or " Don't do that," we must have grasped the situation as it is. It is obvious that this sense of perception, the concrete realization of what is in fact a particular set of circumstances to which a universal principle applies, is an integral part of the virtue of prudence.

It must be equally clear that good reasoning power (*ratio*) is no less a part of this virtue. The very activity of taking counsel (*consiliari*), considering the multiplicity of means, demands this. Not being endowed with angelic intuition, we have to approach our conclusion step by step, by the processes of discursive thought. From general principles we scale downwards to particulars. Accordingly we need facility in reasoning, the power to apply the principles which govern the action to be performed to the manifold conditions of the action itself.

Closely connected with the above-mentioned attributes of prudence is docility. This is the gift of being able to learn from others. Since the matters with which we have to deal in practical life are of infinite variety, no one man can consider them all sufficiently; nor can this be done quickly, for it requires length of time. Hence we ought to profit by the wisdom of others; especially ought we to consult those who are advanced in years, whose judgment has been matured by experience. Aristotle goes so far as to say that, in practical affairs, we ought to pay as much attention to the undemonstrated assertions of the aged as to those for which they advance proof, for the passage of time has given them an insight into principles. St Thomas notes in this context that docility is itself something which has to be learned. " Man has a natural aptitude for docility even as for other things connected with prudence. Yet his own efforts count for much towards the attainment of perfect docility: and he must carefully, frequently and reverently apply his mind to the teachings of the learned (*documenta majorum*), neither neglecting them through laziness nor despising them through pride."[1]

[1] IIa IIae, q. 49, a. 3, ad 2.

A further characteristic of the prudent man is shrewdness (*solertia*). We cannot always take counsel with others. Often we have to act quickly with no opportunity for doing so. As docility leads us to seek advice, so shrewdness enables us to judge for ourselves what is to be done—and rapidly. This combination of shrewdness with alertness is essential to prudence. The scholastics give to it the name *solicitudo*, which, following the etymology of Isidore, they derive from *solers* and *citus*. " A man is said to be solicitious through being shrewd (*solers*) and alert (*citus*); in so far as from a certain shrewdness he is on the alert to do whatever has to be done."[1] The delay counselled by the speculative intellect, if prolonged beyond its due term, is fatal to right action. There are times when almost the whole of virtue lies in our acting promptly. We may have to take time in reviewing the means to be employed but, once they have been decided upon, we should act at once. *Oportet operari quidem velociter consiliata, consiliari autem tarde.*

Three further qualities combine to form our integral conception of prudence: foresight, cautiousness, circumspection. It is noteworthy that there is an element of intelligent anticipation about all our actions. What is past is irrevocable and has now assumed a certain necessity. Nothing can undo what has once been done, even though its effect be nullified by some subsequent counteraction. Similarly with what is actually present; that too is in a measure beyond our control. At the moment of action we have committed ourselves; we have exercised our freedom in the preliminary mental debate but, having finally made our decision, in the precise execution of our choice we cannot but do what we do. By prudence then we have to legislate for the future; it is the act not yet decided upon which we can choose or reject. Hence the importance of foresight (*providentia*); it enables us to look ahead and prepare ourselves for contingencies before they arise.

Linked together with foresight must be a certain cautiousness (*cautio*). This should not be understood in its common English meaning, as implying hesitancy and delay. It is simply a recognition of the fact that appearances are often

[1] IIa IIae, q. 47, a. 9.

deceptive. Just as false is found with true so is evil mingled with good. Through foresight we look for the realization of some good intention, anticipate how best we may act when the appropriate moment arrives; by cautiousness we envisage the possibility of evil, of some interference with our plan, and make preparations accordingly.

That prudence implies circumspection is scarcely in need of proof. It has to do with the highly practical point that what is in itself a good thing to do is not necessarily good in a given set of circumstances. St Thomas states the matter with a succinctness it would be superfluous to paraphrase.

Since prudence is about singular matters of action, which involve many combinations of circumstances, it happens that a thing is good in itself and suitable to the end, and nevertheless becomes evil and unsuitable to the end, by reason of some combination of circumstances. Thus to show signs of love to someone seems, considered in itself, to be a fitting way to arouse love in his heart, yet if pride or suspicion of flattery arise in his heart, it will no longer be a means suitable to the end. Hence the need for circumspection in prudence, namely, for comparing the means with the circumstances.[1]

The fact that prudence adjusts us, morally speaking, to the world as we know it and makes contact with the realities of every-day life should not hide from view its essentially supernatural character. The final end, in the light of which Christian prudence directs our most trivial activities, is the vision of God as known through the theological virtue of faith and loved by charity. For this reason St Thomas conceives it as joined to the gift of the Holy Spirit known as Counsel. "It is proper to the rational creature to be moved through the research of reason to perform any particular action, and this research is called counsel. Hence the Holy Spirit is said to move the rational creature by way of counsel."[2] Even when we are equipped with prudence our range of vision is still limited by the defects of human reason and our path uncertain.

Since human reason is unable to grasp the singular and contingent things which may occur, the result is that "the thoughts of mortal men are fearful, and our counsels uncertain" (Wisdom

---

[1] IIa IIae, q. 49. a. 7.   [2] IIa IIae, q. 52, a. 1.

ix, 14). Hence in the research of counsel, man needs to be directed by God Who comprehends all things: and this is done through the gift of counsel, whereby man is directed as though counselled by God, just as, in human affairs, those who are unable to take counsel for themselves, seek counsel from those who are wiser.[1]

The gift of counsel works on the same material as the virtue of prudence, though with a surer and more delicate touch. Even after forethought and having employed all reasonable means we are not seldom at a loss to know what work we ought to take up, what abandon, how far we should proceed in a certain course of action, how much, in a given situation, we ought to say, how much leave unsaid. It happens sometimes that we have, as we imagine, calculated to a nicety what our attitude is to be, and yet, when the decisive moment arrives, we act differently, and with greater discretion, than we had anticipated. Occasions like these bring home to us the closeness of the Holy Spirit's influence on our actions. The theologians point out that the gift of counsel operates, so to say, at different degrees of intensity. First it directs those choices which are of strict obligation; at a higher level it makes possible the generous practice of the evangelical counsels; highest of all it inspires the performance of those good works which call for heroic sanctity.

It is surely by no arbitrary piece of exegesis that St Thomas following Augustine, connects the gift of counsel and perfect prudence with the Beatitude of mercy.[2] What is here meant is the strong and active showing of mercy, not the eliciting of it from others. Through counsel we are ruled by God; we correspond, more subtly than could unaided human reason, with His government of the world; we co-operate with Him in the execution of His providential plan. Now the dominating aspect of divine providence is God's mercy; He rules over His creatures with loving forbearance. "The Lord is gracious and merciful: patient and plenteous in mercy. The Lord is sweet to all: and His tender mercies are over all His works."[3] The Christian is invited to reproduce in his own conduct mercifulness. Remembering that his actions should be Christlike, an expression of the love of God with

---

[1] ibid., ad 1. [2] IIa IIae, q. 52, a. 4. [3] Psalm 144 (145), 8-9.

which his heart is filled, he will engage in activity with a supernatural gentleness and detachment. He will give to each particular duty the concentration necessary for its due performance, but no more than that. There is nothing on earth which can rightfully claim his entire attention. His dealings with others will be characterized by tolerance and kindliness; not because such is the easier course, but out of love for the brotherhood. Never will he allow himself to be wholly immersed in his activities, to be carried away by the noise and bustle of the hour. Always he will preserve a certain aloofness, the free heart of one whose gaze is fixed upon the everlasting hills. This is the happiness, the beatitude, of the merciful man; who will obtain mercy because he has learned how to show it.

To conclude. All human activity may be regarded as a function either of art or prudence. Of these two the second is of more vital importance, for it regulates the outward expression of art and itself directs our conduct in the only way whereby it is meritorious of eternal life. Supernatural prudence, helped out by the gift of counsel, is the sole sufficient guide to Christian action. When we are wholly submissive to its control there can be no opposition of contemplation to activity, the part of Mary to that of Martha. The harmony between the two is complete; the second is but an epiphany, a showing forth, of the first.

Fittingly, and not without pathos, does the Church, while awaiting the coming of the Redeemer, plead in the name of all humanity for this gift of practical wisdom whereby we may be enabled to serve Him: " O Wisdom Who didst proceed out of the mouth of the Most High, reaching from end unto end, mightily and sweetly ordering all things, come, and teach us the way of prudence "; *O Sapientia, quae ex ore Altissimi prodüsti, attingens a fine usque ad finem, fortiter suaviterque disponens omnia: veni ad docendum nos viam prudentiae.*[1]

---
[1] *Magnificat Antiphon for the* 17*th December.*

Part IV
THE EFFECTS OF THIS LOVE

I

THE PRESENCE

"And I live, now not I: but Christ liveth in me."—*Galatians ii, 20.*

AT the Last Supper Our Lord promised that He would manifest Himself to those who love Him. "And he that loveth Me shall be loved of My Father: and I will love him and manifest Myself to him."[1] From that moment, though He might be hidden from their eyes, He was never to be absent from His friends. The remoteness of God, the divine transcendence, which filled the thoughts of the Jews who rejected Christ as their Messiah, was not to exclude the divine immanence, God's dwelling with His creatures. Of this the Incarnation itself is sufficient proof. This central Christian mystery embraces both the immutability of God, the fact that His assumption of a human nature produced no change in Him, and a new unique presence of humanity to divinity in the closest of all unions, that of a single Personality. In Christ we have a pledge, not only of God's presence on earth at a definite point in history, but of the possibility of our abiding union with Him. Human nature was never again to be separated from God. It is true that only once was man to be united with the Godhead in the manner of Christ's humanity, in a substantial or hypostatic union. Nevertheless, having regard to the fact that each Christian is by adoption what Christ is by nature, a son of God, and "joint-heir with Christ,"[2] it was fitting that God should be present to him in a way corresponding to his presence to His Sole Begotten.

The unique presence of God in the soul which results from sanctifying grace is, like grace itself, the effect of His love for us rather than our love for Him. This must be clear from what we have seen in the preceding chapters; for whatever He finds lovable in His creatures He has first of all given to them. In rewarding us God does no more than crown His own gifts. But this should not lead us to underestimate the worth of the theological virtue of charity whereby we are

[1] John xiv, 21.   [2] Romans viii, 17.

united to God. When possessed of it we are truly capable of a divine love. It is not merely that God loves Himself through us. The desires of our quite human hearts go out to Him as to the one beloved. The humblest soul in grace can make his own the cry of St Peter: " Lord, Thou knowest all things, Thou knowest that I love Thee." We are on terms of friendship with God, and friendship can never be one-sided. Here, as with our human loves, we find those signs by which friendship is always to be distinguished—generosity, the giving of self, above all, the presence of friend to friend. " If anyone love Me he will keep My word. And My Father will love him: and we will come to him and make our abode with him."[1]

A living sense of God's presence is invariably found together with genuine sanctity. The saints, like Adam in the garden of Eden, walk in the company of God. His nearness is more real for them than the air they breathe and the material world which surrounds them. Nor is this conviction the result of a devout imagination, or even of an effort to " place " themselves in God's presence—as if He were ever far away; it is the awakening of the mind to the profoundest of truths. To bring home to ourselves the reality of the divine presence we must pass beyond the evidence of the senses, we must even pass beyond the memories and scenes of Christ's earthly life; for these are over and gone. To form a mental picture of Our Lord in His humanity may at times help our devotion, but we should deceive ourselves were we to suppose that the presence of God within the soul is no more significant than that. At the moment of Communion Christ's human nature comes to the soul, but only then in so far as it is hypostatically one with His Godhead; while that Godhead is already intimately united to the soul in virtue of its state of sanctifying grace. It is the presence of the Triune God, Whose glory is veiled from us in the darkness of our faith, which is the tremendous fact, the mystery of grace underlying all man's experience of Divinity. We approach the Presence, albeit humbly and with bated breath, not by looking outside ourselves, but by turning our gaze inwards upon our own souls and discerning therein the image of that

[1] John xiv, 23.

Trinity with which one day it is to be confronted face to face, *facie ad faciem.*

"Recognize in thyself something within, within thyself. Leave thou abroad both thy clothing and thy flesh; descend into thyself; go to thy secret chamber, thy mind. If thou be far from thine own self, how canst thou draw near to God? For not in the body but in the mind was man made in the image of God. In His own similitude let us seek God: in His own image recognize the Creator."[1] These words, so characteristic of St Augustine who had himself sought God everywhere without to find Him at last within, point out the path which must be followed by those who wish to draw near to God. Not that He is to be found at the end of a process of psychological introspection, for we can have no intuition of Him in this life. But only in self-awareness and tranquillity of spirit does God manifest Himself to His friends in that loving knowledge which, for the want of a better name, we call mystical experience. What has theology to tell us of the manner of God's presence in the soul? And how, since He is everywhere, since, even apart from grace, from the very fact that we are His creatures, " in Him we live and move and are,"[2] can He be present to those who love Him in a way that He is not present to others? We shall now attempt to outline an answer to these questions.

Quite apart from the infusion of sanctifying grace God is already present to the soul[3] by what the theologians call His ubiquity. He is there in the way in which He is present to everything He has made, giving to the soul its being and maintaining it in existence. This presence, it may be noted, is but a logical consequence of the act of creation. There can be no instrument or intermediary for God's creative act; hence He must be intimately present to all His creatures We speak of God being present in this way " by His power " or " through virtual contact "; since, however, the divine power is in reality identical with God Himself it follows that He is present by His very substance in all things. Further,

[1] Augustine, *In Joan. Evang.*, xxiii, 10.   [2] Acts xvii, 28.
[3] The word " soul " is here used as the equivalent of the *mens*. This is the term employed by St Augustine and St Thomas to designate the substance of the soul, considered as the seat of the faculties of intellect and will, so forming a similitude of the Blessed Trinity Itself. It is thus with reference to the *mens* that we are made " to the image and likeness of God."

this presence is not limited to the instant of creation; it must last as long as God preserves His creatures in being, for this conservation is nothing less than the continuance of the creative act. Just as the sun must shine as long as the object it enlightens is to remain illuminated, so God must continue to give each of His creatures its existence without which it cannot continue to be.

The divine ubiquity has nothing to do with space and quantity, as some have thought. It is a gross error to imagine the infinity of God, Who is Being itself, as implying a body without limitations, as though He were like a circle with its circumference everywhere and its centre nowhere. Since He is pure spirit He is above all considerations of space. Though God, by His creative and preservative power, holds all things in existence and is therefore in contact with them, the divine ubiquity is perhaps better conveyed to the mind by the way the voice of a singer is present to those who hear it or the mind to the thoughts which proceed from it than by geometrical imagery.

God is in all things; not, indeed, as part of their essence, nor as an accident; but as an agent is present to that upon which it works. For an agent must be present to that wherein it acts immediately, and touch it by its power; hence it is proved in Aristotle's Physics that the things moved and the mover must be joined together. Now since God is being itself (*ipsum esse*) by His own essence, created being must be an effect peculiar to Himself; as to ignite is an effect peculiar to fire. Now God causes this effect in things not only when they first begin to be, but as long as they are preserved in being; as light is caused in the air by the sun as long as the air remains illuminated. Therefore as long as a thing has being, God must be present to it, according to its mode of being. But being is innermost in each thing and most fundamentally inherent in all things, since it is formal in respect of everything found in a thing. . . . Hence it must be that God is in all things, and innermostly: *Unde oportet quod Deus sit in omnibus rebus, et intime.*[1]

We should note, however, that the soul (*mens*), in its natural state, can have no direct or intuitive knowledge of God's presence within it. It would appear to be certain

---

[1] Ia, q. 8, a. 1.

that, even after the infusion of grace, an intuition of this kind is impossible. Only God, by nature, can know Himself intuitively. In heaven even sanctifying grace is insufficient to enable us to see Him face to face; we need the additional strength given to our intellect by the " light of glory." In this life our knowledge of Him must always be from His effects, and not a vision of Him as He is in Himself. Nevertheless, in virtue of the soul's natural structure—a spiritual essence from which emanate the faculties of intellect and will, so forming a sort of image of the Trinity—there exists an innate capacity for realizing God's nearness which is absent from beings not possessed of consciousness. But this capacity can never be actualized on the merely natural plane. The reason for this is the lack of proportion between the created human intelligence and the divine essence. Moreover we tend naturally in this life to acquire our knowledge through the external senses and the imagination—a fact which places us at a disadvantage in comparison with the angels in gaining knowledge of spiritual realities. Even our consciousness of our own souls is habitual and implicit rather than actual and well-defined. Painfully and with labour do we draw deductions about its inmost nature; we do not see it as we do the objects which fall under our senses.

Notwithstanding these drawbacks, we have sufficient evidence for discerning within ourselves that resemblance to the Trinity by which most of all we are made to the image and likeness of God. It is true that there can be no strict image of the Trinity in the soul without grace, because such a representation of God demands that the soul be raised to the supernatural order. But here, as always, grace builds upon nature—a nature which, as stated above, has an aptitude, an " obediential potentiality," to become the image of the Trinity Itself.

Since man is said to be in the image of God by reason of his intellectual nature, he is the most perfectly like God according to that in which he can best imitate God in his intellectual nature. Now the intellectual nature imitates God chiefly in this, that God understands and loves Himself. Wherefore we see that the image of God is in man . . . inasmuch as man possesses a natural aptitude for understanding and loving God; and this aptitude consists in the very nature of the mind (*mens*) which all men have in common . . .[1]

It is the *mens*, that is,[2] the spiritual soul together with the faculties of intellect and will, which is " the receptive subject of all our divine life; it is the ' exemplar,' the model, and at the same time affords the explanation—in so far as a material cause, a receptive subject, can do so—of the immediate relation between God and the soul which characterizes alike the structure of the justified soul and the mystical experience determined by that structure."[3] We shall consider more closely in the next chapter the nature of the union by knowledge and love between the soul and God; for the moment we must confine our attention to the ontological basis of that union. If God is, from the nature of things, present in the soul in its natural state, what precisely takes place at the infusion of sanctifying grace? What meaning is to be attached to Our Lord's promise that He and the Father would come and make their dwelling with those who love Him? " God is charity," writes St John, " and he that abideth in charity abideth in God, and God in him."[4] Is the divine presence which is so clearly indicated in these words no more than what is implied in God's presence by immensity? If this is so then the presence of God would have no greater fundamental significance for the soul in grace than for the soul in a state of mortal sin—a conclusion which it is impossible to accept.

St Augustine, as might have been expected, shows his awareness of this problem and gives some hint of its solution.

For what is there that is not in Him of whom it is divinely written, " For of Him, and through Him, and in Him, are all things" ? (Rom. xi, 36). If, then, all things are in Him, in whom can any possibly live that do live, or be moved that are moved, except in Him in whom they are? Yet all are not with Him in that way in which it is said to Him, " I am continually with

---
[1] Ia, q. 93, a. 4.
[2] *Mens* in anima nostra dicit illud quod est altissimum in virtute ipsius: unde, cum secundum id quod est altissimum in nobis, *divina imago* inveniatur in nobis, imago non pertinebit ad essentiam animae nisi secundum mentem, prout nominat altissimam potentiam ejus; et sic mens, prout in ea est imago, nominat potentiam animae et non essentiam, vel si nominat essentiam, hoc non est nisi inquantum ab ea fluit talis potentia.—St Thomas, *De Veritate*, q. 10, a. 1.
[3] Gardeil, *La Structure de L'Ame*, I, p. 48.
[4] 1 John iv, 16.

Thee" (Ps. lxxii, 23). Nor is He with all in that way in which we say, The Lord be with you. And so it is the especial wretchedness of man not to be with Him, without whom he cannot be. For, beyond a doubt, he is not without Him in whom he is; and yet if he does not remember and understand, and love Him, he is not with Him.[1]

Elsewhere, and more explicitly, the same thought recurs.

But what is more marvellous is the fact that God, though everywhere complete, does not dwell in all men. For it is not to all men that the Apostle could say: "Know you not that you are the temple of God, and that the Spirit of God dwelleth in you?" (1 Cor. iii, 16). On the contrary, to some he says: "Now if any man hath not the Spirit of Christ, he is none of His" (Rom. viii, 9).... It must therefore be acknowledged that God is everywhere by the presence of His divinity but not everywhere by the indwelling of His grace.... As then God who is everywhere dwells not in all men, so too He does not dwell in all equally.... And if among all the saints some are more saintly than others, it is only because God dwells in them more abundantly....[2]

For further light we must turn to the *Summa Theologica*. St Thomas raises the question whether the coming of the Holy Spirit into the soul depends upon the infusion of sanctifying grace.[3] He answers with an unqualified affirmative, declaring that the Holy Spirit can truly be said to be sent to the soul and to be bestowed upon it as a gift. The famous article which forms his reply is too compressed for summary and is here transcribed in full. It contains in germ the whole of the Thomist mystical theology.

It pertains to a divine person to be sent in so far as He exists in a new way in anyone, and He is given in so far as He is possessed by anyone. And neither of these things comes to pass except through sanctifying grace (*gratia gratum faciens*). For God is in all things by His essence, power and presence, according to His one common mode of being present, namely, as the cause existing in the effects which participate in His goodness (i.e., by His ubiquity). Above and beyond this common mode, however, there is one special mode belonging to the rational nature wherein God is said to be present as the object known is in the knower, and the beloved in the lover—*sicut cognitum in cognoscente, et amatum in amante*. And since the rational creature, by its operation of knowledge and love, reaches to God Himself, accord-

---
[1] St Augustine, *De Trinitate* XIV, xii, 16.
[2] Ep. CLXXXVII, v, 16, 17.   [3] Ia, q. 43, a. 3.

ing to this special mode God is said not only to exist in the rational creature, but also to dwell therein as in His own temple. So no other effect can be put down as the reason why the divine person is in the rational creature in a new mode, excepting sanctifying grace. Accordingly only as a result of sanctifying grace is a divine person sent and does He proceed in the order of time. Likewise we are said to possess only what we can freely use or enjoy: and to have the power of enjoying the divine person can only be according to sanctifying grace. And yet the Holy Spirit is possessed by man, and dwells within him, in the very gift of sanctifying grace. Hence the Holy Spirit Himself is given and sent.

What distinguishes God's presence in the soul by grace from His ordinary presence by ubiquity is the fact that He exists therein, no longer simply as an immanent cause, but "as the object known is in the knower and the beloved in the lover." We shall have some qualifications to make in the next chapter about the knowledge here implied; but that God now objectifies the mind (*mens*) in a manner wholly different from the way in which he is naturally present to it is demanded by the very nature of the transformation which sanctifying grace effects. By grace we are made sharers in the divine nature and friends of God; we are thus intimately related to Him in terms of knowledge and love.

When God is present within a creature in virtue merely of His creative act He still remains infinitely remote from it in the order of being, ontologically. He is present *in* the creature but He is not present *to* it. The created substance is penetrated by the divine action through which it is sustained and moved; *omnia in Ipso constant*, everything depends for its existence on God. But from the point of view of the realities concerned, Creator and creature, the relation between them is one of simple juxtaposition. From the nature of things God is present in a stone, in a piece of wood, in water, but He is present without any answering consciousness on the part of the creature; He is there as a stranger. The created being is incapable of entering into direct relations with the Being on whom it is so absolutely dependent. It cannot communicate or establish any intimacy with Him. The presence of God is as complete as it is possible to conceive, but it operates in an indifference which is no less complete.

How different is God's indwelling in the soul which is united to Him by grace! The Lord is no longer simply *in* us, He is also *with* us. In the indivisible unity of the *mens*, divinized by grace, the divine substance is physically present, as in all things, by immensity; but there now exists over against it, co-ordinated with it, the efficacious tendency of the divine nature as shared by the creature, urging the soul to unite itself with God. The Creator, present in the soul by His immensity, now encounters an energy capable of embracing Him. It is the same indivisible spirit, the *mens*, which contains both: on the one hand, the divine reality towards which the soul aspires, and on the other, the sanctified soul itself whose entire energies are now orientated towards an intimate union with God. It is clear that a new relation has come into being between the grace-endowed soul and God dwelling substantially within it—a unique relation which has nothing in common with the relation which constitutes the presence by immensity, since it is not founded on the divine causality but on the essential ordination of grace to unite us intimately, through the knowledge and efficacious love which emanate from it, to God present substantially within us.

The soul, endowed with grace, owing this gift as well as its natural existence to the divine bounty, turns back by a sort of reflex movement—made possible by the soul's spirituality —towards the God immanent within it. Its relation to God does not now refer to Him as the efficient cause which produces His presence by immensity. What the soul now looks for in God, as dwelling substantially within it, is the object of knowledge and love to which it has been efficaciously ordered by the infusion of grace. The divine presence by immensity provides the ontological foundation for the new mode of indwelling, but it is grace which supplies the characteristic element wholly distinguishing the second kind of presence from the first. Through the infusion of sanctifying grace there results the objective presence of a spiritual reality closely united to a being capable of holding intercourse with it: the divine Spirit united with the created spirit. It is the presence of the very substance of God, not of God as cause, *effector entis*, but of God in His intimate nature, *sub ratione*

Deitatis; no longer is He simply immanent within us, as He is in stone or wood, but He dwells as a guest in the soul now rendered capable of knowing and loving Him, the soul which, through grace, shares in God's own nature.[1] "If any one love Me, ... My Father will love Him; and We will come to him, and will make our abode with him."

It follows from this that our appreciation of the meaning of the presence of God, our sense of His nearness, depends upon what we understand by the object known being present to the knower and the beloved to the lover. We have touched upon the unitive character of knowledge in a previous chapter and we would refer the reader back to what has been said there. But useful, if inadequate, analogies can be drawn from common experience. We know well that to be in close proximity to some object is not the same thing as being aware of its presence. Literally, as well as figuratively, we can have eyes and see not, ears and hear not. Moreover, even when consciousness is aroused, it can exist in varying degrees of intensity. The sight of London at sunrise will leave one man unmoved while inspiring another to poetry. A printed page is for one who can read alive with significance, meaningless for one who cannot. And in our human relationships the truth is still more evident, especially as here it is emphasized by the element of affection. How different we feel in the presence of a friend after years of intimacy from the moment when first we saw him! Physically we are no closer together, but we meet now with an ease and absence of restraint which were not so before. We have learned to know him, to appreciate his good qualities, to hold him in our regard, so that we feel his presence in a mixed company in a way that we are not aware of others. Knowledge and love have transformed a casual contact into a union of spirit which remains unaffected by spatial distance.

It is easy to see the application of all this to the indwelling of God within the soul. The fact that we only know of His presence there by faith weakens, but does not destroy, the force of the parallel. For faith, as we have repeatedly insisted, is a form of knowledge. Further, it will be remem-

---

[1] This and the preceding two paragraphs are taken almost verbatim from Gardeil, *La Structure de L'Ame*, II, pp. 62-65.

bered, that the gifts of the Holy Spirit supply for the deficiencies of faith; their function is to give to the soul a sense of kinship with God, the beginnings of an experimental knowledge of Him whereby the yoke of the Christian life is made easy and its burden light. " O taste, and see that the Lord is sweet."[1]

It goes without saying that the new mode of God's presence, which accompanies the infusion of sanctifying grace, implies a transformation of the human soul (*mens*) but in no way affects the divine changelessness.[2] The soul is raised up to an entirely new relationship with God, that of an adopted son, but He Himself remains unchanged. Nevertheless, as may be gathered from what has been said, the divine Persons of the Son and Holy Spirit can truly be described as *sent* by the Father into the soul. The marvellous life of the Trinity still goes on in the depths of the grace-endowed spirit. By the eternal act of generation the Son comes forth from the Father; and the Holy Spirit proceeds eternally from the Father and the Son. In this way, and by reason of the effects they produce, the second and third Persons of the Trinity can be said to be sent to the soul. With every increase of grace, as well as by its first infusion, the mission (*missio*) of these Persons has effect. Because the Holy Spirit proceeds by way of love, and the Word according to an intellectual generation, an increase of charity in the soul is attributed to the mission of the Holy Spirit, while the illumination of the mind which accompanies charity is ascribed to the mission of the Word.

The soul is made like to God by grace. Hence for a divine Person to be sent to anyone by grace, there must needs be a likening of the soul to the divine Person Who is sent, by some gift of grace. Because the Holy Spirit is Love, the soul is assimilated to the Holy Spirit by the gift of charity: hence the mission of the Holy Spirit is according to the gift of charity. Whereas the Son is the Word, not any sort of Word, but one Who breathes forth love; *est Verbum, non qualecumque, sed spirans amorem*.[3] Hence Augustine says (*De Trin.* ix, 10): " The Word of

[1] Psalm xxxiii, 9.   [2] Ia, q. 43, a. 2, ad 2.
[3] Commenting on this text M. Maritain writes: " In us as well as in God, love must proceed from the Word, that is from the spiritual possession of the truth, in Faith. And just as everything which is in the Word is found once more in the Holy Spirit, so must all that we know pass into our power of affec-

which we speak is knowledge joined with love." Thus the Son is sent, not in accordance with every and any kind of intellectual perfection, but according to the intellectual illumination which breaks forth into the affection of love, as is said (John vi, 45): "Everyone that hath heard from the Father and hath learned cometh to me," and (Ps. xxxviii, 4): "In my meditation a fire shall flame forth." Thus Augustine plainly says (*De Trin.* iv, 20): "The Son is sent whenever He is known and perceived by anyone." Now perception implies a certain experimental knowledge; and this is properly called wisdom (*sapientia*), as it were a sweet knowledge (*sapida scientia*), according to Ecclus. vi, 23: "The wisdom of doctrine is according to her name."[1]

It is impossible to think of God's indwelling within the soul without calling to mind His Eucharistic presence, the special way in which He comes to us in the sacrament of Christ's body and blood. As we have seen, with St Thomas, a sufficient reason for the truth of the Real Presence is that "it is in accordance with Christ's love, out of which for our salvation He assumed a true body of our nature." He continues:

And because it is the special characteristic of friendship for the friends to live together.... He promises us His bodily presence as a reward.... Yet meanwhile in our earthly pilgrimage He does not deprive us of His bodily presence, but unites us with Himself in this Sacrament through the reality of His body and blood. Wherefore He says (John vi, 57): "He that eateth My flesh and drinketh My blood abideth in Me and I in Him." Hence this Sacrament is the sign of supreme charity, and the uplifter of our hope, from such familiar union of Christ with us.[2]

But if our devotion to the Blessed Sacrament is to be founded on Catholic dogma, we must understand Our Lord's entry into the soul at the moment of Communion in the light of what we have seen concerning God's presence within us by sanctifying grace. It is possible for even the

tion by love, finding only there its resting place. Love must proceed from Truth, and Knowledge must bear fruit in love. Our prayer is not what it ought to be, if either of these conditions is wanting. And by prayer we understand no other thing than that supreme prayer which is made in the secret depth of the heart—in so far as it is directed to contemplation and union with God." (*De la Vie d'Oraison* par Jacques et Raïssa Maritain, p. 11).

It is well to be reminded that the sublime mystery of the Blessed Trinity can teach us truths of very practical value.

[1] Ia, q. 43, a. 5, ad 2.   [2] IIIa, q. 75, a. 1.

relatively well-instructed to have ideas on this matter which would not bear close examination. Admittedly it is difficult to exclude spatial images from our thoughts about the Eucharist, but it is of obvious importance that we should view the mystery without prejudice to God's absolute changelessness and the impassibility of Christ's sacred humanity. The divine presence, as contained under the appearances (*species*) of bread and wine, is unique; equally so the process of change by which it is brought about, so aptly named *transubstantiation*. It is true that at the reception of the sacred species we may think of Our Lord coming into the soul, but it is worth while considering what this means; or rather, since it is easier to speak of a mystery in negative terms, what it does not mean.

"Just as Christ by coming visibly into the world gave to it the life of grace, so by coming sacramentally into man He sets the life of grace in operation."[1] The formal effect of receiving the Eucharist is to nourish the divine life of the soul, to proffer spiritual refreshment. It is not intended to confer that life in the first instance, since it is a sacrament of the living and presupposes life, nor to bring about a new mode of God's presence in the soul. It should be noted that the reality signified by this sacrament, *res sacramenti*, namely, the grace by which we are united to Christ, can be had by the desire for Communion apart from the act itself.[2] For the reality in question is but another name for the eternal life without which none can be saved, while salvation is not made dependent upon the actual reception of the sacramental species. Because the Eucharist contains Christ Himself it is the greatest of the sacraments and the one to which all the others are ordered as to their consummation; they are but the passing instruments of God's power, but in this sacrament Christ abides permanently, as long as the accidents of bread and wine remain. If, however, we would appreciate the special effects of Holy Communion it is better to think of it in terms of spiritual nourishment, rather than attempt to visualize a presence of God within the soul other than that already due to it by the infusion of sanctifying grace.

As with the other sacraments, so with the Eucharist, its

[1] IIIa, q. 79, a. 1.   [2] IIIa, q. 73, a. 3.

peculiar graces are given to us through the instrumentality of Our Lord's human nature. But His human nature does not, if we may so speak, confer grace in its own right; it is only in virtue of its union with the Godhead that it can do so.[1] God alone is the author of grace; Christ's humanity is the principal instrument of its bestowal upon us (*instrumentum divinitati conjunctum*), and, subordinately, the sacraments (*instrumenta separata*) instituted by Christ. Now, in view of what has been said above, it must be clear that even before receiving Communion Christ in His Godhead is already present in the soul. He is there as the second Person of the Trinity; and indeed, it is only by reason of His being one in essence with the Father and the Holy Spirit that it is possible for the Incarnate Word to be intimately united to the soul at all. From the nature of things the Trinity alone can dwell within the mind: *sola Trinitas menti illabitur*.[2] Even while the adorable Humanity is inseparably united as one hypostasis with the Person of the Word, a distinction must remain between the presence of the divinity in the soul and that of the humanity.

Moreover, although after the words of consecration have been pronounced, Christ's body is really and substantially present, as signified by the accidents of bread and wine, it is not there in any sense which could imply its being confined in space: *nullo modo corpus Christi est in hoc sacramento localiter*.[3] This truth may be somewhat baffling to the imagination; it is, however, of the first importance, though sometimes overlooked in popular works of piety. The picture of Our Lord as a prisoner in the tabernacle, at the mercy of His creatures, has no doubt a certain pathos calculated to inspire devotion, but it does little justice to the realities involved. Christ is ascended into heaven and the days of His suffering are over; He reigns gloriously with the Father on high beyond the reach of human malice. To insult the Blessed Sacrament is truly an affront to Our Lord Himself; but it does not touch Him in the way that the malevolence of His enemies affected Him during the days of His earthly life. The conversion (*conversio*) brought about through transubstantiation means

[1] Ia IIae, q. 112, a. 1, ad 1 et ad 2. [2] IIIa, q. 8, a. 8, ad 1.
[3] IIIa, q. 76, a. 5.

that the substance of Christ's body and blood, and, concomitantly, His soul and divinity, have been substituted for the substance of bread and wine. Thus, after the consecration, the presence of Christ is as truly signified by the externals of bread and wine as was formerly the substance of which they are the normal accidents. There is, however, an all-important difference to be noted.

The accidents of bread and wine do not bear the same relation to the substance of Christ's body as they did to their proper subject of inherence (i.e., the bread and wine themselves). Christ is wholly present, but "substantially," *per modum substantiae*—and therefore unspatialized. This presence implies, not only that the substance of His body is there, but the accidents also, though existing, by divine intervention, in a substantial mode of being. For this reason —and for many others—it is unthinkable that the accidents of bread and wine should in any way inhere in Christ's body. In fact these accidents are kept in being, miraculously, without any subject of inherence at all. Accordingly, when it is recalled that location in space is only possible on a basis of the accident known as dimensional quantity, is itself therefore fundamentally an accident, it must be seen that the Real Presence is something outside the category of space. Undoubtedly we can point to a consecrated Host, wherever it may be, and say with truth: "Christ is there," because the appearances of bread and wine now signify His presence. But we cannot say that Christ is circumscribed by the space which surrounds the accidental species; nor is it in the strict sense true to say, when the Host is moved on the altar or carried in procession that Christ is passing from one place to another. Christ's body is related to the place occupied by the spatialized accidents of bread and wine precisely by means of these, that is, by dimensions which are not its own, *mediantibus dimensionibus alienis*. While "the proper dimensions of Christ's body are compared with that place through the medium of substance; which is contrary to the notion of a located body. Hence in no way is Christ's body locally in this sacrament."[1]

It should be unnecessary to say that these remarks are not intended to lessen our conviction of Our Lord's presence

[1] IIIa, q. 76, a. 5.

within us at the moment of Communion. Words are in fact incapable of expressing how vital that presence is. But it is desirable that we should avoid any materialistic notion of the divine indwelling and realize what is its ultimate foundation, namely, the natural immanence of God in the soul and the special mode of His presence which accompanies the infusion of sanctifying grace. Consequently we should think of Our Lord's coming into the soul at Communion as an invisible mission of the Word, the sending forth by the Father which corresponds to the eternal act whereby He generates the Son, rather than as a change of state in Christ Himself. In this way the emphasis is thrown on what, so far as man is concerned, is the most important element in the Eucharist: its effect upon the soul, what the theologians call the "reality" of the sacrament, the *res*. And the *res* of this sacrament is the grace conferred on the one who receives it.[1] While it is true that the Real Presence is in no way affected by the dispositions of the recipient, and is independent of the effects produced in his soul, nevertheless the spiritual eating, *spiritualis manducatio*, of Christ's body—which alone is of any profit—is precisely that "by which one receives the effect of this sacrament, whereby a man is spiritually united with Christ through faith and charity."[2] The material reception of the sacramental species, involving as it must the Real Presence of Our Lord within us, is not in itself the union with Him effected through Communion. "It is the spirit which quickeneth: the flesh profiteth nothing."[3] The supernatural vitality of the Godhead, communicated to us through Christ's sacred Humanity, is what gives to our Communion its inward meaning. And this is nothing else but the nourishing of the life of grace, the building up of our union with Christ Himself and with the members of His Mystical Body, the Church.

It is well for us constantly to recall the essential truth about the Eucharist, that it is the bread of life, the food of our souls. It bears the same relation to the life of the soul as material nourishment to our corporeal life. So close is the analogy that theologians teach that when it is not treated

[1] IIIa, q. 73, a. 1, ad 3.   [2] IIIa, q. 73, a. 1, ad 3.
[3] John vi, 64.

precisely as food it does not produce its effects. Correspondingly, it is just at the moment of consumption, when the Host is being used as nourishment, that the sacramental graces are conferred.

We need not here enumerate the effects of the sacrament of the Eucharist; they are all included in what is meant by the strengthening of the soul's supernatural life. The fulfilment to which it leads is the union with Christ by charity. Unlike earthly food, which we assimilate and transform into our own bodies, this heavenly and spiritual food changes us into itself.[1] For the Eucharist is the banquet of love, the *agape*, and by love we do not appropriate the beloved object to ourselves, but rather submit to its influence and are transformed into it. " And I live, now not I : but Christ liveth in me."[2]

It is illuminating to bear in mind that, in eating Christ's flesh and drinking His blood, we as wayfarers partake on earth of the food which the angels enjoy in heaven. *Ecce panis angelorum, factus cibus viatorum*, sings the Church on the feast of Corpus Christi.

The receiving of Christ under this sacrament is ordained to the enjoyment of heaven, as to its end, in the same way as the angels enjoy it; and since the means are gauged by the end, hence it is that such eating of Christ whereby we receive Him under this sacrament is, as it were, derived from that eating whereby the angels enjoy Christ in heaven. Consequently, man is said to eat the *bread of angels*, because it belongs to the angels to do so first and principally, since they enjoy Him in His proper species; and secondly, it belongs to men, who receive Christ under this sacrament.[3]

Perhaps no passage in St Thomas's treatment of the Eucharist is more significant than the one just quoted. It makes clear what certain presentations of sacramental theology can sometimes allow us to forget, that nothing can bring God close to man, in the only sense that counts, except love enlightened by knowledge. We must be preoccupied with God, have our minds fixed, by faith and charity, upon that Object Which is the eternal delight of the

[1] IIIa, q. 73, a. 3, ad 2.
[2] Galatians ii, 20.
[3] IIIa, q. 80, a. 2, ad 1.

blessed in heaven. For God is not to be found at the end of any ordinary search; only by desire do we draw near to Him. "Whom we approach by the affections of the soul, not by the movement of the body"; *cui non appropinquatur passibus corporis, sed affectibus mentis.*[1]

[1] IIa IIae, q. 24, a. 4.

II

UNION

"But he who is joined to the Lord is one spirit."—1 *Corinthians vi*, 17.

And it is to be observed, if one would learn how to find this Spouse (so far as may be in this life), that the Word, together with the Father and the Holy Spirit, is hidden essentially in the inmost centre of the soul. Wherefore the soul that would find Him through union of love must issue forth and hide itself from all created things according to the will, and enter within itself in deepest recollection, communing there with God in loving and affectionate fellowship, esteeming all that is in the world as though it were not.'[1]

THESE words of St John of the Cross, which could be paralleled by passages from St Augustine and the great tradition of Christian mysticism, lead us to consider more closely the nature of the soul's union with God. This union takes place in "the inmost centre of the soul," that is, the *mens*. The soul, being immaterial, has, strictly speaking, neither centre nor height nor depth; it is all spirit. Nevertheless the descriptive language of the mystics, which applies to it these terms, is not without meaning. Although the spiritual substance of the soul contains within itself the principles of even our animal and sentient life—for man is a unity, not a heterogeneous compound of spirit and matter—it can be considered as more fundamentally spiritual, more truly itself, when we prescind from its animal and sentient activities and look at it with reference to those operations which are wholly its own, its acts of knowledge and love. It is when viewed from this standpoint, as a spiritual essence from which there emerge the powers of intellect and will, that we perceive in the soul an image of the Trinity.

By the *mens* is meant the highest power of the soul; wherefore, because the divine image is to be found in us according to what is highest in our soul, the image will only pertain to the essence of the soul, when viewed as the *mens*, in so far as this signifies its highest power. Thus the *mens*, as comprising the image, desig-

---
[1] St John of the Cross, *Spiritual Canticle*, stanza 1, 4; p. 33 (Works, Vol. II)

nates the power of the soul and not its essence; or if it implies the essence, it does so only in as much as this power flows out from it.[1]

In other words, as has already been pointed out, the image of the Trinity in the soul consists in its spiritual essence, considered as the source from which proceed the faculties of intellect and will. It is here that the divine life has its interior source within us, here that fellowship with God has its only true meaning, here that our union with Him will reach its consummation, when the soul will be all but transformed into God Himself. " Dearly beloved, we are now the sons of God: and it hath not yet appeared what we shall be. We know that when He shall appear we shall be like to Him: because we shall see Him as He is."[2]

It is by means of knowledge and love, the most characteristic activities of man, that union with God takes place. By knowing God as He is and by conforming our wills to Him, both as an object of desire and as the ruler of all our actions, we enter into communion with Him. We have seen much in the foregoing pages of the approach to God by the knowledge of faith, and the love which is charity, and of sanctifying grace which is at the roots of both. In this chapter we shall attempt to examine more closely the object of this knowledge and the oneness of our will with His which is but another name for love.

To speak first of knowledge. What is the precise object of the cognitive experience which accompanies the higher degrees of charity? Is there given to the mystics in this life an intuition of God Himself? Though St Augustine and, following him, St Thomas, seem to have held that Moses and St Paul enjoyed a momentary vision, *per modum transitus*, of the divine essence while on earth, nothing can safely be generalized from these cases. The theology of sanctifying grace, the virtues and the gifts, would appear to rule out, rather than include, the possibility of man attaining to any true vision of God in this life. Under the present dispensation we live by faith, and faith is, by definition, of things unseen. Faith, no doubt, is progressively strengthened and

[1] *De Veritate*, q. 10, a. 1. (See page 210, footnote 2.)
[2] 1 John iii, 2.

enlightened by that kinship with its object which comes through charity, but it is never done away with. The raptures and visions which occasionally accompany mystical experience—sometimes unfortunately identified with the experience itself—prove nothing against this conclusion. In no manner can God be seen in the imagination or with the bodily eyes. It is for this reason that St John of the Cross, while extolling the treasures to be found in the " dark night " of faith, was so distrustful of visions and ecstasies. These last are not in themselves proof of genuine holiness. It is true that in many hagiographies the disproportionately large place given to mystical phenomena, visions, locutions, ecstasies and the like, is apt to hide from view their relative unimportance. They are undoubtedly to be found in the lives of the Christian saints, but they are to be found also in the lives of those whose moral conduct shows them to be very far from saints. With justice the theologians teach that preternatural manifestations of sanctity are either *gratiae gratis datae*, that is, graces given for the benefit of others or the Church as a whole, or signs of the body's incapacity to adapt itself to the interior elevation of spirit. In either case they are not of the essence of holiness. It may be noted that Our Lord Himself was never in ecstasy; for any of His followers to wish such a thing for themselves is illusion and vanity.

The fact that the phenomena of mysticism do not necessarily presuppose supernatural grace and can often be explained by natural causes suggests a further question: Can there be a mystical union with God on the purely natural plane? Have the intuitions of a philosopher like Plotinus, or the experiences of a poet such as Wordsworth, to do with the same realities as the loving knowledge of the Christian contemplative? There are some who apparently find no difficulty in admitting an affirmative answer to this question. The abstract speculation of the neo-Platonist and Christian contemplation differ only in degree. The thesis has even been maintained that though the poet, unlike the contemplative, may fail in the perfection of charity, and is therefore a " broken-down mystic," the vision towards which he moves is essentially the same as that of the saints.

It would be out of place at this point to enter into a full discussion of the question. But it must be obvious that, if the principles set out in the earlier chapters of this book are true and their development valid, then no such view can be advanced here. This is not to deny the genuineness of poetical and philosophical experience; the poets are unquestionably the recipients of some sort of inspiration not given to ordinary mortals, and one has not to search far among their writings to discover passages analogous to the accounts the mystics give of their own experiences. But if theology—in particular the theology of St Thomas—has anything to teach us on the matter, we have slight grounds for accepting such resemblances on their face-value. If the distinction between grace and nature is not to be reduced to one of mere words, it would seem of the highest importance to insist that what is granted as a co-relative of grace is not to be acquired on a basis of nature. For the point in question is not confined in its interest to speculative theologians; nothing less than the inner significance of the Incarnation and the Redemption is at issue. It is hard to see how those who hand over so lightly the treasures of the saints to the philosophers and poets do not empty our concept of divine grace of its unique content, being unconsciously guilty of that intellectual *evacuatio crucis* which is the inevitable result of confusing the supernatural with the natural order. If the experience which Christian theology teaches to be an outflowing of the supernatural virtues of faith and charity can be shown to be inherent in man, be he poet or philosopher, what peculiar meaning is to be attached to that superabundant life of knowledge and love which Christ came to bring? Or alternatively, if the most glorious of human achievements have only been possible through the intervention of grace, how, on such a view, can we avoid either depriving man of his native dignity by denying him his triumphs or lowering the function of grace to that of perfecting nature in its own order?

It is surely a *refugium in mysterium* unworthy of a philosopher to seek to solve a problem in aesthetics by appealing to supernatural revelation. The metaphysics and epistemology of Aristotle and his followers have been shown to offer conclusions about the nature of artistic sensibility more satisfying than those obtained by trespassing on the domain of theology. No doubt the causes which lead to philosophical ecstasy and the intoxication of the poets in their high moments defy complete analysis and are not to be explained in purely intellectual terms, but there is no warrant for allying them with mystical experience. The element of the unknown which surrounds these processes would seem to be only an extreme case of the natural mystery which lies at the root of all our communication with the extra-mental world. We know that we know, though the precise way in which knowledge comes about escapes us. But we have no reason to maintain that the insight of even the greatest among the poets exceeded in richness and profundity the vision of Plato gazing upon the world, " the spectator of all time and all existence," or that the most uncompromising neo-Platonist ever reaches at the term of his ascesis a vision more illuminating than that of *being*, τὸ ὄν, which led Aristotle to describe metaphysics as a quasi-divine science. And neither Plato nor Aristotle knew the elements of what Catholic tradition understands by sanctifying grace.

The truth is that a knowledge of the highly fascinating literature of Christian mysticism is not a sufficient qualification for pronouncing on its inner nature. Verbal resemblances between the writings of the mystics and those of the poets are as likely to mislead as prove illuminating. Nor does the final word rest with the philosopher, whose province lies within the boundaries marked out by natural reason. If the experiences of the saints are not an epiphenomenon of sanctity, but its harmonious outflowing, then we must attempt to account for them in the light of the supernatural truths by which these chosen souls professedly lived and whose mysteries formed the object of their contemplation. In other words it is theology, the science of revealed truth, that is the final court of appeal.

Clearly we cannot here set out the full theological arguments which lead us to the conclusion that there can be no true experience of God in the natural order. This conclusion is, however, but a deduction from what has been said in regard to the twofold knowledge and love of God, on the natural and supernatural planes, and His peculiar presence in the soul resulting from the infusion of sanctifying grace. Gladly we make our own the views expressed in the following passage by M. Maritain who, while in no way diminishing the rightful claims of reason, has the rare distinction of being able to enlighten an admirable philosophy by the guiding lights of theology.

The precise property of grace, that infused quality which engrafts in us a new spiritual nature and turns us face to face with God, of the proper and special presence of the Trinity in the just soul as a gift and object of fruition, is *to render possible* a passion of the divine reality, an experience of the deep things of God. *To realize* this experience of God is the peculiar end of those gifts of knowledge and wisdom which, under the inspiration of the Holy Spirit, raise the mind to the object presented to it by faith in a superhuman way due to the kinship effected with it by charity. It is thus the precise function of the supernatural to permit of an experimental knowledge of God.

To admit in any degree, even in the simplest conceivable form, an authentic experience of the deep things of God on the natural plane would necessarily imply:

Either confusing our natural intellectuality, which is made specific by being in general, with our grace-endowed intellectuality, which is made specific by the divine essence itself;

Or confusing the presence of immensity, whereby God is present in all things in virtue of His creative power, with the holy indwelling of God, by which He is specially present as an object (of knowledge and love), in the soul in a state of grace;

Or again mixing up in the same hybrid concept the wisdom of the natural order (metaphysical wisdom) and the infused gift of wisdom;

Or finally, attributing to the natural love of God what belongs exclusively to supernatural charity.

Whatever way we look at it, this would be to confound what is absolutely proper to grace with what is proper to the order of nature.

There can be no "immediate seizure" of God in the natural order; authentic mystical contemplation in the natural order is a contradiction in terms; an authentic experience of the deep things of God, a felt contact with Him, a *pati divina*, can only take place in the order of sanctifying grace and by its means.[1]

---

[1] J. Maritain, *Les Degrés du Savoir*, pp. 533-534 (English tr. pp. 332-333).

On the other hand, to maintain that true mystical experience, that is, some kind of experimental union with God Himself through knowledge and love, is conditioned by sanctifying grace and the theological virtues of faith and charity is not to assert that genuine mysticism has never been found outside orthodox Christianity. There is, of course, an antecedently stronger case in favour of the claims of the Catholic mystics on account of their explicit faith; but the Church recognizes that divine grace is not a prerogative of those who are in visible communion with the Apostolic See; and where sanctifying grace is present the way is open to intimate union with God.

There appear to be instances in the earlier stages of the Sufic movement in Islam which have every right to be compared with the states reached by St Teresa and St John of the Cross. These cases must, however, be as sharply distinguished from the natural "mysticism" of certain philosophers and poets as those of the Catholic saints. For Mohammedan mysticism at its best period, before it degenerated into a pantheistic quietism, presupposed asceticism and moral purification. Thus Rabi'a, the saintly freedwoman of Basra, used to pray upon the house-top at night: " O my Lord, the stars are shining and the eyes of men are closed, and the kings have shut their doors and every lover is alone with his beloved, and here am I alone with Thee."[1] And then she would spend the whole night in prayer. Again the life and death of al-Hallâj,[2] the great martyr of Sufism, exhibit all the signs of the intense personal sanctity and supernatural faith without which true mystical experience is not possible. Although the explicit articles of the Christian revelation may not have been proposed to them, these saintly non-Christians seem at least to have made their act of faith in the two principal truths of the supernatural order which implicitly contain all the rest.

Without faith, we learn from the Epistle to the Hebrews,[3] it is impossible to please God. The minimum of faith (*fides*

---

[1] Quoted from Christopher Dawson's essay, "Islamic Mysticism," in his *Enquiries*, p. 161.
[2] Cf. "The Problem of Mystical Grace in Islam," in *Studies in the Psychology of the Mystics* (p. 241) by Joseph Maréchal, S.J.
[3] xi, 6.

formata) required as a condition for the infusion of sanctifying grace would seem to be a belief in God, as the author of the supernatural life, and in His wish to save those who seek Him. "For he that cometh to God must believe that He is: and is a rewarder to them that seek Him." How explicit this assent should be is disputed by the theologians. Clearly, the faith of those to whom God's authentic revelation has been unequivocally made known through the voice of the Church should be immeasurably more alive than the belief of those not so highly favoured. Nevertheless the insistence by the Church on the Pauline teaching that Christ died for all men, and the explicit condemnation of the view that grace is not conceded to those outside the visible fold, point to the possibility that true faith can exist without a knowledge of all the articles of the creeds. But however few the truths to be believed, they cannot be dispensed with altogether. There must be that surrender to God, an acceptance of truth, not as recognized by reason but as coming direct from Him, in default of which the mind cannot be raised to the supernatural level. By faith, as we have seen, our intelligence has over against it, as an object to be contemplated (though "in a glass darkly"), the mind of God Himself, First Truth, *Veritas Prima*. It is from this source that the mystics, in common with the faithful at large, receive the light which gives point to their vision. For it is the material furnished by faith, the revealed truths (the *revelata*), which forms the object of their contemplation.

It is in virtue of this faith that the apparent infidels of saintly life partake of the grace of the redemption. They are brought into invisible communion with Christ's Church, outside of which intimate union with God is not possible—a fact of which the Catholic mystics themselves were fully aware. Though they are sometimes represented as choice souls chafing at the bonds of an all too rigid orthodoxy, partisans of the religion of the spirit as distinct from the religion of authority, the picture is a caricature. No one who is in the least familiar with the writings of Bernard of Clairvaux or Teresa of Avila can fail to be impressed by their passionate concern for sound doctrine and their hatred of heresy. St Catherine of Siena, surrounded by the corrupt ecclesiasticism of fourteenth century Italy, could yet speak of her visions in these terms:

For the light of the mind had mirrored itself in the Eternal Trinity; and in that abyss was seen the dignity of the rational being, and the misery into which man falls by fault of mortal sin, and the necessity of Holy Church, which God revealed to His servant's bosom; and how no one can attain to enjoy the beauty of God in the abyss of the Trinity but by means of that sweet Bride; for it befits all to pass by the door of Christ crucified, and this door is not found elsewhere than in Holy Church. She saw that this Bride brought life to men, because she holds in herself such life that there is no one who can kill her; and that she gave fortitude and light, and that there is no one who can weaken her, in her true self, or cast her into darkness. And she saw that her fruit never fails, but increases for ever.[1]

The fundamentally contemplative character of the virtue of faith has been insisted on in another chapter. The act of belief is not terminated by the words in which the articles of the creeds are formulated but by the ontological truth, the *thing*, which they express: *actus autem credentis non terminatur ad enuntiabile sed ad rem*.[2] It is because the intellectual content of the contemplative act is sufficiently provided for by the object of faith that the theologians deny the necessity of an infusion of new ideas, or *species*, to make mystical experience possible. No doubt the revelations and intellectual visions which accompany certain of the mystical states imply the presence of such species, but neither revelations nor intellectual visions are to be regarded as the essence of the experience. Contemplation is itself, of course, an infused supernatural gift; but what is infused is not new ideas to be contemplated—for they are already supplied by the revealed truths—but the " light " in which these are apprehended: a " light " produced in the mind by the operation of the infused virtues of faith and charity and the gifts of the Holy Spirit. The intelligence, in contemplation, does not take on the intuitive power of the angels; it remains human with human limitations. This is why St Thomas teaches that infused contemplation does not entirely exclude those

---
[1] Letter to Master Raimondo of Capua; from *Letters of St Catherine of Siena* translated by Vida D. Scudder, p. 342.
[2] IIa IIae, q. 1, a. 2, ad 2.

imaginative elements which are bound up with all man's understanding. The images may be all but imperceptible and, for practical purposes, disregarded, but they are there.

The concepts or ideas through which the mystic contemplates God are derived from faith It is the presence of these concepts—a necessity of our thought until the Beatific Vision is reached—which rules out the possibility of any intuitive knowledge of God Himself in this life. Not that conceptual knowledge is to be regarded as an unworthy substitute for immediate and intuitive knowledge, though there are some who appear to hold this view. It is simply a law of created intelligence that it must know in this way. In God alone the act of knowledge is identical with the essence of the knower. God *is* His knowledge, but the creature *has* his knowledge. Though knowledge, even in its created modes, involves a complete identity between the knower and the thing known, nevertheless, the act by which the creature knows is not his own essence, but a modification or accident of that essence. The most perfect forms of knowledge outside the divine mind, the angelic self-consciousness, the separated soul's knowledge of itself, involve the presence of a concept. The same must also be said of the experimental knowledge of the mystics. We should note, however, that its conceptual character does not diminish the reality of their knowledge, so far as it goes, though it shows that they do not directly see God Himself. The reason for this is that the divine essence cannot be represented in any created concept; *nullo modo per aliquam speciem creatam repraesentari potest.*[1] This is why, in the Beatific Vision, the divine essence itself fulfils the function of the concept.

But if this experimental knowledge is ultimately based upon concepts representative of revealed truths, this does not mean that the mystics need be explicitly aware of the fact. The language in which they describe their experiences would seem to point the other way. Yet the " dark night " and the " cloud of unknowing " in which they find themselves can be explained by the excess of light coming from the object towards which their gaze is directed. They are like birds of the night awakening to the full rays of the noon-day sun.

[1] Ia, q. 12, a. 2.

For the mind knows the thing represented by the concept, so far as it is revealed thereby, before it knows the concept itself; indeed the concept, as such, is only known by a process of reflection. And the saints are too much of lovers to be able to engage in reflection of this kind. It is the affective quality of their experience which makes it so hard to analyse. They are more conscious of warmth than light. The content of the experience is regulated by faith, but the experience itself is governed by love. And the love of God, which is charity, unlike faith, brings to the mind the very being of God Himself. In this life at least, " by love he can be gotten and holden, but by knowledge never."

The following passage from John of St Thomas states perhaps as accurately as the subject-matter will allow the relation between the cognitive and affective elements at this stage of the soul's union with God.

Although faith regulates love and our union with God in as much as it proposes its object, nevertheless, from this union itself, in which the affection reaches God immediately and is united to Him, the intellect is moved by a certain affective experience to judge in a higher way about divine things than the obscurity of faith permits. And the reason for this is that the intellect discerns and knows that more lies hidden in the things of faith than faith makes known, because it loves more therein and tastes more in its affective power. From this greater knowledge it judges more surely (*altius*) of divine things, relying rather on its affective experience than on the bare testimony of belief, together with the instinct of the Holy Spirit which strengthens and moves the intellect more surely (*altiori modo*).[1]

The transforming union, which is the term of the unitive way, places the soul on the brink of the Beatific Vision; it is ready to pass without further purification into the region of everlasting light. St John of the Cross teaches that when this stage is reached the soul is confirmed in grace;[2] and the theologians suggest that the assurance it brings would be for its possessor equivalent to the " special revelation " required by the Council of Trent as a warrant for the absolute certainty of being in a state of grace.[3] But even at this point the

---
[1] *Cursus Theol.*, t. vi, q. 70, disp. 18, a. 4 ; § xiv. (Vivès ed. p. 638).
[2] *Spiritual Canticle*, stanza xxii, 3 (Works, Vol. II, p. 308).
[3] Garrigou-Lagrange, *L'Amour de Dieu*, t. I, p. 189.

substance of God is not directly perceived, for the veil of faith remains. He is indeed known as He is in Himself, *in seipso*—for it is the function of supernatural faith to produce such knowledge—but He is not yet known according to His own ineffable mode of being, *sicuti est*. God is known, not face to face, but through the effects which He works in the soul; by the effects of filial love, *per effectum amoris filialis*, as St Thomas glosses the text: " For the Spirit Himself giveth testimony to our spirit that we are the sons of God."[1] Not that God is known only by inference from these effects. This would make the knowledge remote and indirect and would furthermore be against all the evidence. The divine " touches," and the tasting-knowledge (*sapida cognitio*) resulting from them, are not realities which, being first of all known, lead the mind on to recognize the closeness of its union with God. Like intellectual concepts, their function is primarily representative; they are the media through which the divine essence presents itself objectively to the mind in all but tangible form. Thus the knowledge of God can be described as immediate, though imperfectly so, on account of the residue of obscurity which only direct vision can remove. Not until heaven is reached will the soul be wholly transparent to God. Accordingly the experimental character of the mystics' knowledge is not quite unqualified; it is a *quasi*-experimental knowledge: *cognitio ista est quasi experimentalis*.[2]

Again John of St Thomas gives us what may well be the ultimate statement of the manner in which the soul is transformed into the object of its love by the very operation of love itself.

Love and affection can be considered in a twofold way. First, as applying itself and other powers to their operation, and in this way its function is that of an efficient and executive cause. Secondly, as drawing its object to itself and uniting itself therewith and rooting itself therein by a certain fruition and kinship and proportion with this object, so that it knows it, as it were experimentally, by a certain affective experience, according to what is said in Ps. xxxiii: " Taste and see that the Lord is sweet." And thus the affective power passes into the condition of

---

[1] Romans viii, 16.   [2] 1 *Sent.*, d. 14, q. 2, a. 2, ad 3.

the object, *affectus transit in conditionem objecti*, in so far as, by reason of this affective experience, the object is rendered more closely conformed and proportioned and united to the person who loves, and more becoming to him. In this way the understanding bears upon its object, as experiencing and touching it; and thus love moves in the manner of an objective cause, *in genere causae objectivae*, for by the aforesaid experience, *tale experimentum*, the object is, in diverse ways, made proportionate and becoming. ...[1]

It may be doubted whether the unifying of the lover and the beloved is patient of profounder analysis than is contained in this brief and unemotional passage from one of the very greatest theologians. We are enabled to glimpse something of what we ask for when we pray with the author of the *Imitation*: "O God Who art Truth, make me one with Thee in everlasting charity."[2]

But union with God means far more than an intimate personal relationship with Him. It means not only an identification of our will with His in love, but a complete correspondence therewith on the plane of action. We have to enter into God's scheme of things and co-operate with Him in the working out of His providential plan. In other words, a love-union with God implies the entire abandonment of the creature's will to divine providence. The words of Our Lady at the Annunciation perfectly express what should be the Christian's attitude in the face of the recognized will of God: "Be it done unto me according to Thy word."[3] In proportion as her state of mind becomes our own will be the closeness of our union with God.

The doctrine of abandonment to the will of God is founded on the gospels and is traditional in the Church, though it has sometimes been misunderstood. Experience goes to show that it is not always easy to steer a middle course between the Scylla of quietism and the Charybdis of activism. In practice, of course, the golden mean is only reached with the achievement of sanctity itself; but it is possible at the outset to appreciate where the dangers lie. We must, on the one hand, avoid the spiritual sloth and tacit disparagement of the moral struggle which often accompany a sense of the divine

---

[1] *Cursus Theol.*, loc. cit., §xi (pp. 637, 638).   [2] Bk. i, ch. 3.
[3] Luke i, 38.

changelessness and omnipotence and, on the other, the agitation and disquiet of those who feel that God's will is in some way frustrated if they do not do all the good which lies to their hand.

To gain a balanced view of the position and, in particular, as a corrective to undue anxiety and distress over the evils and uncertainties which surround us, three principles must be kept in mind.[1] First, everything that happens has been foreseen by God from all eternity, and has been willed or at least permitted by Him. Secondly, nothing can be willed or permitted by God that does not contribute to the end He purposed in creating, which is the manifestation of His goodness and infinite perfections and the glory of the God-Man Jesus Christ. St Paul supplies us with our third principle: "We know that to them that love God, all things work together unto good, to such as according to His purpose are called to be saints."[2] From the company of those who love God no one need be excluded; and to the perfecting of those who are to love Him always every event in history is ordered. *Etiam peccata*, says St Augustine, even sins.

In order, however, to ensure that, under pretext of submission to the will of God, the moral life does not degenerate into a practical quietism, a further principle must be stated. Abandonment to providence, far from excluding, necessarily implies, the unceasing effort to fulfil God's will as made known in the commandments and counsels and the events of life. The point will be better understood by observing the distinction drawn by St Thomas between God's "will of good pleasure," *voluntas beneplaciti*, and His "expressed will," *voluntas signi*.

This distinction, which is made in order to aid our understanding of what is in the last analysis a mystery, is of the first importance if we are to grasp what is meant by submission to the will of God. In God Himself there is but one act of willing, "the will of good pleasure," entirely above and beyond the comprehension of any created mind; but that will is expressed in the events of every-day life as they affect

---

[1] The teaching outlined in the next few pages owes much to Père Garrigou-Lagrange's *Providence*.
[2] Romans viii, 28.

us. Now it is before the will of good pleasure that the attitude of the Christian must be one of submission and indifference; but to the divine will as expressed he must respond by the performance of some duty. It is the teaching of such spiritual masters as St Francis of Sales and Bossuet that God's will of good pleasure is the domain of trusting surrender, whereas the expressed will of God is the domain of obedience.

St Thomas tells us[1] that when we say in the Our Father "Thy will be done," it is to the divine will as expressed that we refer. Indifference is out of the question when the expressed will of God is concerned; for such would not be a virtue but a plain neglect of our obligations. And the will of God expresses itself in innumerable ways: in the duties of our state, in each dictate of conscience, in the commands of superiors, in the obligations of charity to the brethren, in every impulse of grace. To all these we must reply, not with a gesture of submission to God's will—like the man in the parable who said "I go, sir" and went not—but with action, prompt and obedient. Here we are in the realm of the daily task, the duties of the hour, the "small things" to which the saints attached so great importance. "Every moment," says St Francis of Sales, "comes to us pregnant with a command from God, only to pass on and plunge into eternity, there to remain for ever what we have made it."

But, do what we will, we cannot live for the little daily task. Our eyes are on the future, and beyond the future—for that too will be in time. What part are we destined to play in the great drama of creation? What is to be the fate of all the things which interest us most? What success is to attend the plans we make for ourselves and others who are given to our charge? How much happiness and sorrow, good fortune and suffering, lies waiting for us in the years that are to come? Above all, when and where and in what circumstances are we to die? All these questions have their answer in God's will of good pleasure. Here the summons is not to strenuous action, still less to anxiety and pointless questioning, but to complete abandonment to the lovingkindness of the God Who is more solicitous for our welfare than we are ourselves. "Are not five sparrows sold for two farthings, and

[1] Ia, q. 19, a. 11.

not one of them is forgotten before God? Yea, the very hairs of your head are all numbered. Fear not therefore; you are of more value than many sparrows."[1]

The theologians make it clear that the act of self-abandonment to God's providence has its source, not in a special virtue, but in the three theological virtues of faith, hope and charity joined with the gift of piety. A little reflection on what has already been said in regard to the theological virtues will throw light on the significance of this fact. By the theological virtues, flowing as they do from sanctifying grace, we know and love God, not merely human-wise but divinely, sharing in the knowledge and love proper to the three Persons of the Blessed Trinity. Accordingly submission to God's will does not simply mean the passive acquiescence in something which lies beyond our ken; " Do not also the heathens this? "; it implies the salutary acts of faith and confidence in God Himself. Above all it implies the love of God, which is but another name for the union of our will with His. It is thus that we make the divine will of good pleasure our own, for we embrace it with our minds and hearts. This is the secret of the passionate devotion of the saints to the will of God; they saw in their unceasing submission to it the supreme means of being drawn into ever-deepening union with Him. God's will remains obscure, for our faith is of things not seen, but it is obscure from an overflow of light. We move in the darkness of the night, yet it is the " night more lovely than the dawn."

It must be obvious that the practical conclusions to be drawn from the doctrine of Christian providence are of universal application. They bear no more immediately on the few who are called to the cloister than on the majority who are leading an every-day life in the world. Thus, as we have suggested above, a misguided " submission to the will of God " can very easily induce a state of quietistic inertia in the face of the Christian realities. We can adopt an attitude of critical detachment where there is immediate need for action, the arm-chair approach when our place is in the thick of the fray. A modern Catholic philosopher has justly complained of those who make of the eternal truths a

[1] Luke xii, 6-7.

pillow on which to go to sleep. Apart from any grave dereliction of duty, it is surely possible for those who have seriously at heart the good of religion to fail lamentably in this respect. The aesthetic and philosophical viewpoint is notoriously prone to overstress the importance of the spectator's part, and we are cast for the rôle of actors. " Now these things you ought to have done, and not to leave the others undone." Whatever be the value of speculation and philosophy for their own sake—and the writer of these pages can scarcely be accused of underrating it—it would truly be rashness for anyone to hold himself exempt from service as a simple labourer in the vineyard. It is well to reflect that, according to the great tradition, each man is called to be a co-operator with God—an office " than which nothing can be more divine."

At the other extreme, an over-anxious preoccupation with the passing events of the hour can lead us to disregard, in the practical order, the very existence of providence. The shallowness and irrational speed of modern life invite to such an attitude, while the secularism of our day pays little heed to any divinely appointed scheme. It is sometimes forgotten that if the life of action—most of all, of Catholic action—is to be of profit it must observe the exigencies of the creature's ontological subordination to God. Thus the vain precipitancy, the pushing and hustling methods which occasionally disfigure the noblest causes, must give place to action which waits on the signs of God's will and is not the mere indulgence in our own. To act otherwise is to become victims of the illusion that our contribution is of value for its own sake, that we are really augmenting God's essential glory, presenting Him with something. Whereas our task is to work under His guidance, and in our own measure, to perfect in the world of space and time the plan which has existed in the divine mind from eternity.

It need hardly be said that true abandonment to the will of God is founded upon supernatural faith. For it presupposes the conviction that " all things work together unto good " in the lives of those who love God. It was this faith which enabled Job to cry out in the midst of his sufferings: " The Lord gave, and the Lord hath taken away. . . .

Blessed be the name of the Lord."[1] Nevertheless it is formally by the will, the faculty of love and desire, that we are united to God in this world. And this union takes place, as we have seen, according to the will's twofold function: first, as desire, for it has over against it as an object to be embraced, God Himself; and then as regulating human action, so that all we do is in perfect harmony with the will of God. This is the union which the faithful soul most of all desires. When it is attained the supernatural life within us has reached its full fruition.

Perhaps no happier commentary on the meaning of this union can be found than St John of the Cross's exposition of the 37th stanza of his *Spiritual Canticle*:

There wouldst thou show me That which my soul desired[2]

This desire is the equality of love which the soul ever desires, both naturally and supernaturally, because the lover cannot be satisfied if he feels not that he loves as much as he is loved. And as the soul sees the truth of the vastness of the love wherewith God loves her, she desires not to love Him less loftily and perfectly, to which end she desires present transformation, because the soul cannot reach this equality and completeness of love save by the total transformation of her will in that of God, wherein the two wills are united after such a manner that they become one. And thus there is equality of love, for the will of the soul that is converted into the will of God is then wholly the will of God, and the will of the soul is not lost but becomes the will of God. And thus the soul loves God with the will of God, which is also her own will; and thus she will love Him even as much as she is loved by God, since she loves Him with the will of God Himself, in the same love wherewith He loves her, which is the Holy Spirit, Who is given to the soul, even as the Apostle says in these words: "The charity of God is poured forth in our hearts by the Holy Spirit Who is given to us" (Romans v, 5).... And thus the soul loves God in the Holy Spirit together with the Holy Spirit, not by means of Him, as by an instrument, but together with Him, by reason of the transformation ... and He supplies that which she lacks by her having been transformed in love with Him."

[1] Job i, 21.
[2] Works, Vol. II, p. 172. Professor Allison Peers has the following: "The saint adds in the margin this note, which he expounds with some fullness in the second redaction: 'Although it is true that glory consists in the understanding, the end of the soul is to love'." The above passage is taken from the *Spiritual Canticle* in its first form.

III

THE MIND OF CHRIST

"But we have the mind of Christ."—1 *Corinthians ii*, 16.

It is fitting that we should lead the thoughts which have occupied us in the foregoing pages to their conclusion by some brief reflections on the inner meaning of man's conformity with Christ Our Lord. Such an epilogue finds here its natural place, for the final issue of God's love for us is that we should become like to Him Who is the "firstborn among many brethren."[1] And it is by having the mind of Christ that we most of all resemble Him. This is the gift that St Paul wished for his beloved Philippians: "For let this mind be in you which was also in Christ Jesus."[2] Likewise, at the end of the second chapter of his first epistle to the Corinthians he boasts that, in distinction from the folly and sensuality of the world, the Christian has the true wisdom: "But we have the mind of Christ."[3]

This last text is of interest because, as the exegetes point out, the term St Paul uses is νοῦς instead of πνεῦμα, which might have been expected. It would be unjustifiable to read into the word *nous* at this stage the implications of later theology, though those implications are clearly not to be excluded. That our human and merely rational ways of seeing things are in some manner replaced by the thought processes of Christ Himself is the obvious meaning of what is said. The new wisdom of the Christians "takes its inspiration from the 'sense of Christ,' from the judgments which exist in the rational faculties of the man Jesus.... For Christ lives in them and communicates to them, in human measure, His own knowledge."[4] And the knowledge with which Christ enlightens His followers is a knowledge joined with love: knowledge and love of the Father and, through Him, of all mankind. We are here at the fountainhead of faith and charity and all the elements which make man's union with God the unique relationship it is.

---

[1] Romans viii, 29.   [2] Philippians ii, 5.   [3] 1 Corinthians ii, 16.
[4] Allo, *Première Épître aux Corinthiens* (II, 16), p. 50.

Not that Christ, like ourselves, saw God only as veiled by faith. It would appear certain that there was present to His human mind at all times the vision of the Father. Although He allowed Himself to learn things in a new way, and could accordingly feel surprise and wonder, the perfection of an intelligence hypostatically united to the Godhead is incompatible with anything that could be described as ignorance. The theologians approach the mystery of Our Lord's knowledge with great caution, for it is hardly possible to state in rational terms the subtleties involved. But in grounding the divine assurance behind the Master's message on His insight into the mind of His heavenly Father the Church is but giving the obvious meaning to Christ's words: "Amen, amen, I say to thee that we speak what we know and we testify what we have seen."[1]

Our Lord's unceasing contemplation of the face of God is the explanation of the absolute conformity of His own will with the will of the Father. We saw in the last chapter how it is precisely by this union of wills that the love of God is consummated. Be it remembered that it was in order to give to the world the perfect example of love for the Father that Christ allowed Himself to be crucified. "But that the world may know that I love the Father: and as the Father has given Me commandment, so do I."[2] Never should the intense love of Christ for His Father be lost sight of. We have no difficulty in appreciating, at least theoretically, His love for mankind; nor, in view of the New Testament evidence, can we fail to realize something of the inexhaustible love of the Father for His only begotten Son. But it is possible to overlook the way in which the paternal love was reciprocated. The fact that Christ was the victim for our sins, that He paid the price of our redemption, may emphasize for us the presence of a certain reluctance and bitterness of spirit in a way that obscures the essential element of love. It should always be borne in mind that the sacrifice of Calvary was a love-offering to the Father before it could ever be of profit to the human race. The human will and desires of Christ were fixed upon God in a way that make them the model and exemplar-cause of all Christian charity; for by

[1] John iii, 11. [2] John xiv, 31.

charity we first of all love God, and only secondarily, and in relation to Him, our neighbour.

"With desire I have desired to eat this pasch with you."[1] The new pasch and what it signified were the fulfilment of Our Lord's mission on earth. He had looked forward to the moment of their accomplishment as the hour when the manifestation of His love of God should be complete. When that time came He could cry out in triumph to the Father: "I have glorified Thee on the earth; I have finished the work which Thou gavest Me to do."[2] From the beginning His human will had been united with the will of God, wholly submissive to it. "... I do nothing of Myself.... And He that sent Me is with Me: and He hath not left Me alone. For I do always the things that please Him."[3] In other words, that state of perfection which we have seen to be the culmination of the experience of the saints belonged to Christ in a supereminent degree throughout His life. Nor should it be forgotten that it is His human nature and mind, those realities which He shares with us, of which we speak. We can say with truth that His soul (*mens*) was perfected—though, by reason of the Hypostatic Union, immeasurably more profoundly—in the same way as ours; that is to say, by the infusion of grace and charity. Through grace and charity, then, we ourselves have the first beginnings of the "mind of Christ"; in proportion as they are intensified within us do we become like to Him. Never, of course, can we be so united with God as to form one personality with Him; nor, in the present life, can we be sustained by the vision of the divine essence. But, by way of compensation, we are given that creaturely participation in the divine nature which is sanctifying grace; and, to correspond with Christ's knowledge, we receive the supernatural illumination of faith and the gifts of wisdom and understanding.

From these thoughts we are led easily to the conclusion that the imitation of Christ consists essentially in knowing and loving, in our own measure, what He knows and loves. From this knowledge and love Christlike action will follow; for we have seen how these two immanent activities dictate all human behaviour. We must have before our eyes the

[1] Luke xxii, 15.   [2] John xvii, 4.   [3] John viii, 28, 29.

vision by which He lived and in our hearts the desires which motivated all His actions. It is thus, and not otherwise, that we are united to Him. How close that union may become we have already tried to show. Only with the saints does it reach the stage in which the lover is virtually identified with the Beloved. " And I live, now not I; but Christ liveth in me. . . . I live in the faith of the Son of God, Who loved me and delivered Himself up for me."[1]

It would be an error to interpret this insistence on what essentially unites us with Our Lord as an indirect disparagement of the devout imitation of the particular circumstances and actions of His historic life. Every detail of that career is of eternal moment to the truly Christian soul. For it was by no accident that the earthly days of the Incarnate Word had their peculiar local and temporal setting. He came to His own people in " the fullness of time "[2] after centuries of waiting. The places where He taught and preached, every footstep of the journeys He made, the hills and valleys on which He gazed hold for all who claim to be His followers an irresistible fascination. The external minutiae of His life have a meaning which can never be ignored. Though human nature cannot form an adequate medium of self-expression for a divine Personality, we know that it came nearest to doing so during those thirty odd years passed by the God-Man in Palestine. The choice of a carpenter's trade, of personal poverty, the preference of the company of the weak and the despised, the state of unmarried chastity, incidents such as the visit to the marriage feast and the washing of the disciples' feet, have in their way as much significance for us as each miracle that Christ performed and every word that He uttered.

It is for this reason that the saints have wished to reproduce in themselves, so far as may be, the physical conditions of the life of Him they serve. While a St Jerome and many another betake themselves to the Holy Land itself that their imitation may be the more complete, there is none who does not strive to give to the gospel a personal and very literal interpretation. Especially have these souls been moved to emulation by the story of the Passion; for it is by suffering that love for

[1] Galatians ii, 20.   [2] Galatians iv, 4.

the Crucified receives its unmistakable seal. " Always bearing about in our body the mortification of Jesus, that the life also of Jesus may be made manifest in our bodies."[1]

Nevertheless it would be a mistake to allow what is accidental and adventitious to obscure the essential. Though we may meditate upon the scenes and actions of Our Lord's earthly life, we should not allow the mind to stop there. The love-union with God does not depend upon our representing to ourselves events of past history, even of sacred history. Such a preoccupation can engender day-dreaming and a certain romanticism in religion which dissipate the spirit. Be it recalled that the Person of Christ, since it is divine, is, and has always been, outside all considerations of space and time. " Jesus Christ, yesterday, and to-day, and the same for ever."[2] To communicate with Him our minds must be uplifted above what St Augustine calls the *nunc fluens*, the sequence of temporal events, and enter into the *nunc stans*, the " eternal now " of the God " with Whom there is no change nor shadow of alteration."[3] Though the senses and imagination have a very definite part to play in religious worship, they cannot of themselves form the medium of a vital and intimate contact with Christ. This is possible only for the mind (*mens*) which, by reason of its spirituality, is itself liberated from time and movement and therefore able, in some degree, to be admitted into a participation of the divine eternity. It is in our mind, and only there, that we hold communion with the " mind of Christ."

The stress which has been laid in recent years on the doctrine of the Church as the Mystical Body of Christ surely emphasizes this truth. The Church is itself the Body of Christ, the veritable prolongation of the Incarnation.

The Church, especially as described in the Epistles of the captivity, is the fulfilment, the fullness, ($\pi\lambda\acute{\eta}\rho\omega\mu a$) of Christ, as Paul repeats. She is in the same relation to Christ as a building to its foundations, as the stem to the root, as an organism to the life which animates it. The Church continues Christ; she expresses Him; she develops all the powers of sanctification that are His. Without her, Christ would be incomplete, like a head

---

[1] 2 Corinthians iv, 10. [2] Hebrews xiii, 8. [3] James i, 17.

without a body. The expression is strong; but the Apostle says it over and over again: without the faithful Christ has not His fullness.[1]

The truth underlying the doctrine of the Mystical Body is of vast importance, though the language which is occasionally used to describe it is not without its difficulties for the more thoughtful. It has to be kept in mind that the phrase "Mystical Body" (never, incidentally, employed by St Paul) is a metaphor and the modes of speech in which the dogma has found expression in the fathers and theologians are, for the most part, figurative and not literal. This is, of course, only to be expected, since there are truths so sublime that glimpses of them can only be conveyed to the understanding by means of the metaphorical and picturesque. But we can sometimes be misled as well as instructed by metaphors. It is possible to forget St Thomas's warning in this connection, that the comparison suggested by the metaphor is not to be too strictly applied: *in metaphoricis locutionibus non oportet attendi similitudinem quantum ad omnia.*[2] Thus a too literal interpretation of the Pauline and patristic language about the Body of Christ can lead us to conceive of the unity of the Church in terms of a sort of "panchristism" which is as unacceptable as the pantheism which lies behind it. Not only does an oversimplification of the doctrine involve speculative error, but the possibility of defective morality as well. We may be tempted to suppose that, since Christ works in us and by us, we are dispensed from any personal effort to co-operate with Him. In other words, the way is open to quietism and the variety of mistakes which can be made by those who regard grace as a substitute for nature, instead of its perfection and elevation.

In the monumental work from which we have just quoted Père Mersch makes some valuable introductory remarks, warning us, in a matter of such importance, to rely more on reason and faith than on imagination and sentiment.

Some, for example, absolutely insist on picturing the Mystical Body to themselves, by means of an image which they consider to be a perfect representation of the reality. Certainly we need

[1] Émile Mersch, S.J. *Le Corps Mystique du Christ,* tome I, pp. 158-159; translated into English under the title *The Whole Christ* by John R. Kelly, S.J., p. 121. [2] IIIa, q. 8, a. 1, ad 2

images; we cannot think without phantasms, and Scripture provides many of them in connection with the doctrine of the Mystical Body. The error lies in mistaking the image for a definition and in thinking that just because they are able to conceive some huge ethereal and invisible organism or a kind of living atmosphere in which men's souls are somehow fused together, they therefore possess a perfect knowledge of the mystery of the Head and members. It goes without saying that whoever allows himself to be so misled by his imagination is exposing himself to every sort of aberration.

It has been necessary in every age to put the faithful on their guard against false mysticism, and in our day the warning is, to say the least, as indispensable as ever. It is unnecessary to describe all the forms which the illusion takes, but one can see how the doctrine of the Mystical Body might well serve it as a mask. The angel of darkness has always loved to disguise himself as an angel of light.[1]

Surely the fundamental truth which the Church would have us appreciate in her teaching on the Mystical Body is that the life which is proper to Christ Himself is shared by His followers in a multiplicity of ways, that "there are diversities of graces, but the same Spirit."[2] That is to say, the grace and charity which unite the human soul of Christ to God form the prototype, the exemplar-cause, of the innumerable modes in which essentially the same grace and charity are reproduced in the members of the Church throughout history. Our Lord's own life, perfect though it was in every respect, was nevertheless limited in its range and influence. This was part of the divine plan, that the infinite God, while retaining His own nature, should yet assume creaturely limitations. He " emptied Himself by taking the form of a slave and becoming like unto men."[3] The individual human nature of Christ, though perfected by the Personality of the Word, was not itself divine; accordingly, to this degree, Our Lord could but act in human fashion and His work could claim no more of immortality than attends the achievements of every great man. The extent of His activities was limited to a small area of the earth's surface during the space of a short lifetime, His personal contacts to a few thousand souls. But God's arm was not thereby

[1] Mersch, op. cit., pp. xxi-xxii. [2] 1 Corinthians xii, 4. [3] Philippians ii, 7.

shortened. It was His design to overpass the limits of space and time and bestow the Christ-life on all the world, " to bring all things to a head (ἀνακεφαλαιώσασθαι) in Christ."[1] And this is done by imparting to each soul the grace won for it by Christ—the process whereby we become the members of Christ's Body, the Church, and have Him for our Head.[2]

It is impossible to gain any adequate understanding of the teaching on the Mystical Body apart from the theology of grace on which it is founded. The act by which man is justified, that is, by the infusion of sanctifying grace, is the means whereby He is incorporated into the Body of Christ. As grace is a quality most intimate to each of us, rooted in the very essence of the soul, it effects the transition from the natural to the supernatural life without in any way infringing the rights of the individual personality. While grace does not adapt itself to the soul, but rather adapts the soul to itself, it nevertheless does its work without destroying the natural perfection of the subject in which it inheres. *Gratia non destruit sed perficit naturam.* As a result, each man is raised to the supernatural order without being despoiled of those qualities which are peculiarly his own. The process whereby we are made conformable to the image of God's Son[3] does not issue in a colourless uniformity which bears no relation to the wealth and variety of human life as we know it. On the contrary the distinctive contributions of each, arising from differences of temperament and character, are taken account of and endowed with supernatural value. What was impossible for Christ as a single individual, namely, the presentation in human form of the life of the Son of God in all places and throughout all ages, is made possible by the imparting of that life to all men according to their respective functions in the divine plan. " And Himself ' gave ' some as apostles, some as prophets, some as evangelists, some as shepherds and teachers, for the perfecting of the saints in the work of the ministry, unto the building up of the body of Christ, till we all attain to the unity of the faith and the full knowledge of the Son of God, to the perfect man, to the full measure of the stature of Christ."[4]

---

[1] Ephesians i, 10.   [2] vid. IIIa, q. 8, a. 1: *Utrum Christus sit Caput Ecclesiae.*
[3] Romans viii, 29.   [4] Ephesians iv, 11-13.

The position of Christ Himself is unique: He is the Head. His human nature is united to the Person of the Word and the grace whereby His soul is justified is itself the grace, *gratia capitalis*, by which He claims the headship of the Church.[1] The degree of subordination of the " members of the body " to their Head can scarcely be expressed in words. It was no doubt St Paul's recognition of the relative insignificance of the members in comparison with the Head which led him to make a point which is worth pondering. He implies that whatever be the part played by individuals in the life of the Church, in respect of their importance there is no distinction to be drawn between them, so that God's good pleasure be observed.

For the body also is not one member but many. If the foot should say, because I am not the hand, I am not of the body, is it therefore not of the body? And if the ear should say, because I am not the eye, I am not of the body: is it therefore not of the body? If the whole body were the eye, where would be the hearing? If the whole were hearing, where would be the smelling? But now God hath set the members every one of them in the body as it hath pleased Him. And if they all were one member, where would be the body? But now there are many members indeed, yet one body. And the eye cannot say to the hand: I need not thy help; nor again the head to the feet: I have no need of you. ... Now you are the body of Christ, and members of member.[2]

It would be unjustifiable to interpret St Paul here as countenancing in the Church anything less than the best, especially as a few verses later he begins his great hymn in praise of charity—the " more excellent way." But it surely suggests to us that, in practice, the number of possible interpretations of the mind of Christ is greater than we might sometimes be led to suppose. Not a few of the more abstract treatments of the spiritual life appear to find little room, in their clearly marked divisions, for those who, though full of human weakness and inconsistency, have yet dedicated themselves wholeheartedly to God's service. We should never allow ourselves to forget that it does not all work out according to plan—even the theological plan. The efforts of many, whom it would be pharisaical to think of as

[1] IIIa, q. 8, a. 5.   [2] 1 Corinthians xii, 14-21, 27.

"weaker brethren," who are confessedly oppressed by the weight of the moral struggle, may well be informed by greater charity, not to say humility, than the poise and self-mastery of the one who feels himself to be mounting rung by rung the ladder of the spiritual life.

Furthermore it must be acknowledged that, while the saint is the masterpiece of God's handiwork, He did not intend all men to be eligible for canonization at their death. Our Lord came on earth to lead mankind to the heights of holiness; but He dealt with us according to our native feebleness and poverty. The ideal was above all things desirable, but not here and now, if it meant breaking the bruised reed or extinguishing the smouldering flax.[1] All without exception are required to tend towards the perfection of charity, but it is comforting to reflect that this precept is fulfilled so long as the soul is in a state of grace. The perfection of charity is the end to be attained; but, precisely because it is the end, we observe the precept of loving God above all things on condition that we do not cease to move towards the end. And we can be said to do this so long as charity is not extinguished by mortal sin.[2] Nor should we fail to recall that the glorious and unblemished Church of which St Paul speaks[3] is the ideal and heavenly Church, not the Church of this world. "To be a Church without spot or wrinkle is the final end to which we are led by the passion of Christ; wherefore this will be in heaven, not on earth, in which ' If we say we have no sin we deceive ourselves ' (1 John i, 10.) "[4]

The saints are the glory of the world, but the rest of us have each our contribution to make, slight though it be, to the harmony and beauty of the finished plan. It is interesting to reflect that St Thomas assigns as the primary reason for the inequality of graces given to men the fact that such an arrangement makes for the excellence of God's design as a whole.

Whence the first cause of this diversity comes from God Himself, Who dispenses the gifts of His grace in various ways so that the beauty and perfection of the Church may result from

---

[1] Matthew xii, 20.   [2] Cajetan in IIam IIae, q. 184, a. 3, v.
[3] Ephesians v, 27.   [4] IIIa, q. 8, a. 3, ad 2.

these various degrees; even as He instituted the various conditions of natural things, that the universe might be perfect. Hence after the Apostle had said: "To every one of us is given grace, according to the measure of the giving of Christ" (Ephesians iv, 7), having enumerated the various gifts, he adds: (verse 12) "For the perfecting of the saints ... for the building up of the body of Christ."[1]

. . . . .

To the reader who has persevered through the foregoing chapters it will perhaps appear strange that we should have chosen to end on what he may feel to be a note of anticlimax. We have attempted to outline, as objectively as possible, the nature of the love of God and the practical conditions of its achievement, only to conclude by demanding much less than the ideal. It might even seem that we are suggesting that, in practice, men can rest content with the half-hearted and second best. In reply to such misgivings we would answer that what has been attempted is an exposition of doctrine rather than an exhortation to practice. When it comes to action and fidelity to grace and our own conscience we are answerable for the least defection. And as Newman has well said, no one has the right to take another's lower standard of holiness for his own. It is of faith that every man receives sufficient grace to be saved, in other words, to reach, here or hereafter, the perfect love of God. But it is no less certain that all do not receive the same degree of grace, that some stars are destined to shine more brightly in the firmament of sanctity than others. The practical importance of this truth is not so obvious, but it is surely there.

No one is more convinced than the present writer that the modern world is crying out for saints. One such is of incalculably greater benefit to mankind than a thousand mediocrities. Furthermore no one may rest assured that the call to practise heroic sanctity has not been given to him. Nevertheless not only do we need the saints but a Christian society as well. That is, we need what was once a historic fact, a social order which is informed by grace, which, dimly and feebly it may be, has "the mind of Christ." In a world of paganism there is a demand for "ordinary" Christians as well as for the heroes. Hence it is important that, while having our

[1] Ia IIae, q. 112, a. 4.

hearts set on the ideal, we should know also what is the acceptable and tolerable. To attempt sublimation outside its proper context is to invite disaster. To expect from others more than they are in a position to give is to offer hindrance rather than help. God's grace undoubtedly supplies for natural deficiencies, but nature must be led, not forced, to what is supernatural. The standard must be kept aloft—it is hoped that no word in these pages has done anything to lower it—but the highest is not to be uncompromisingly demanded of all, lest those who " labour and are burdened "[1] (the specially invited) be turned away.

Without a return to the " mind of Christ " there is little hope for the world in which we live. Already, for want of unity, western civilization is in danger of going down to destruction in blood and ruins. The life-giving knowledge of human destiny and a desire for the rule of God, that is, faith and charity, are the conditions of the earthly as well as the heavenly peace. This knowledge and love, man's only imperishable treasure, have their ideal form in the sacred humanity of Christ. Next in order comes the Mother of God, she who was uniquely " full of grace." Thereafter are the saints, so many embodiments of the eternal ideas of what man should be. And then the ranks of the faithful, insignificant by comparison, but of the same company, since they too drink of the waters springing up unto life everlasting. This is the assembly which makes up the " fullness of Christ," His Mystical Body. Its members have been admitted into the divine secrets; their ultimate worth and the influence they exercise upon others are to be reckoned by the depth of their love. For it is the love of God which brings to us the only immortality that counts. When the day breaks and the shadows retire and the Incarnate Word has delivered up His Kingdom to the Father, it is by love that we shall possess the vision that is ours.

[1] Matthew xi, 28.